100 SCIENCE PUZZLES

JANE YOUNG & COLIN McCARTY

UNWIN

HYMAN

Published by
UNWIN HYMAN LTD
15/17 Broadwick Street
London W1V 1FP

First published 1987 by Longman Cheshire Pty Limited

First published in Great Britain 1989

ISBN 0 04 448163 2

Typeset by Cambridge Photosetting Services
Printed in Great Britain by
The Alden Press Ltd., Oxford and bound by
Hunter & Foulis Ltd., Edinburgh

CONTENTS

Index

For each puzzle, the Index identifies related Attainment Target(s) and Level(s) of the National Curriculum for Science. Answers to puzzles appear at the end of the book.

Page	Title	Type of Puzzle	Attainment Target(s)	Level(s)
40	Petroleum Puzzle	Finding words to fit descriptions relating to petroleum industry	6 7 8	10 9 10
41	Clued Up on Carbon	Crossword on carbon chemistry	7	5, 6
42	Compound Conundrum	Choosing formulae to fit descriptions of compounts	7 8	4 7
43	Polymer Puzzle	Finding words to fit descriptions of polymers	7	7, 9
44	It's a Gas	Matching gases to their uses in industry	6 7 17	10 7 4, 6
45	Metals and Man	Crossword on metal uses and extraction	6 7	8 7
46	$E = mc^2$	Crossword about the nucleus and nuclear reactions	8	7, 8, 9
47	State Secrets	Finding definitions about the states of matter	8	5, 6
48	In the Balance	Balancing chemical equations	8	9
49	Displacement	Completing displacement equations	8	8
50	Getting Physical	Classifying changes into physical/ chemical/nuclear	6 8	4 6, 7
51	Symbol Search	Matching elements to symbols to follow a maze	8	7
52	Family Fun	Identifying odd-one-out in groups of elements	6	8, 9
53	Ferreting Out Formulae	Matching compounds to formulae to follow a maze	8	7
54	Formula Fun	Crossword of chemical formulae	8	7
55	The Mole-Hole Game	Following a maze by doing mole calculations	8	9
56	Chemical Conundrum	Finding words to fit descriptions about bonding	8 17	8 4, 5, 6
57	Togetherness	True/false statements about bonding	6 8	6, 8, 9, 10 8
58	Particle Puzzle	Unscrambling words on bonding fit them into a matrix	8	8
59	Watery Words	Unscrambling words about rivers and seas	8 9	6 6
60	Atmospherics	Crossword on the atmosphere	9	6

Preface

Tackling the puzzles in this book should be an enjoyable way for pupils to build and reinforce their knowledge and understanding of science. The puzzles are intended to complement the good teaching that occurs in most school laboratories. All the National Curriculum Attainment Targets are covered in order, and the puzzles reflect the emphasis on the knowledge and understanding component. The Index pages list the puzzle titles and give a short description of each, together with the related Attainment Targets and Levels. I have tried to give enough detail to help teachers make an informed choice of puzzles.

The flavour of the puzzle book is best described in the following excerpts from the original "Notes for Teachers" written by Jane Young in Australia.

> My first idea was to subtitle this production 'What to do with General Science last period on a wet Friday afternoon when their regular teacher has collapsed with a migraine'. But my publisher objected that (a) it was a little cumbersome, and (b) it lowered the tone. He was probably right – these puzzles really aren't designed as 'busy work' for Friday afternoons, wet or otherwise. I hope there will be times when you find them useful in an emergency, for instance that unexpected supervision; but primarily they aim to provide worthwhile learning experiences.
>
> A number of puzzles may strike you as being rather heavy on facts. However, the facts are often being used to underpin a concept. Personally I don't think it matters too much whether or not pupils can name 20 famous scientists and their discoveries, or 10 industrial gases and their uses. What **does** matter is that they develop some appreciation of the range of scientific enquiry, and the importance of science in everyday life.
>
> Using puzzles for library research, with students working either singly or in small groups, can supplement or substitute for 'chalk-and-talk' lessons on a large variety of topics. They can also be used as a starting point for further project or assignment work, e.g. on the history of science.
>
> Some puzzles involve identification of specimens from drawings or written descriptions. These could be used in conjunction with laboratory work, especially in areas that require learning and recall which many students find less than enthralling.
>
> Try setting puzzles as homework assignments – you may find that you don't have as many defaulters the next lesson. You could even use some of them for assessment; there's no law against kids actually enjoying a test!
>
> A puzzle needn't always be given to the whole group. The harder ones can be useful as extension activities for the bright spark who comes to you ten minutes before the end of the lesson to say, 'I've finished all my work – what do I do **now**?'. The easy puzzles can be given to the slower students in the group who need a dose of extra practice in basic skills, but respond better if the pill is sugar-coated.

Modifying these puzzles to be useful to hard-pressed teachers in Britain has been a rewarding experience. I have had fun in doing the questions and trying to solve the riddles and I feel confident that our pupils will also find them a refreshing change and challenge.

Anything that brings variety to the learning experience must be welcome. Enjoyable contributions such as these puzzles give both 'taste' and 'nutrition' to the academic diet.

COLIN McCARTY

BEAKERS AND BUNSENS

1.					■	■	■	2.	■	■	■
	■	■	■	■	■	3.					4.
5.					■	■	■		■	■	
	■	■	■	■	■	6.				■	
■	7.		8.			■	■		■	■	
■		■		■	■	■	9.	■	10.	■	
11.				■	12.						■
■		■	■	■	■	■		■		■	13.
14.			15.				■	16.			
■		■		■	■	■	■	■		■	
17.	■	18.						■		■	
	■	■		■	■	■	■	■	■	■	
19.							■	20.			

ACROSS

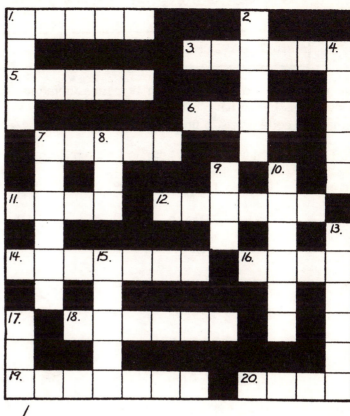

1. Do not test chemicals by using this sense
3. Colour of a smoky bunsen flame
5. Sensible footwear for the lab
6. Dangerous to do this to people in the lab
7. Laboratory accidents that should be treated with cold water
11. This solid can be used to put out small laboratory fires
12. Beakers or flasks are stood on this when they are heated
14. General name given to a laboratory chemical
16. Colour of a hot bunsen flame
18. Laboratory burner
19. Used for transferring small quantities of liquids
20. Chemical with a low pH

DOWN

1. What you have to do to a hypothesis
2. A conical piece of glassware
4. Should be applied immediately if chemicals get in the eye
7. Container for heating liquids
8. Used for stirring
9. Mixed with gas for a hotter flame
10. Controls the gas mixture in a bunsen
13. You do this with the results of experiments
15. Use this when heating a beaker or flask on a tripod
17. Unit of electrical current

UNDERSTANDING UNITS

WHAT HAPPENED TO THE WOLF WHO FELL INTO THE WASHING MACHINE ?

We often have to be able to change measurements from one set of units to another. Not all the conversions below have been done correctly. Cross out the ones which are wrong. Read down the remaining code letters to find the answer to the riddle.

NOTE: 1 dm^3 is 1 litre, 1 l and 1 cm^3 is 1 ml, a millilitre.

1.	10 mm = 1.0 cm	H	26.	15 mm = 1.5 cm	A
2.	750 g = 0.075 kg	D	27.	0.2 cm^3 = 0.02 dm^3	V
3.	12.0 dm^3 = 120 cm^3	F	28.	23 cm^3 = 0.023 dm^3	N
4.	6.2 cm = 62 mm	E	29.	0.1 cm^3 = 0.0001 dm^3	D
5.	23 mm = 0.23 cm	R	30.	16.4 cm = 1640 mm	I
6.	340 mg = 3.4 g	L	31.	50 mm = 0.5 cm	C
7.	2.7 g = 2700 mg	B	32.	0.0025 dm^3 = 2.5 cm^3	W
8.	0.15 kg = 150 g	E	33.	2.5 g = 250 mg	S
9.	2500 g = 25 kg	N	34.	3780 g = 37.8 kg	T
10.	16.8 dm^3 = 1680 cm^3	O	35.	248 cm = 0.248 m	G
11.	0.1 dm^3 = 100 cm^3	C	36.	15.3 dm^3 = 15 300 cm^3	E
12.	437 g = 0.437 kg	A	37.	0.01 cm = 0.1 mm	R
13.	0.1 cm = 1 mm	M	38.	18 mm = 1.8 cm	E
14.	0.1 m = 100 cm	S	39.	4560 cm = 456.0 m	D
15.	1.7 kg = 170 g	I	40.	16.8 g = 1680 mg	B
16.	163 cm = 1.63 m	E	41.	0.95 dm^3 = 9500 cm^3	U
17.	3.5 dm^3 = 3500 cm^3	A	42.	0.075 dm^3 = 75 cm^3	W
18.	2.0 m = 2000 cm	P	43.	0.023 kg = 230 g	Y
19.	0.02 cm = 0.2 mm	W	44.	2500 g = 25 Kg	A
20.	155 mg = 0.155 g	A	45.	0.4 cm = 40 mm	M
21.	0.30 m = 300 cm	O	46.	397 cm^3 = 0.397 dm^3	O
22.	0.034 kg = 34 g	S	47.	0.0037 dm^3 = 3.7 cm^3	L
23.	0.95 dm^3 = 9500 cm^3	J	48.	42 mm = 0.42 cm	G
24.	65 cm = 0.65 m	H	49.	73 cm^3 = 0.73 dm^3	K
25.	15 mm = 0.015 cm	G	50.	0.034 kg = 34 g	F

KIDS' STUFF

WHICH BRANCH OF THE ARMY DO BABIES JOIN ?

Calculate the average of the results obtained in each of the experiments below. Find the number in the key list and write the corresponding letter next to the number of the question. Read off the letters down the page.

1. The time it takes a mouse to learn to run through a maze.
   Results: 3 h, 6 h, 4 h, 2 h, 10 h

   Average: . . . . hours

2. The height bean plants grow to.
   Results: 45cm, 30 cm, 27 cm, 37 cm, 42 cm, 29 cm

   Average: . . . . centimetres

3. The gas pressure that bursts a balloon.
   Results: 12 kPa, 9 kPa, 12 kPa, 11 kPa, 12 kPa, 11 kPa, 10 kPa

   Average: . . . . kilopascals

4. The volume of acid needed to neutralise 10.0 cm^3 of sodium hydroxide solution.
   Results: 10.2 cm^3, 10.1 cm^3, 10.3 cm^3, 10.1 cm^3, 10.3 cm^3

   Average: . . . . cubic centimetres

5. The force needed to bend a piece of paper.
   Results: 1.3 N, 1.0 N, 1.1 N, 0.9 N, 1.3 N, 1.2 N, 0.9 N

   Average: . . . . newtons

6. The lowest concentration of toxin that will kill a rat.
   Results: 0.015%, 0.020%, 0.019%, 0.022%

   Average: . . . . %

7. The counts per minute from a uranium sample.
   Results: 69, 85, 92, 67, 83, 72, 83, 78, 81, 80

   Average: . . . . counts/minute

8. The number of fruit flies that entered a trap in a one hour period.
   Results: 24, 28, 25, 32, 22, 19

   Average: . . . . fruit flies/hour

9. The concentration of calcium ions in a water sample.
   Results: 0.85 g/dm^3, 0.75 g/dm^3, 0.64 g/dm^3, 0.80 g/dm^3

   Average: . . . . grams/cubic decimetre

10. The percentage of copper in an ore sample.
    Results: 0.63%, 0.64%, 0.59%, 0.61%, 0.60%, 0.61%, 0.63%, 0.57%

    Average: . . . . %

11. The concentration of glucose in human plasma.
    Results: 0.105%, 0.112%, 0.106%, 0.108%, 0.105%, 0.112%, 0.108%

    Average: . . . . %

KEY LIST

F.	0.019	T.	0.76	S.	4	I.	10.2	H.	35
S.	0.020	B.	0.78	T.	5	E.	11	D.	70
D.	0.106	O.	1.0	R.	10.0	V.	11.1	G.	78
Y.	0.108	N.	1.1	J.	10.03	N.	25	A.	79
R.	0.61	L.	2	T.	10.1	F.	30	E.	80

FOR WOOLLY THINKERS

WHY DO WHITE SHEEP EAT MORE THAN BLACK SHEEP ?

The professor is carrying out an experiment on sheep. She wants to find out if they grow more quickly when fed on 'Baa-Lamb' food supplement. Her control group is fed on grass only. Plot her results on the grid and join up the points. The curves pass through the letters which spell out the answer to the problem.

AVERAGE MASS OF LAMBS (kg)

Week	Experimental Group	Control Group
1	5.0	5.0
2	5.6	5.2
3	5.8	5.4
4	6.4	6.0
5	7.2	6.3

AVERAGE MASS OF LAMBS (kg)

Week	Experimental Group	Control Group
6	7.5	7.0
7	8.0	7.3
8	8.2	7.5
9	9.2	8.5
10	9.6	8.7

GRAPHS SHOWING MASS GAINS OF LAMBS WITH DIFFERENT DIETS

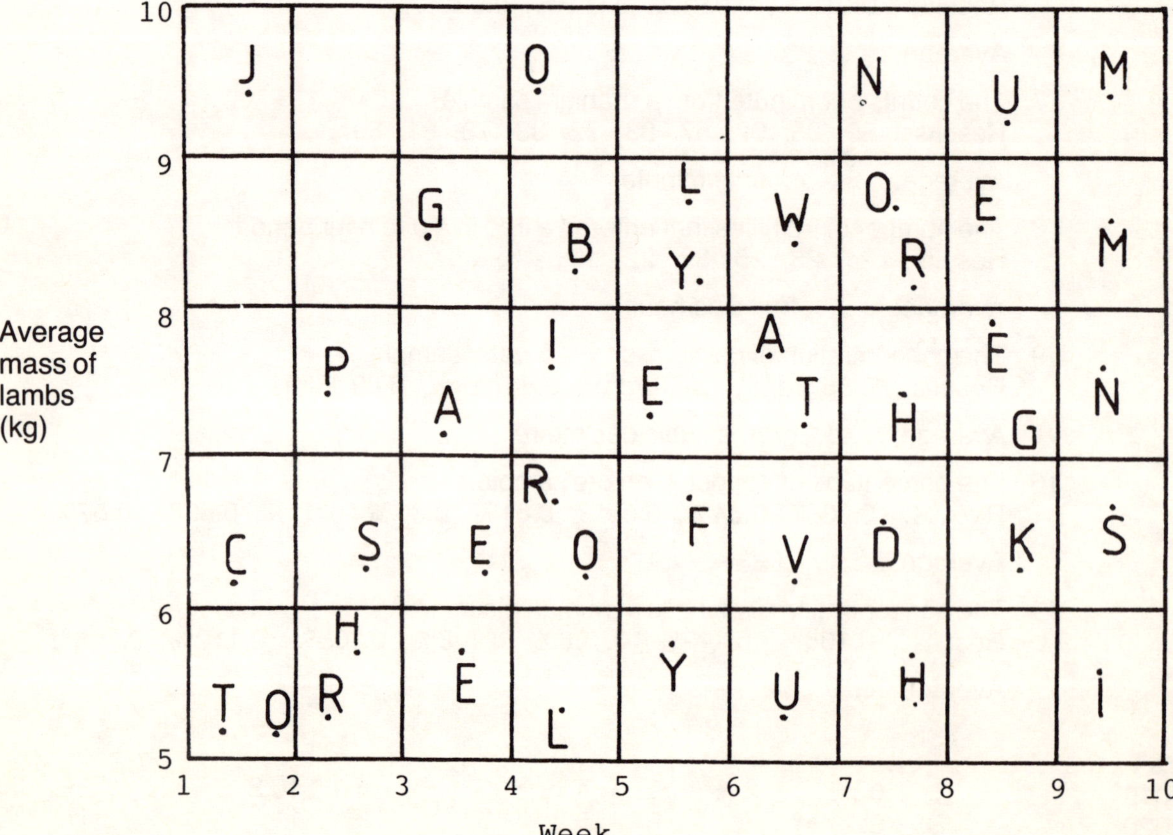

TOY TIME

WHY WOULDN'T ANYONE PLAY WITH THE BABY VAMPIRE ?

Each set of diagrams shows part of the scale of a measuring instrument. Record the reading shown on each instrument with its correct units. Find the corresponding letter in the key list and write it next to the number of the question. Read off the letters, in order, to get the answer to the riddle.

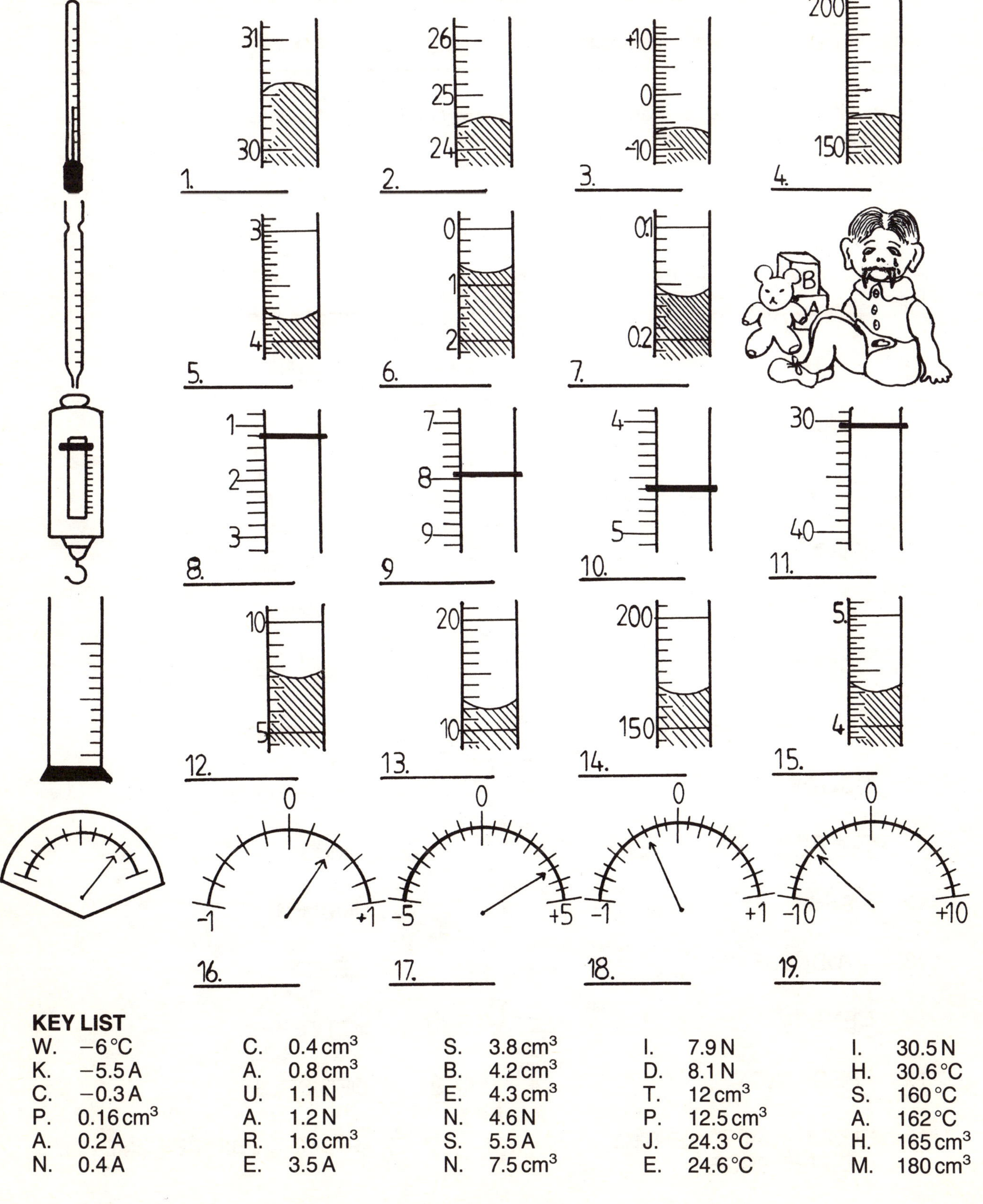

KEY LIST

W.	−6 °C	C.	$0.4\ cm^3$	S.	$3.8\ cm^3$	I.	7.9 N	I.	30.5 N
K.	−5.5 A	A.	$0.8\ cm^3$	B.	$4.2\ cm^3$	D.	8.1 N	H.	30.6 °C
C.	−0.3 A	U.	1.1 N	E.	$4.3\ cm^3$	T.	$12\ cm^3$	S.	160 °C
P.	$0.16\ cm^3$	A.	1.2 N	N.	4.6 N	P.	$12.5\ cm^3$	A.	162 °C
A.	0.2 A	R.	$1.6\ cm^3$	S.	5.5 A	J.	24.3 °C	H.	$165\ cm^3$
N.	0.4 A	E.	3.5 A	N.	$7.5\ cm^3$	E.	24.6 °C	M.	$180\ cm^3$

MEASURING MONSTERS

WHAT INSTRUMENT WOULD YOU USE TO EXAMINE MONSTERS?

Draw a line connecting each quantity with its correct units. Circle the letters through which the lines pass. Read down the circled letters to find the answer. No. 1 is done for you.

Quantity	Letters	Units
1. LENGTH	(T) H	DEGREES
2. TEMPERATURE	A	SECONDS
3. FORCE	S	METRES
4. TIME	E L O N	OHMS
5. ELECTRICAL RESISTANCE	H A	NEWTONS
6. VOLUME	D P E	PASCALS
7. VELOCITY	O F R R	WATTS
8. PRESSURE	W L	CUBIC DECIMETRES
9. ELECTRIC CURRENT	G O U	METRES/SECOND
10. POWER	R I W	KILOGRAMS
11. ENERGY	A S	AMPS
12. MASS	K T	JOULES
13. LOUDNESS	N	HERTZ
14. DENSITY	C M O	VOLTS
15. FREQUENCY	P A E	DECIBELS
16. ELECTRICAL POTENTIAL DIFFERENCE	J D	GRAMS/CUBIC CENTIMETRE

TUBULAR TANGLE

It's a hot day, and this seems the hard way to be making water for a drink. Label the pieces of laboratory apparatus.

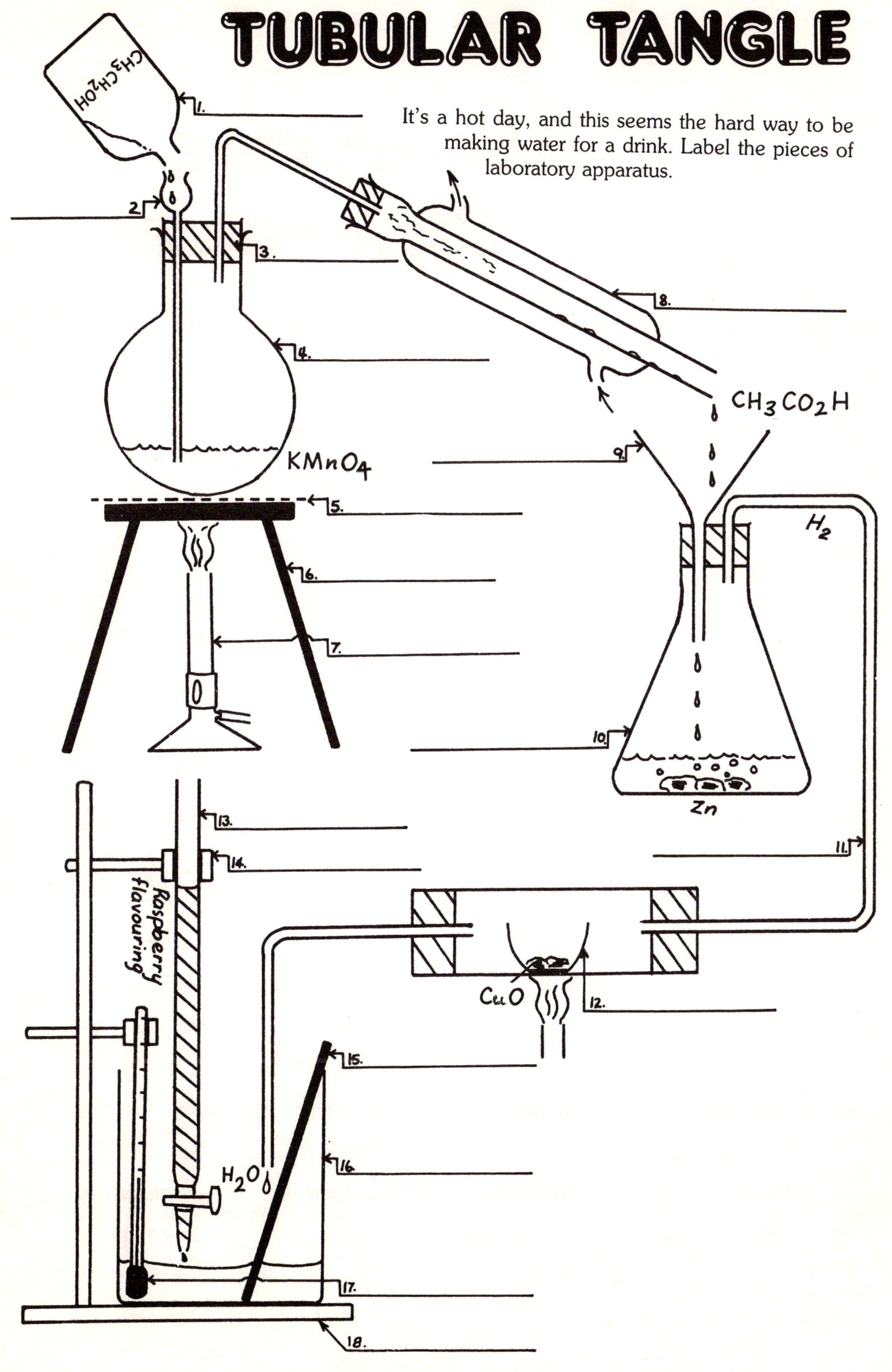

Discovering Differences

WHAT ARE THE FINEST ANIMALS ON EARTH?

Each set of four animals contains one member which is not classified in the same group as the others. Circle the letter next to the odd-man-out in each set. Read the circled letters down the page to find the answer.

1.	A.	Sting ray	T.	Stone fish	C.	Dog fish	R.	Hammerhead shark
2.	M.	Hawk	O.	Emu	H.	Bat	F.	Parrot
3.	E.	Turtle	X.	Newt	U.	Salamander	N.	Frog
4.	P.	Otter	W.	Beaver	T.	Platypus	C.	Tiger
5.	B.	Tortoise	S.	Dinosaur	D.	Snake	H.	Toad
6.	L.	Deer	G.	Porcupine	R.	Starfish	V.	Armadillo
7.	W.	Polar bear	Z.	Killer whale	A.	Sea-lion	E.	Tiger shark
8.	N.	Sheep	E.	Lion	Q.	Cow	B.	Goat
9.	F.	Whiting	S.	Electric eel	G.	Sting ray	D.	Plaice
10.	Y.	Toad	J.	Salamander	P.	Frog	R.	Mud skipper
11.	O.	Magpie	X.	Badger	N.	Rabbit	Q.	Monkey
12.	U.	Lamprey	I.	Haddock	M.	Cleaner fish	Z.	Angler fish
13.	K.	Snake	N.	Earthworm	B.	Possum	F.	Eel
14.	N.	Antelope	R.	Sperm whale	D.	Penguin	S.	Seal
15.	M.	*Archaeopteryx*	Z.	*Tyrannosaurus*	P.	*Diplodocus*	W.	*Brontosaurus*
16.	S.	Chimpanzee	I.	Rhesus monkey	T.	Gorilla	U.	Orang-utan
17.	E.	Deer	M.	Buffalo	V.	Cow	C.	Horse
18.	E.	Leopard	G.	Fox	J.	Wolf	A.	Pekinese

Fish, Feathers and Fur

WHY DON'T THEY HAVE FROGS IN THE ARMY ?

Identify the group to which each animal, or part of an animal, belongs. For each one find the corresponding letter from the key list and put it in the box with the number of the drawing.

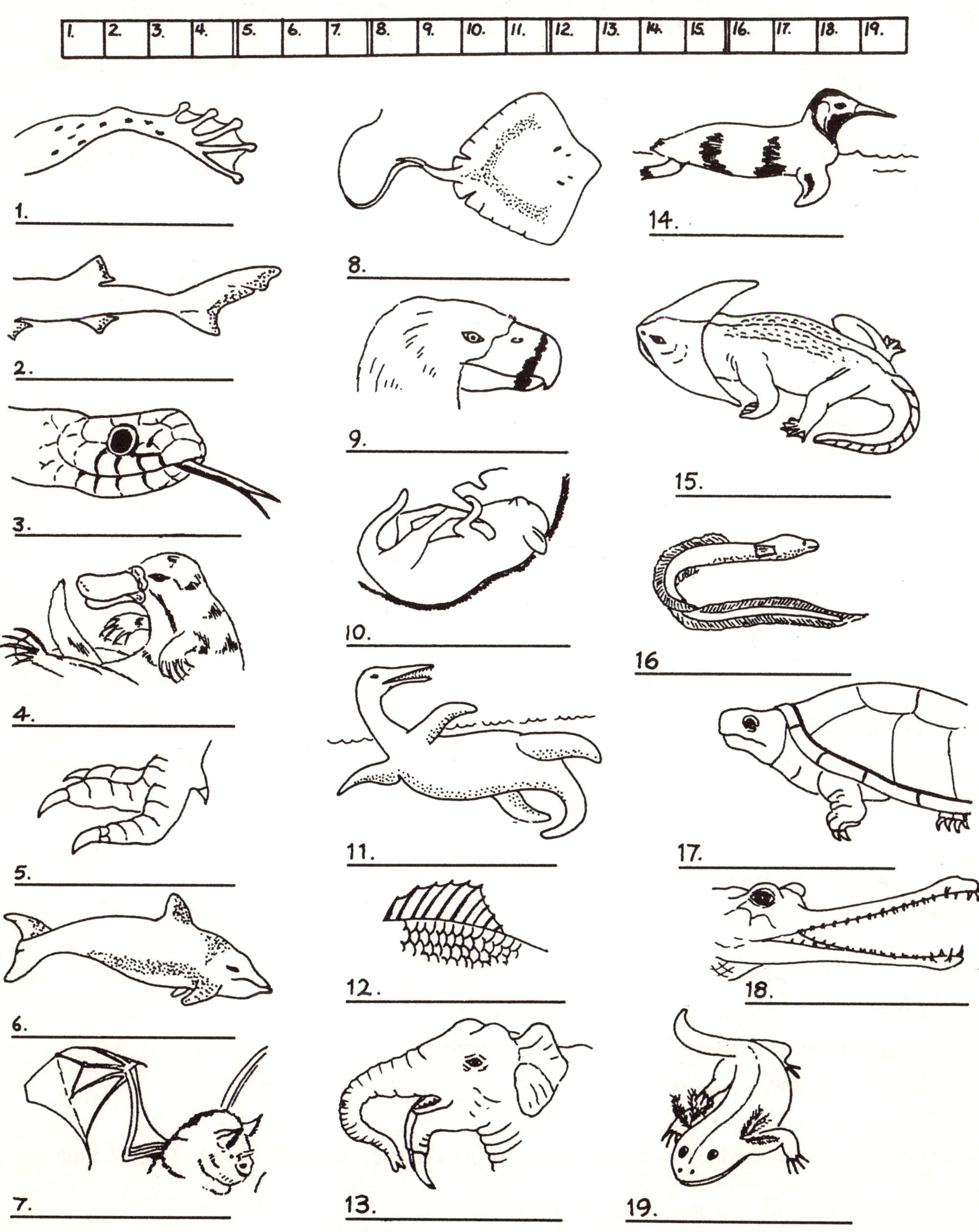

KEY LIST

H. Cartilaginous fish (the shark family)
F. Bony fish
T. Amphibians
E. Reptiles
A. Birds
Y. Monotremes (a type of mammal; egg layers that suckle their young)
V. Marsupials
L. True mammals

The Food Chain Game

WHAT IS GREEN, HAS TWO LEGS AND A TRUNK ?

Select the food chain which **best** fits each description below. For each one write the code letter for the food chain next to the number of the question. Not all food chains need to be used; some may be used more than once. Read down the letters to get the answer to the riddle.

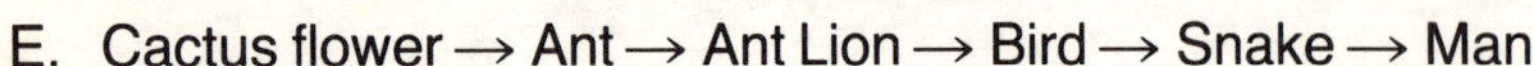

E. Cactus flower → Ant → Ant Lion → Bird → Snake → Man

K. Phytoplankton → Krill → Small fish → Large fish → Man

C. Seaweed → Man

I. Lettuce → Snail → Man

U. Phytoplankton → Zooplankton → Anchovy protein supplement → Cow → Man

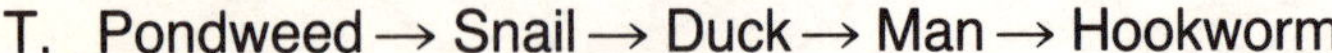

T. Pondweed → Snail → Duck → Man → Hookworm

S. Lichen → Caribou → Man

R. Banana → Bird → Monkey → Man

A. Phytoplankton → Zooplankton → Small fish → Large fish → Seal → Polar bear → Man

D. Leaf → Caterpillar → Chicken → Man

O. Mushroom → Man

M. Potato → Pig → Man

1. The greatest percentage of energy is lost between the primary producer and the top consumer.
2. The first member of the food chain is made up of two different organisms living together in a symbiotic relationship.
3. Man is a fifth order consumer.
4. Man would be at the greatest risk of accumulating mercury if the marine environment became polluted with this element.
5. Man is most likely to accumulate strontium-90 if the environment were exposed to radioactive fall-out.
6. Man is feeding on an invertebrate.
7. Least energy is likely to be lost through the food chain.
8. The organisms are found in an Antarctic environment.
9. There is a parasite in the food chain.
10. There is no primary producer.
11. Man is likely to be making the most wasteful use of food resources and having the most harmful effect on a natural ecosystem.
12. There are two primates in the food chain.
13. French cuisine?!
14. Man is likely to have the wolf as a competitor.
15. Man is not the top consumer.

WEB OF WORDS

ACROSS

2. Organism which can make its own food
5. Gas needed by most living things
7. Environment which may have a low oxygen concentration
8. Useful for observing animals in their habitats
10. Important consumer in the soil
13. Decomposers
14. Every organism lives in one of these
15. Part of a nuclear reactor which could cause major pollution
16. Introduced species?
18. Too much of this ion pollutes water (formula)
19. Number of consumers in this food chain: alga → periwinkle → seagull
20. Harmful rodents
22. Unit of radiation dosage
23. A decomposer of bread
25. Network of interrelationships between living things
26. Important substance in any environment, without which life dies
27. Freshwater ecosystem

DOWN

1. Likely soil problem when vegetation is removed
2. This unbalances an ecosystem
3. Number of producers in this food chain: grass → antelope → lion
4. Organism which can't make its own food
6. Ion needed by plants for protein production
8. Place where an organism lives
9. An organism which breaks down dead plants and/or animals
11. An animal which gets its food by entering other animals
12. Metal pollutant
14. The sun is the source of .... for almost all living things
17. May be done when making a population count of wild animals
21. Parasite that sounds like a clock
24. Insecticide banned in many countries because of pollution problems

Researching Relationships

WHAT DO WELL-DRESSED FROGS WEAR?

Next to each of the following statements write **T** if the statement is always true, **F** if it is always false, and **S** if it is sometimes true and sometimes false. Each group of three questions codes for one letter. Check the code list and write the letters in the numbered boxes.

1	2	3	4	5	6	7	8	9

1A. A dog and a tick have a happy relationship.
1B. Oxygen is produced during photosynthesis. … … …
1C. Decomposition occurs more rapidly in warm, moist conditions.
2A. Food chains start with green plants.
2B. Energy is lost going up a food chain. … … …
2C. Living organisms need light for growth.
3A. A pig and a tapeworm have a symbiotic relationship.
3B. Rain forest soil is very fertile. … … …
3C. Carbon dioxide is produced during aerobic respiration.
4A. Both organisms in a parasitical relationship cannot survive alone.
4B. A parasite lives inside another animal. … … …
4C. In the food chain Plant plankton → Krill → Whale the krill is a primary consumer.
5A. Bacteria are decomposers.
5B. Green plants make sugar from carbon dioxide and water. … … …
5C. Every organism has its own ecological niche; that is, place in nature.
6A. Living organisms need nitrogen in the form of nitrates.
6B. Polar bears are carnivores. … … …
6C. The top consumer is the largest organism in a food chain.
7A. A cow has a symbiotic relationship with the cellulose-digesting animals normally found in its gut.
7B. Flatworms are parasites. … … …
7C. Primary producers are green plants.
8A. Cold water contains more nutrients than warm water.
8B. Chimpanzees are heterotrophs. … … …
8C. An animal's habitat describes what it does.
9A. Living organisms need oxygen.
9B. Two different species cannot share the same ecological niche. … … …
9C. In the food chain Wheat → Cow → Man man is a secondary consumer.

CODE LIST

A.	TTT	F.	TFS	K.	FTF	P.	FST	U.	STS	Z.	SSF
B.	TTF	G.	TST	L.	FTS	Q.	FSF	V.	SFT		
C.	TTS	H.	TSF	M.	FFT	R.	FSS	W.	SFF		
D.	TFT	I.	TSS	N.	FFF	S.	STT	X.	SFS		
E.	TFF	J.	FTT	O.	FFS	T.	STF	Y.	SST		

Population Problems

ON WHAT SORT OF LIFEBOATS WOULD YOU EXPECT TO FIND SHIP-WRECKED VAMPIRES ?

H.M.S. 'Disaster' has sunk near an uninhabited desert island. Fifty men and fifty women survive. Calculate the changes in the population of the island during the next twelve years and plot the points on the axes below. Your curve should pass through the letters which spell out the answer to the riddle.

Year	Events	Population
1.	There is a 12% birth rate but 2% of the adults are taken by sharks.	....
2.	The birth rate is 10% this year. Another 4 castaways arrive.	....
3.	At the beginning of the year 4% of the population die from scurvy. The birth rate is again 10%	....
4.	8 babies are born at the beginning of the year, then 5% of the population are fatally injured by falling coconuts.	....
5.	7 babies are born and there is 1 death. 9 of the inhabitants take a boat out fishing and are never seen again.	....
6.	10% birth rate – no deaths this year.	....
7.	Another quiet year – except for the nurse – 17 babies are born.	....
8.	A 5% birth rate, but 7.5% of the population expire through sheer boredom.	....
9.	4 babies are born, and 20 survivors from yet another shipwreck are washed ashore.	....
10.	Birth-rate is 5%. There are fears of overcrowding.	....
11.	Yet another 11 babies are born. A lottery is drawn and 10% of the population have to start swimming for another island. Overcome by despair, 5% of the remainder commit suicide.	....
12.	Rescue! But sadly the HMS 'Recovery' only has room for 71 passengers; the rest must stay on their island home.	....

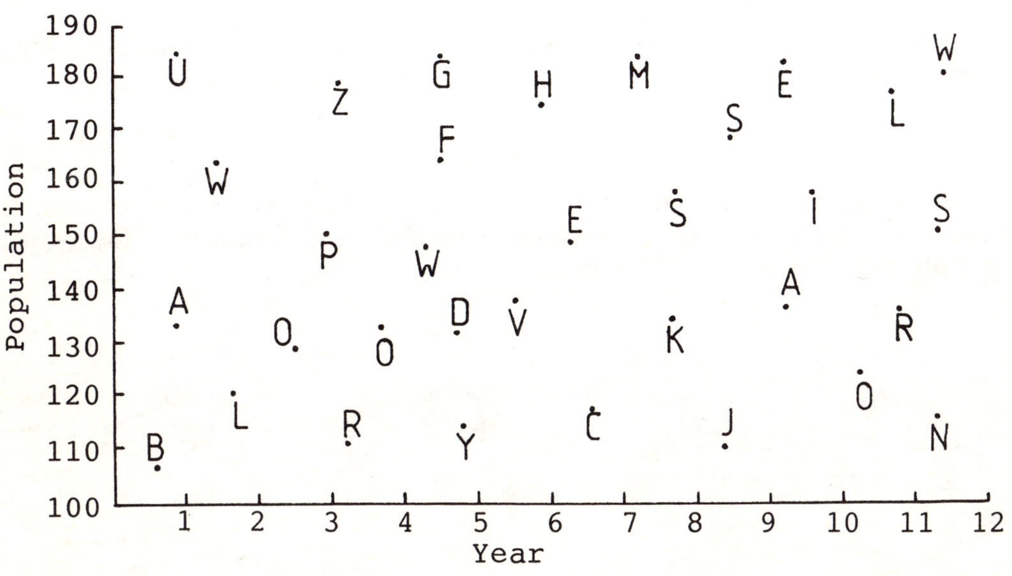

What am I ?

1. The first European who saw me thought that I was born inside mum's pouch. How wrong can you be! Mind you, I'm very tiny when I'm born, and once I get into mum's pouch it's a long time before I see the light of day again.

   I am a ....

2. Some people don't like my soft moist skin but I'm kind of attached to it. Besides, it helps me to get the oxygen I need. My early days were spent in water, but now I get around on land quite a lot. But if I want to start a family I'll have to go back to the pond.

   I am a ....

3. None of this nasty wet stuff for me. I'm above all that. When I lay my eggs they've got a good hard shell. I'm warm-blooded too, and though I live in the tropics I've got relatives who hang out in the antarctic.

   I am a ....

4. I guess I'm not really a very lovable character. My rows of teeth just keep growing, and you wouldn't want to cuddle up to my sandpapery skin. 'Cold-blooded' they call me, and I guess they could be right.

   I am a ....

5. The say I'm cold-blooded too, but give me a chance to wriggle into the sun and I'll be the hottest thing around. I'm better off than Fred Frog; he doesn't have my super scaly water-proof skin.

   I am a ....

6. I am a pretty exclusive character. Only found in Australia, and despite my rows of spines, I'm an egg-layer like our feathered friends. Oh, yes . . . just to complicate things, I feed my young on milk.

   I am a ....

7. I'm much more successful than my sharky relations. Swim bladder for buoyancy, protective plate over my gills, and . . . sad to say . . . I'm one of the best food sources you humans have got.

   I am a ....

8. Well, what have that lot got to boast about? **I'm** the most advanced vertebrate around. Body temperature? Under perfect control. And none of this nonsense about eggs or pouches. **My** babies get the best of care and attention before and after birth.

   I am a ....

A TALL STORY

HOW DOES AN ELEPHANT GET TO THE TOP OF AN OAK TREE ?

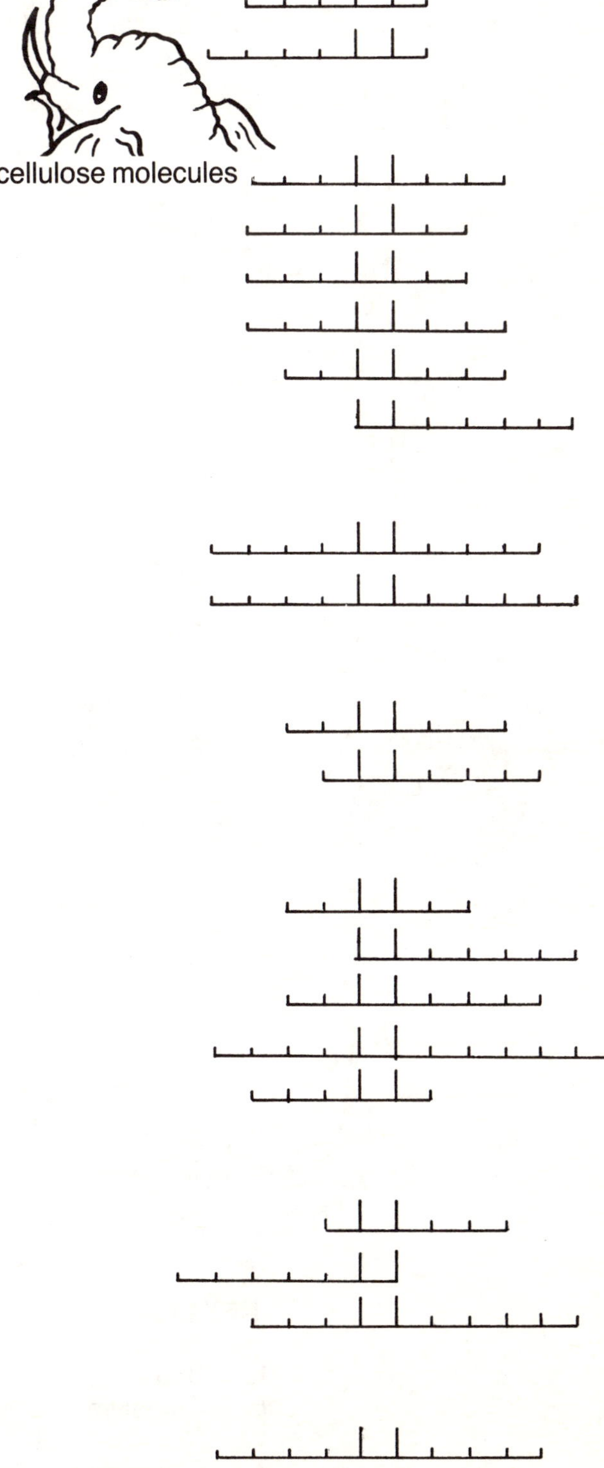

1. Radiant energy needed by plants
2. Gas produced during photosynthesis

3. Simple sugar which is a building block of starch and cellulose molecules
4. Female reproductive cells in flowering plants
5. Chemical used to test for starch
6. Tiny openings on underside of a leaf
7. Stage of plant development within the seed
8. Asexual reproductive cells of ferns

9. Chemical which makes up plant cell walls
10. Important element needed by plants

11. Carbohydrate which plants use as an energy store
12. Part of the flower which produces pollen

13. Cells which surround a stoma
14. } Gas used in photosynthesis
15. }
16. Green plant pigment
17. Transport system in 'higher' plants

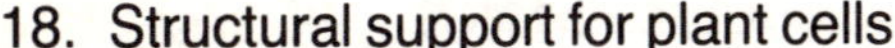

18. Structural support for plant cells
19. Male reproductive cells of flowering plants
20. Outer layer of cells in a leaf

21. Used to test for carbon dioxide
22. Photosynthesis sites of plants
23. Peas hold on with these
24. 'Fruit sugar'
25. These take in water and minerals

FLOWER POWER

WHAT GOES 'CLOMP, CLOMP, CLOMP, SQUISH ....
CLOMP, CLOMP, CLOMP, SQUISH ....' ?

Use the words from the key list to label the diagrams below. For each one, write the letter that is next to the word from the key list in the box with the same number as the label. (Each label is used only once.)

1.	2.	3.	4.	5.	6.	7.	8.	9.	10.	11.	12.	13.	14.	15.	16.	17.	18.	19.	20.	21.	22.	23.	24.	25.

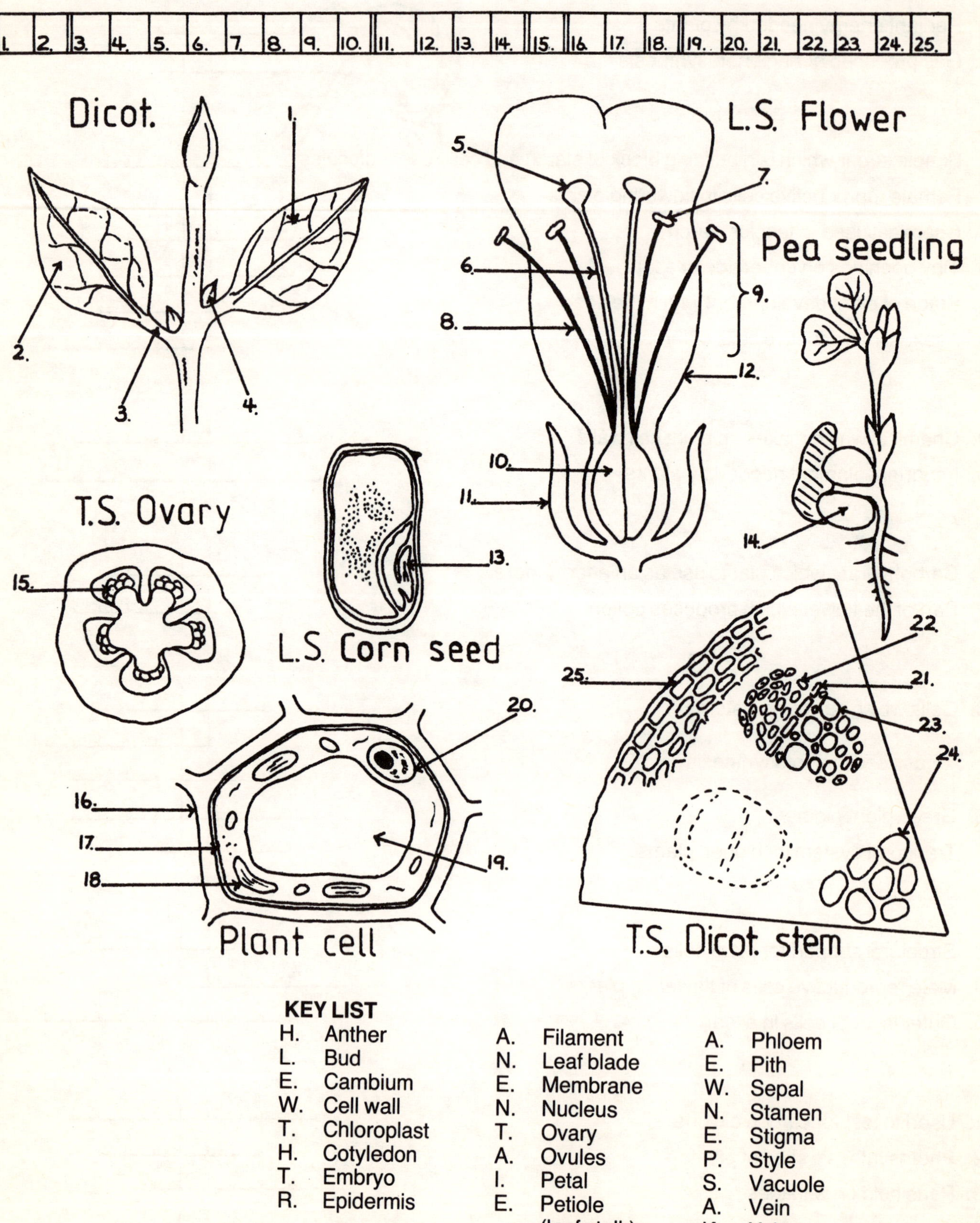

KEY LIST

H.	Anther	A.	Filament	A.	Phloem
L.	Bud	N.	Leaf blade	E.	Pith
E.	Cambium	E.	Membrane	W.	Sepal
W.	Cell wall	N.	Nucleus	N.	Stamen
T.	Chloroplast	T.	Ovary	E.	Stigma
H.	Cotyledon	A.	Ovules	P.	Style
T.	Embryo	I.	Petal	S.	Vacuole
R.	Epidermis	E.	Petiole (leaf stalk)	A.	Vein
				K.	Xylem

VERTEBRATE VIBES

Next to each of the following statements write **T** if the statement is always true, **F** if it is always false, and **S** if it is sometimes true and sometimes false. Each group of three questions codes for one letter. Check the code list and write the letters in the numbered boxes.

WHO ATE ITS VICTIMS TWO BY TWO?

Code List

A	TTT	D	TFT	G	TST	J	FTT	M	FFT	P	FST	S	STT	V	SFT	Y	SST		
B	TTF	E	TFF	H	TSF	K	FTF	N	FFF	Q	FSF	T	STF	W	SFF	Z	SSF		
C	TTS	F	TFS	I	TSS	L	FTS	O	FFS	R	FSS	U	STS	X	SFS				

1	2	3	4	5	6	7	8	9	10

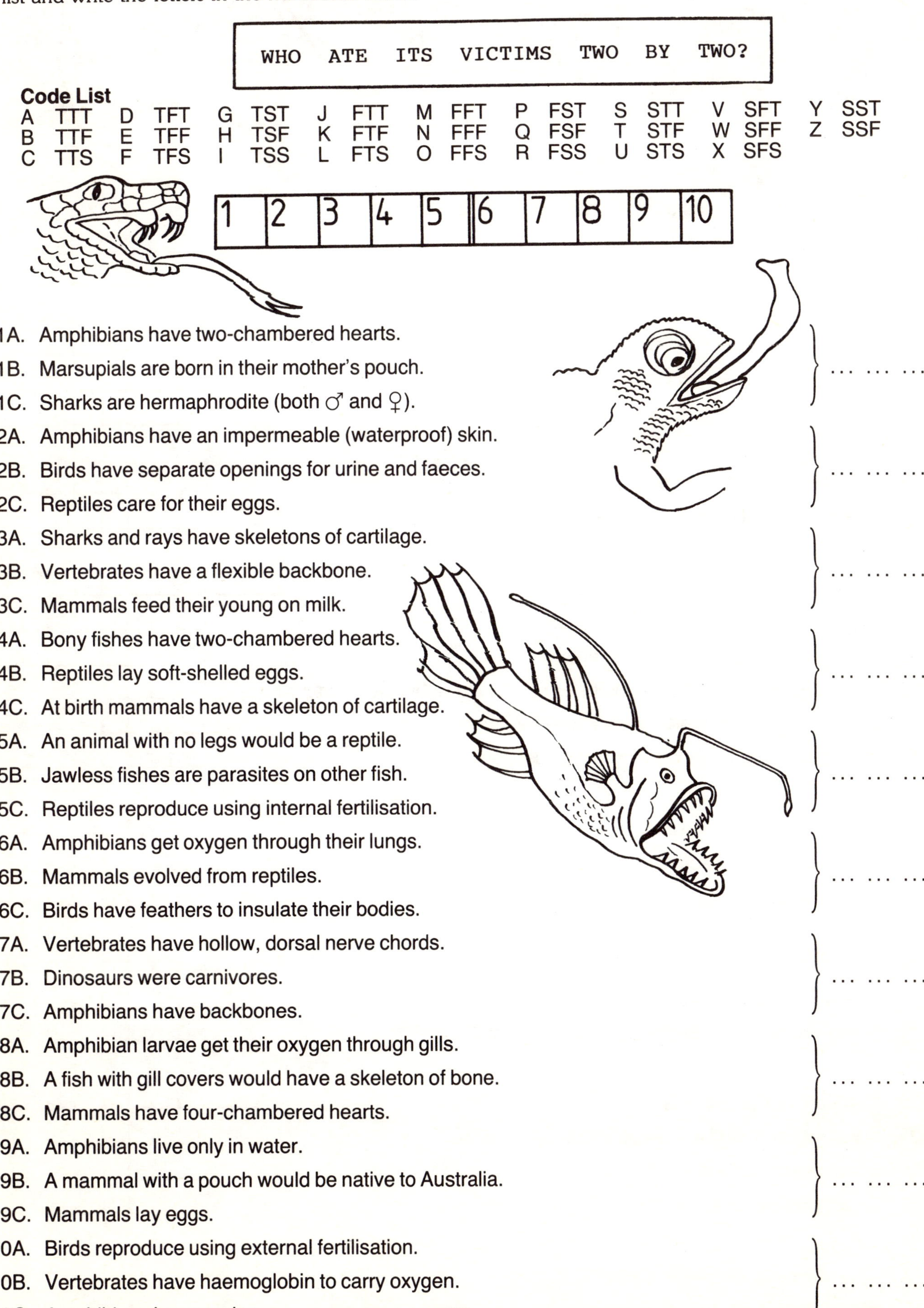

1A. Amphibians have two-chambered hearts.
1B. Marsupials are born in their mother's pouch.
1C. Sharks are hermaphrodite (both ♂ and ♀). } ... ...

2A. Amphibians have an impermeable (waterproof) skin.
2B. Birds have separate openings for urine and faeces.
2C. Reptiles care for their eggs. } ... ...

3A. Sharks and rays have skeletons of cartilage.
3B. Vertebrates have a flexible backbone.
3C. Mammals feed their young on milk. } ... ...

4A. Bony fishes have two-chambered hearts.
4B. Reptiles lay soft-shelled eggs.
4C. At birth mammals have a skeleton of cartilage. } ... ...

5A. An animal with no legs would be a reptile.
5B. Jawless fishes are parasites on other fish.
5C. Reptiles reproduce using internal fertilisation. } ... ...

6A. Amphibians get oxygen through their lungs.
6B. Mammals evolved from reptiles.
6C. Birds have feathers to insulate their bodies. } ... ...

7A. Vertebrates have hollow, dorsal nerve chords.
7B. Dinosaurs were carnivores.
7C. Amphibians have backbones. } ... ...

8A. Amphibian larvae get their oxygen through gills.
8B. A fish with gill covers would have a skeleton of bone.
8C. Mammals have four-chambered hearts. } ... ...

9A. Amphibians live only in water.
9B. A mammal with a pouch would be native to Australia.
9C. Mammals lay eggs. } ... ...

10A. Birds reproduce using external fertilisation.
10B. Vertebrates have haemoglobin to carry oxygen.
10C. Amphibians have scales. } ... ...

Camel Capers

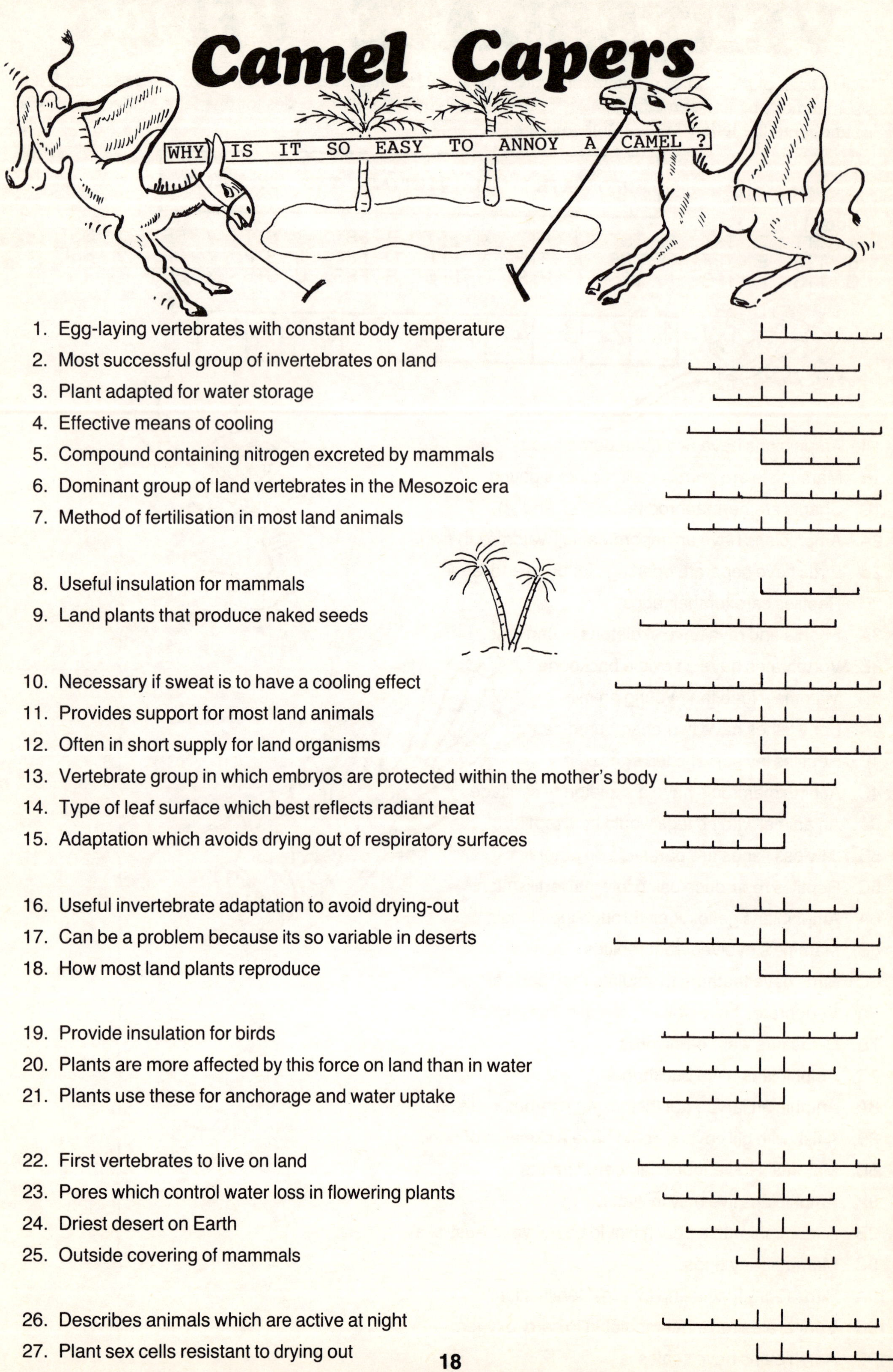

WHY IS IT SO EASY TO ANNOY A CAMEL ?

1. Egg-laying vertebrates with constant body temperature
2. Most successful group of invertebrates on land
3. Plant adapted for water storage
4. Effective means of cooling
5. Compound containing nitrogen excreted by mammals
6. Dominant group of land vertebrates in the Mesozoic era
7. Method of fertilisation in most land animals
8. Useful insulation for mammals
9. Land plants that produce naked seeds
10. Necessary if sweat is to have a cooling effect
11. Provides support for most land animals
12. Often in short supply for land organisms
13. Vertebrate group in which embryos are protected within the mother's body
14. Type of leaf surface which best reflects radiant heat
15. Adaptation which avoids drying out of respiratory surfaces
16. Useful invertebrate adaptation to avoid drying-out
17. Can be a problem because its so variable in deserts
18. How most land plants reproduce
19. Provide insulation for birds
20. Plants are more affected by this force on land than in water
21. Plants use these for anchorage and water uptake
22. First vertebrates to live on land
23. Pores which control water loss in flowering plants
24. Driest desert on Earth
25. Outside covering of mammals
26. Describes animals which are active at night
27. Plant sex cells resistant to drying out

IT'S CYTOLOGICAL

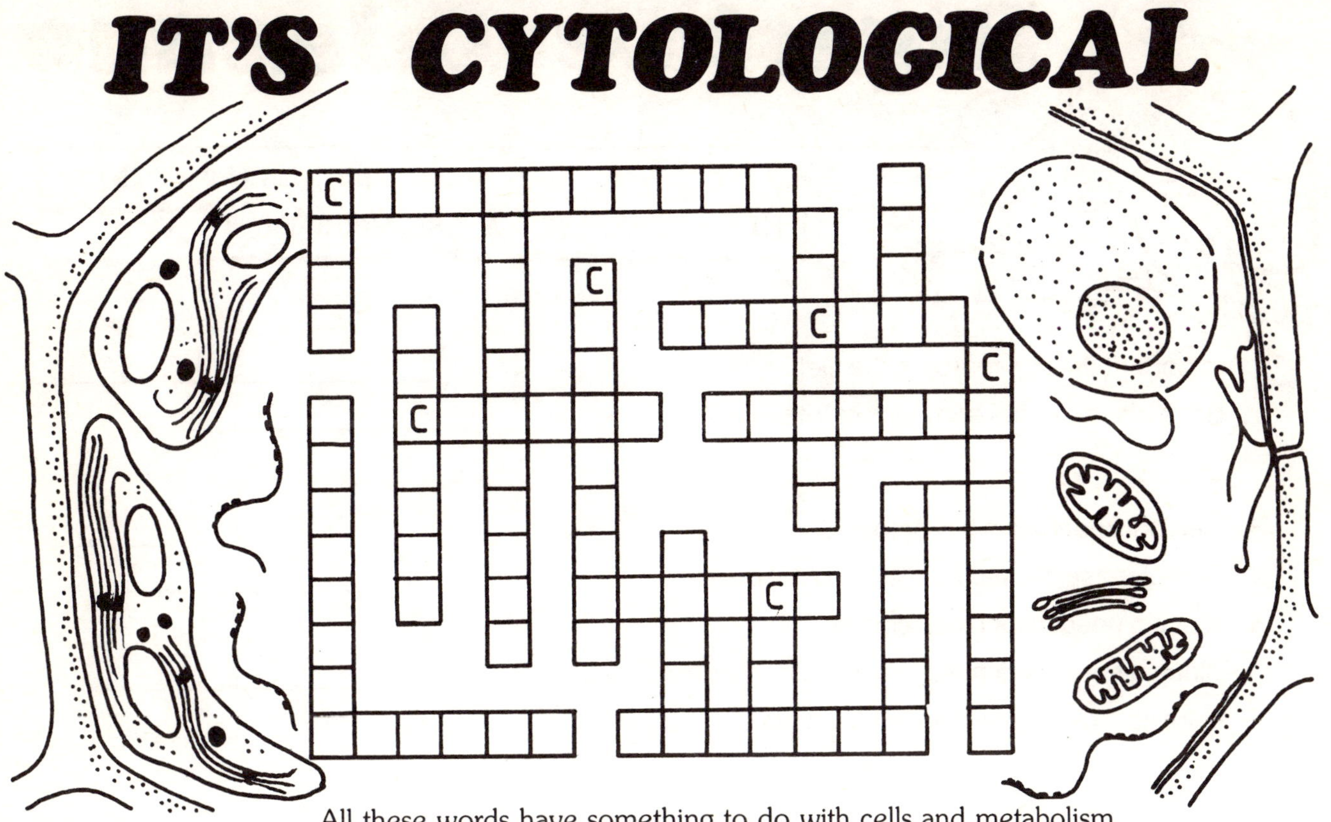

All these words have something to do with cells and metabolism.
Can you unscramble them and fit them into the puzzle?
There are clues to help you.

	Clue	Scrambled	Answer
1.	Building block of living things	LECL	....
2.	Makes up plant cell walls	LECLUSOLE	....
3.	Green plant pigment	ROCHLOYPHLL	....
4.	Gas used in photosynthesis	RACNOB XIODIDE	....
5.	Part of cell outside the nucleus	OTYCSALPM	....
6.	Obtained by process of respiration	GERNEY	....
7.	Used for energy storage in animals	SAFT	....
8.	Surrounds all cells	BEMRANEM	....
9.	High-energy compound in seeds	LOI	....
10.	Most abundant chemical in a cell	TAWRE	....
11.	Control-centre in the cell	LUNCSEU	....
12.	Immediate source of energy for animals	CULGSOE	....
13.	Storage depot in a cell	UCAVOLE	....
14.	Stops red cells escaping from a cut	TOLC	....
15.	Compound which stores energy in plants	RATSCH	....
16.	Complex molecule made up of amino acids	TORPINE	....
17.	Releases energy from food	PERSRIATION	....
18.	Gas needed by most living things	NEOXGY	....

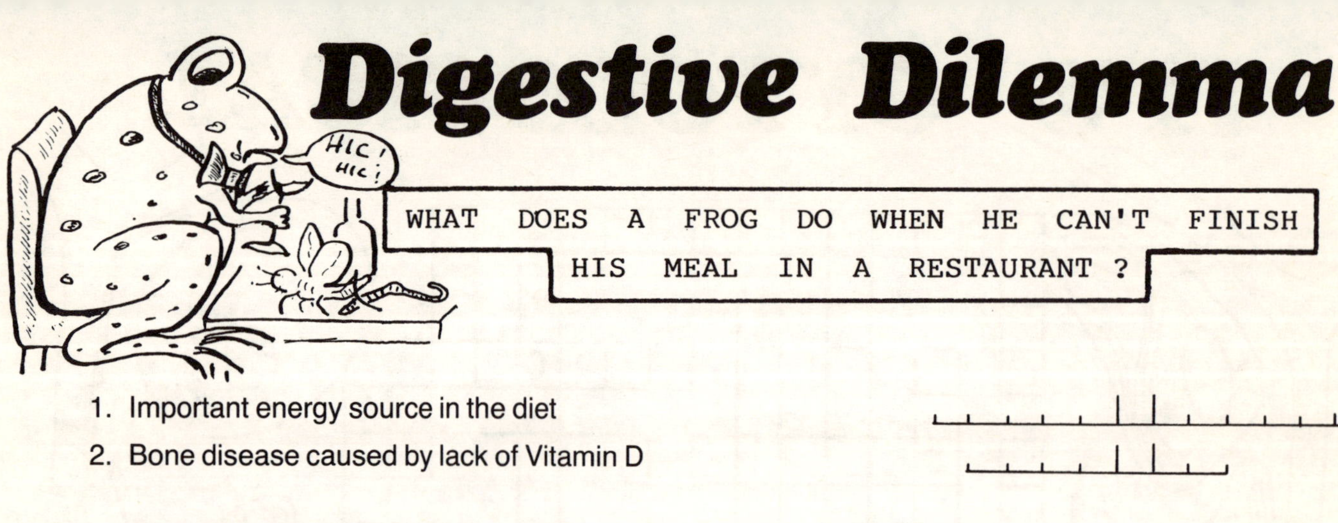

Digestive Dilemma

WHAT DOES A FROG DO WHEN HE CAN'T FINISH HIS MEAL IN A RESTAURANT ?

1. Important energy source in the diet
2. Bone disease caused by lack of Vitamin D
3. Nutrients needed in tiny amounts
4. Skin disease caused by vitamin B deficiency
5. Vitamin needed for blood clotting
6. Blood disease which may be caused by iron deficiency
7. Caused by severe shortage of vitamin C
8. Mineral needed for functioning of thyroid gland
9. Needed to make enzymes, and for growth and repair
10. Part of the brain which controls appetite
11. Unit for measuring energy content of food
12. Responsible for much spoilage of stored foods
13. Protein-digesting enzymes
14. Severe protein deficiency disease
15. Mineral needed for production of haemoglobin
16. Mineral needed for healthy bones and teeth
17. Acid which is an important B vitamin needed for iron absorption
18. Inorganic nutrients
19. Important mineral but excess may cause high blood pressure
20. Thyroid disease caused by iodine deficiency
21. 'Blood sugar'
22. Proteins that speed up chemical reactions in living organisms
23. Important acid found in many fruits and vegetables
24. Deficiency of this vitamin may result in night blindness
25. Process by which food is broken down into small enough particles to be absorbed

Filling in Facts

WHERE WOULD YOU FIND A FROG DENTIST ?

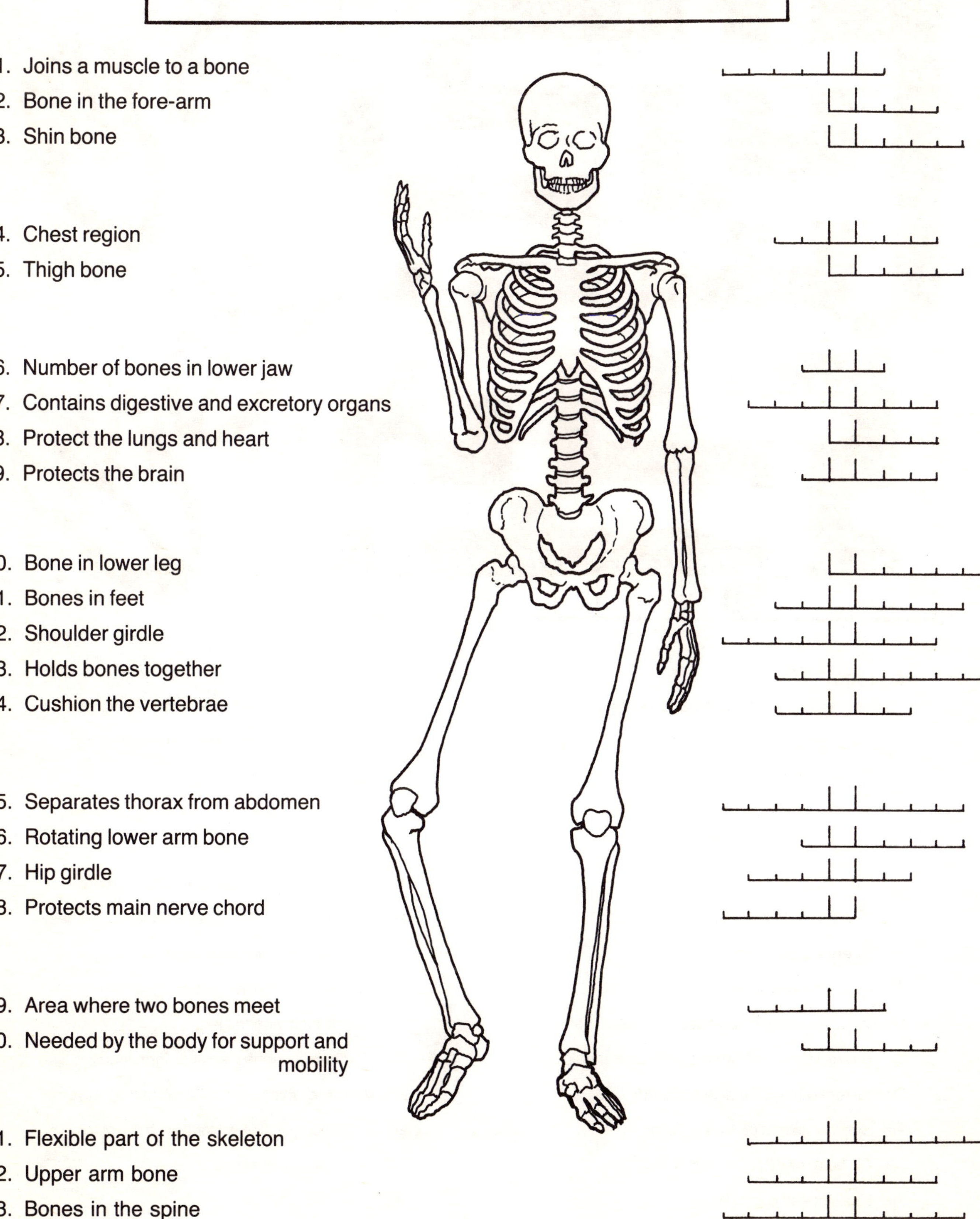

1. Joins a muscle to a bone
2. Bone in the fore-arm
3. Shin bone
4. Chest region
5. Thigh bone
6. Number of bones in lower jaw
7. Contains digestive and excretory organs
8. Protect the lungs and heart
9. Protects the brain
10. Bone in lower leg
11. Bones in feet
12. Shoulder girdle
13. Holds bones together
14. Cushion the vertebrae
15. Separates thorax from abdomen
16. Rotating lower arm bone
17. Hip girdle
18. Protects main nerve chord
19. Area where two bones meet
20. Needed by the body for support and mobility
21. Flexible part of the skeleton
22. Upper arm bone
23. Bones in the spine
24. Broken bone
25. Type of joint in elbow

HAVE – A – HEART

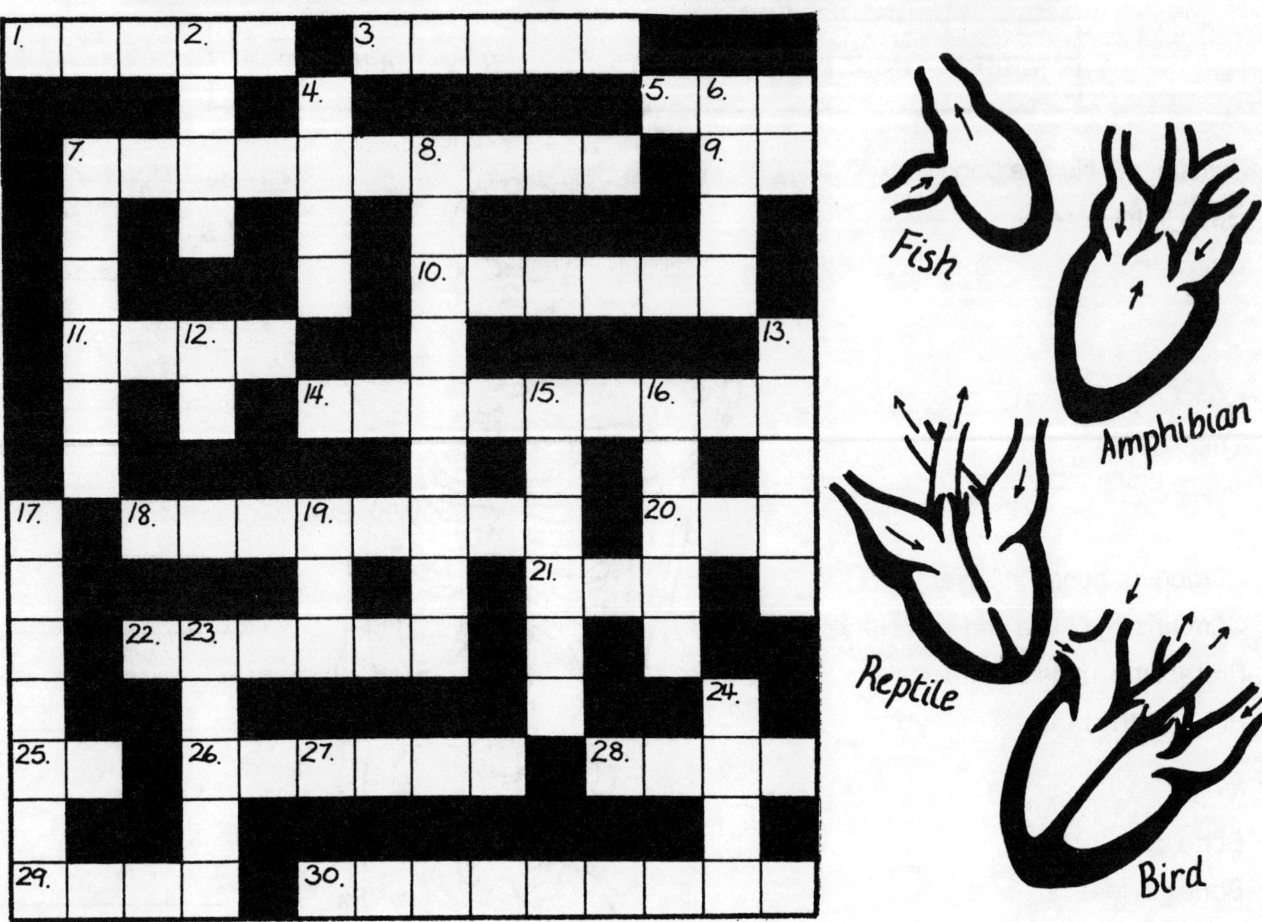

ACROSS

1. Prevents back flow of blood in a vein
3. Cells which fight infection
5. Study of heart's electrical activity
7. Main pumping chambers of the heart
9. Uncommon blood group
10. Liquid part of the blood
11. Carries blood back to the heart
14. Artery supplying the lungs
18. Artery supplying the heart
20. Possible effect of too much smoking
21. Needs increased blood supply after meals
22. Vessel with high pressure blood
25. Negative blood grouping factor
26. Globular protein in blood or muscle
28. Basic unit of living things
29. Auricle which receives blood from the lungs
30. Cell fragments involved in clotting

DOWN

2. And 6: Largest vein in the body (2 words)
4. Element needed to make haemoglobin
6. See No. 2 Down
7. They keep a one-way flow through the heart
8. Microscopic blood vessel
12. Shorthand of way for giving transfusions
13. Fluid which must be drained back to the heart
15. Gas carried by haemoglobin
16. Largest artery in the body
17. Artery supplying the leg
19. Number of arteries leaving right ventricle
23. Ventricle which pumps blood to the lungs
24. May cause a stroke if lodges in the brain
27. Common blood group

Circulation Challenge

How does a glucose molecule get from your mouth to a muscle in your leg where it is used to provide energy? Assume that the molecule takes the most direct path possible. Select, in order, from the key list below the names of the eighteen parts of the body through which the molecule will travel. Not all the parts in the key list have to be used, and you may use the same part more than once. Note that, for simplicity, the arterioles, venules and capillaries have been left out. Each time you select a part of the body, continue the line joining up the corresponding letters on the mystery diagram which shows a popular source of carbohydrate.

KEY LIST

A. Aorta
B. Carotid artery
C. Carotid vein
D. Coronary artery
E. Femoral artery
F. Gall bladder
G. Hepatic portal vein
H. Hepatic vein
I. Kidney
J. Large intestine
K. Left auricle
L. Left ventricle
M. Leg muscle
N. Liver
O. Lungs
P. Mouth
Q. Oesophagus
R. Pancreas
S. Pulmonary artery
T. Pulmonary vein
U. Renal artery
V. Right auricle
W. Right ventricle
X. Small intestine
Y. Stomach
Z. Vena cava

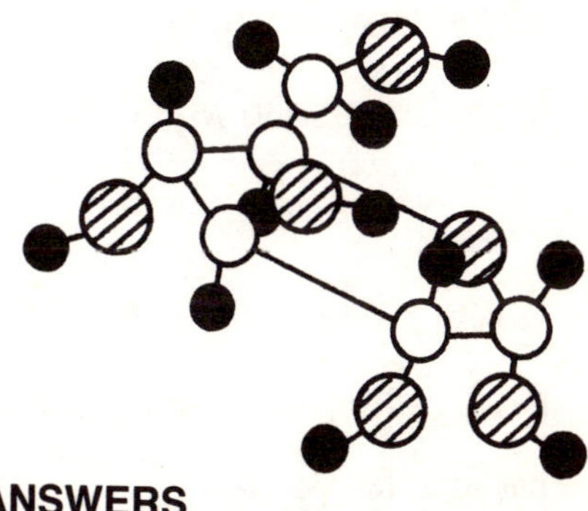

ANSWERS

1. ....
2. ....
3. ....
4. ....
5. ....
6. ....
7. ....
8. ....
9. ....
10. ....
11. ....
12. ....
13. ....
14. ....
15. ....
16. ....
17. ....
18. ....

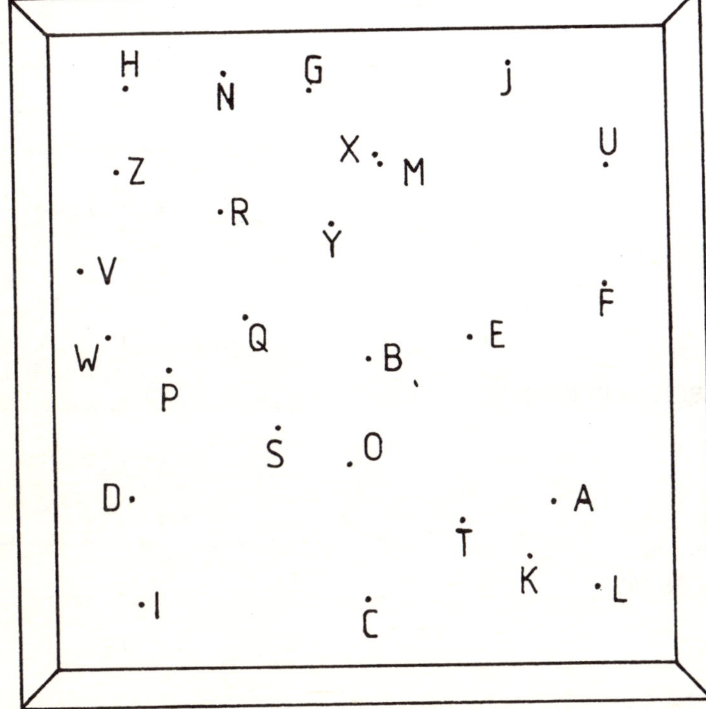

A Breathtaking Mystery

WHY ARE VAMPIRES UNWELCOME IN BLOOD BANKS ?

1. Ventricle which pumps blood to lungs
2. Tubes carrying air to lungs from trachea
3. Blood flows from the lungs to the heart in the pulmonary ....
4. Lung disease in which the air sacs collapse

5. Sugar which is oxidised in respiration
6. Artery carrying blood to lungs
7. Protein which carries oxygen
8. Gas needed by all living cells in the body

9. Disease which fills lungs with fluid
10. Air passage from mouth to bronchi
11. Larynx is necessary for this form of communication
12. Air sacs

13. Produces red blood cells
14. Process that releases energy from food
15. Serious bacterial lung disease
16. Sheet of muscle needed for breathing
17. Blood cells which carry oxygen
18. Ion produced when carbon dioxide dissolves in plasma
19. Contains lungs, heart and ribs
20. Produced during respiration
21. Blood vessels where gas exchange takes place
22. Tiny 'hairs' lining bronchi
23. Problem if too much in lungs

A Growing Problem

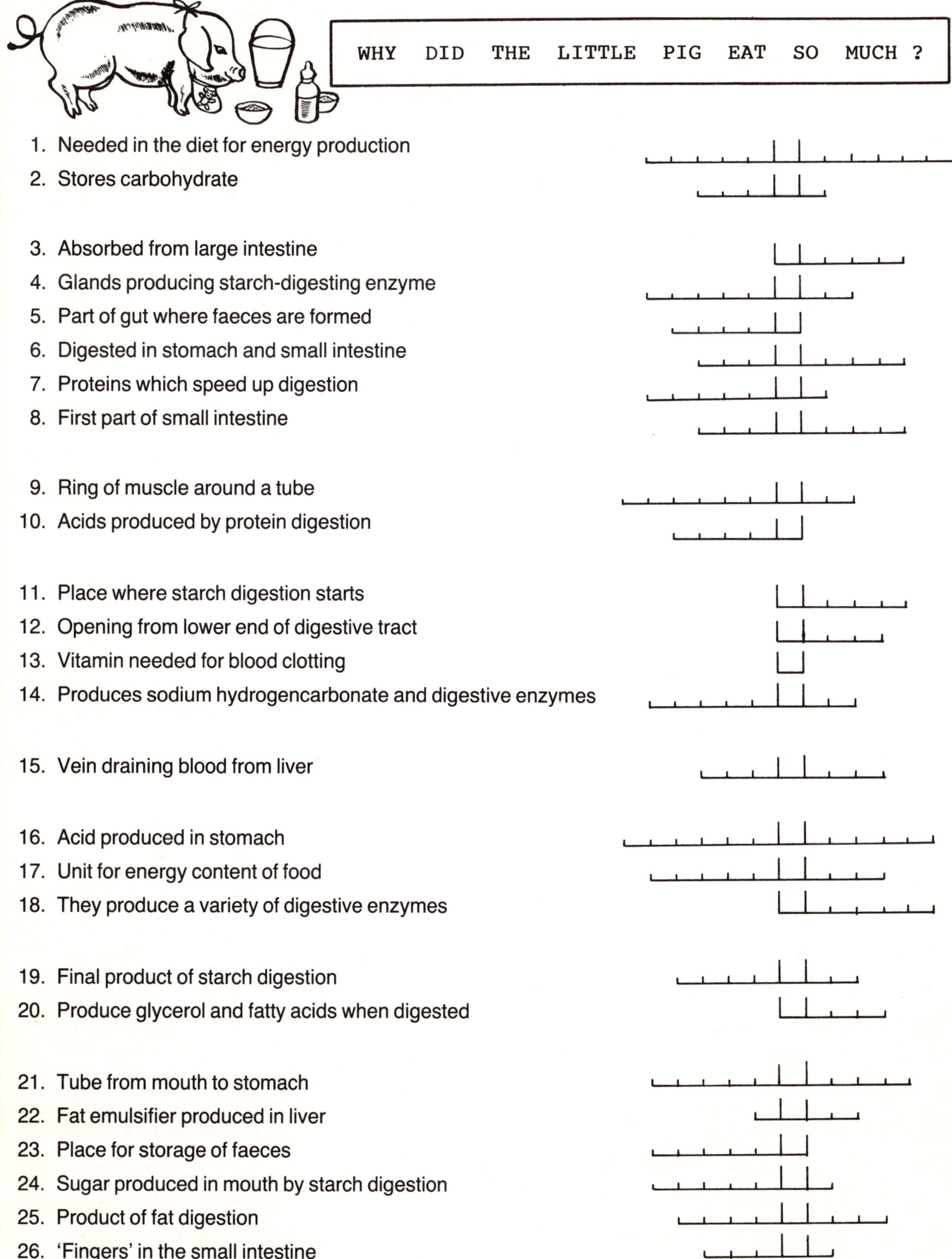

WHY DID THE LITTLE PIG EAT SO MUCH ?

1. Needed in the diet for energy production
2. Stores carbohydrate
3. Absorbed from large intestine
4. Glands producing starch-digesting enzyme
5. Part of gut where faeces are formed
6. Digested in stomach and small intestine
7. Proteins which speed up digestion
8. First part of small intestine
9. Ring of muscle around a tube
10. Acids produced by protein digestion
11. Place where starch digestion starts
12. Opening from lower end of digestive tract
13. Vitamin needed for blood clotting
14. Produces sodium hydrogencarbonate and digestive enzymes
15. Vein draining blood from liver
16. Acid produced in stomach
17. Unit for energy content of food
18. They produce a variety of digestive enzymes
19. Final product of starch digestion
20. Produce glycerol and fatty acids when digested
21. Tube from mouth to stomach
22. Fat emulsifier produced in liver
23. Place for storage of faeces
24. Sugar produced in mouth by starch digestion
25. Product of fat digestion
26. 'Fingers' in the small intestine
27. Mineral needed to prevent anaemia (symbol)

The Facts of Life

WHAT DID THE MOTHER EAR OF CORN TELL HER BABY WHEN HE ASKED, 'MUMMY, WHERE DID I COME FROM?'

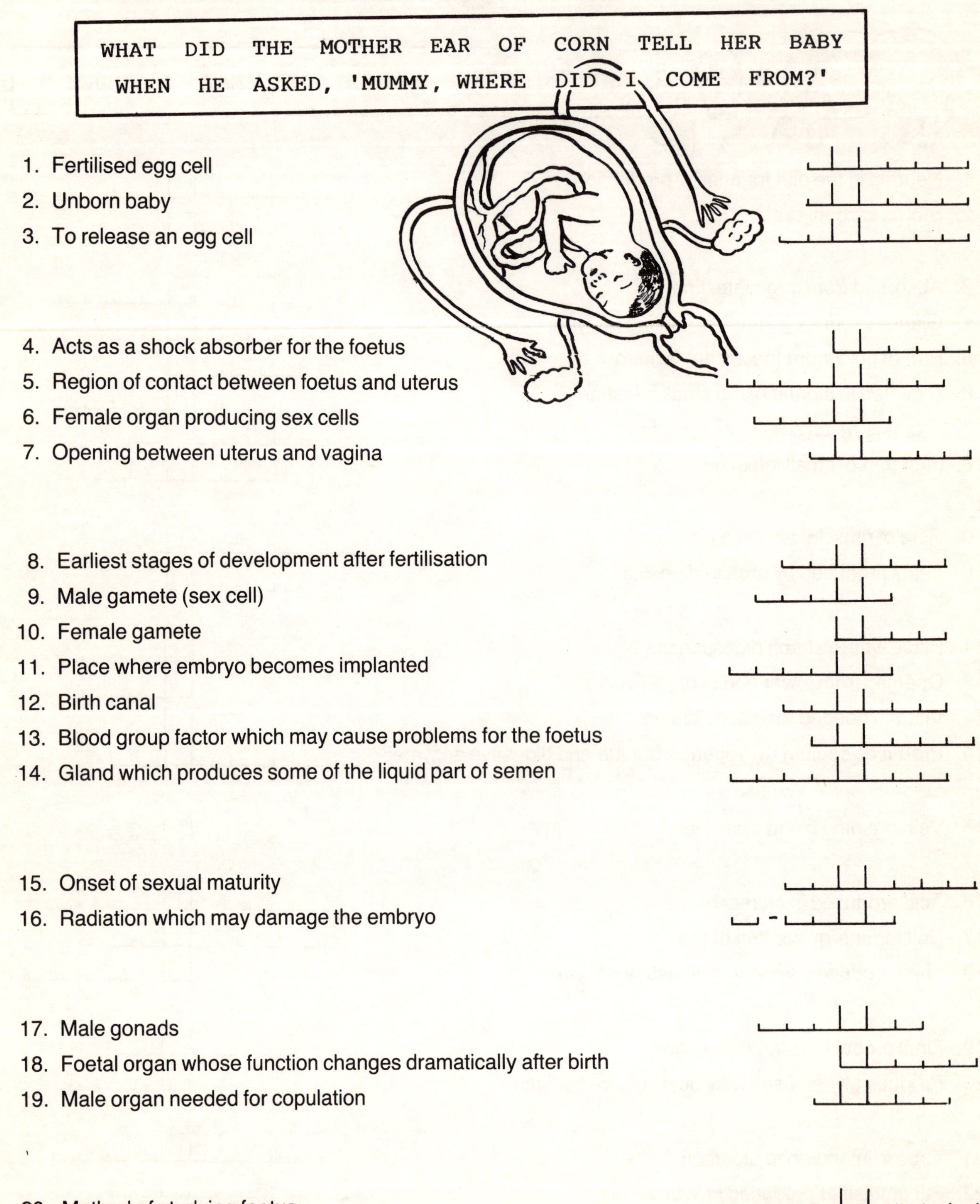

1. Fertilised egg cell
2. Unborn baby
3. To release an egg cell

4. Acts as a shock absorber for the foetus
5. Region of contact between foetus and uterus
6. Female organ producing sex cells
7. Opening between uterus and vagina

8. Earliest stages of development after fertilisation
9. Male gamete (sex cell)
10. Female gamete
11. Place where embryo becomes implanted
12. Birth canal
13. Blood group factor which may cause problems for the foetus
14. Gland which produces some of the liquid part of semen

15. Onset of sexual maturity
16. Radiation which may damage the embryo

17. Male gonads
18. Foetal organ whose function changes dramatically after birth
19. Male organ needed for copulation

20. Method of studying foetus
21. Fertilisation 'in glass' (test-tube babies)
22. Period of development before birth
23. Tube where fertilisation takes place
24. Drug habit which results in lower birth weight babies

Hybrid Humour

WHAT DO YOU GET WHEN YOU CROSS A SHEEP AND A KANGAROO?

Work out the answers to these problems. For each one, find the corresponding letter from the key list and write it next to your answer. Read off the letters going down the page.

1. How many chromosomes are there in a human sperm cell? ......
2. Mr. and Mrs. Jones have two sons. What is the probability (chance) that their next child will be a boy? ......
3. How many chromosomes are there in a human zygote? ......
4. How many sperm cells are produced from the original parent cell when meiosis is completed? ......
5. How many chromosomes are there in a human red blood cell? ......
6. In mice black coat is dominant over brown coat. A homozygous black male (**BB**) is mated with a heterozygous black female (**Bb**). Eight pups are born. How many would you expect to be brown? ......
7. How many chromosomes are there in the cells of a person who suffers from Downs Syndrome? ......
8. A man has haemophilia caused by a sex-linked recessive gene. What is the probability that he will pass on the gene to his daughters? ......
9. In guinea pigs rough coat (**R**) is dominant over smooth coat (**r**). A male and female are mated. Both are heterozygous. If they have four offspring, how many would you expect to have rough coats? ......
10. Mr and Mrs Smith have two children. What is the probability that they are both girls? ......
11. In sweet peas, round seed is dominant over wrinkled. Two heterozygous plants are crossed and produce 200 offspring. Approximately how many would you expect to have wrinkled seeds? ......
12. In cattle, polled is dominant to horned. A heterozygous polled bull is mated with homozygous horned cows. 20 calves are born. How many would you expect to have horns? ......
13. How many chromosomes are there in the cells of a woman who suffers from Turner's syndrome? ......

KEY LIST

L.	0	D.	0.75	O.	4	C.	20	Y.	47
S.	0.125	J.	1.0	T.	5	A.	23	I.	48
M.	0.25	V.	2	B.	8	R.	45	P.	50
W.	0.5	U.	3	E.	10	O.	46	N.	100

MYSTERY MONGREL

WHAT DO YOU GET WHEN YOU CROSS A GERMAN SHEPHERD WITH A CHIHUAHUA ?

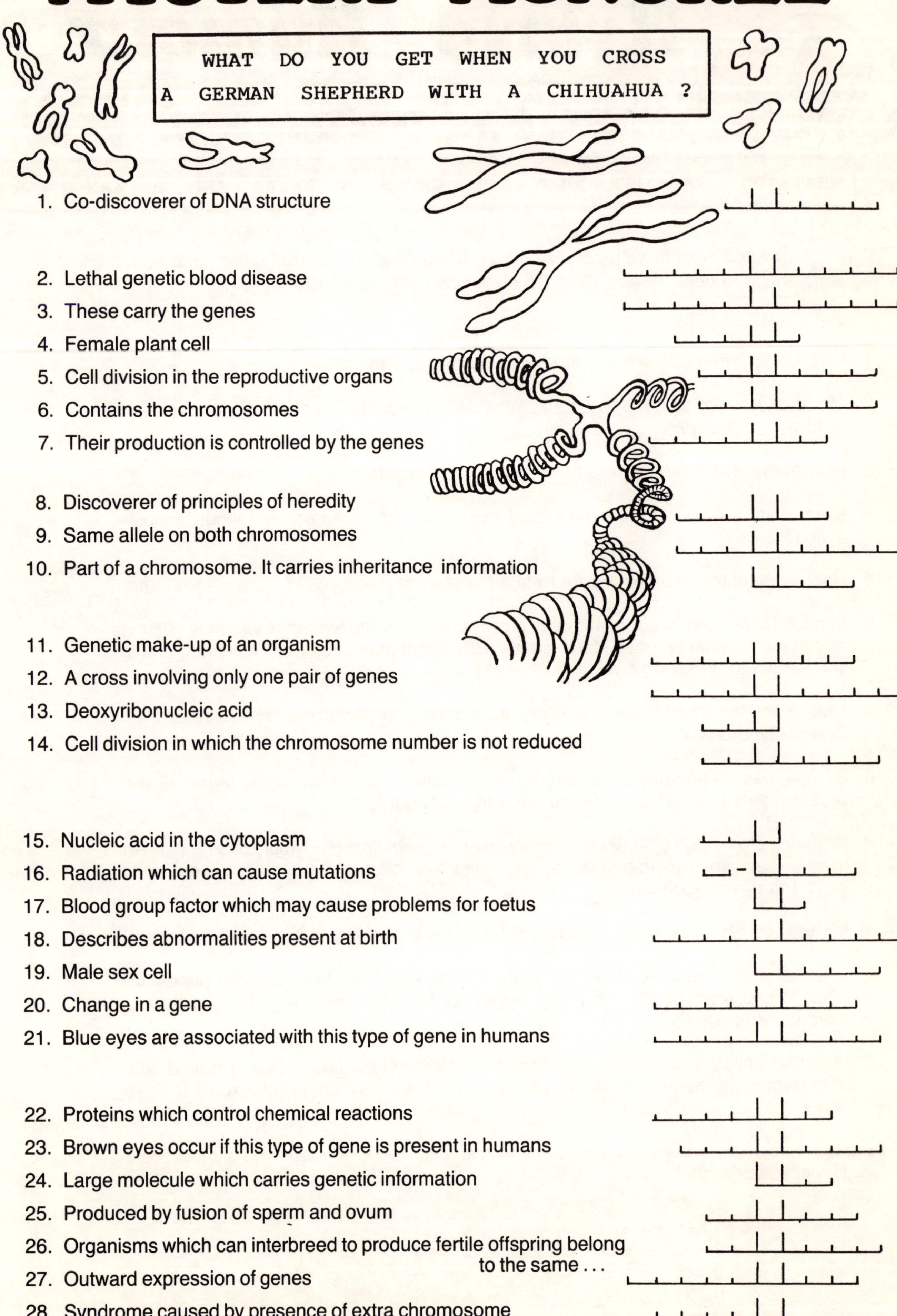

1. Co-discoverer of DNA structure

2. Lethal genetic blood disease
3. These carry the genes
4. Female plant cell
5. Cell division in the reproductive organs
6. Contains the chromosomes
7. Their production is controlled by the genes

8. Discoverer of principles of heredity
9. Same allele on both chromosomes
10. Part of a chromosome. It carries inheritance information

11. Genetic make-up of an organism
12. A cross involving only one pair of genes
13. Deoxyribonucleic acid
14. Cell division in which the chromosome number is not reduced

15. Nucleic acid in the cytoplasm
16. Radiation which can cause mutations
17. Blood group factor which may cause problems for foetus
18. Describes abnormalities present at birth
19. Male sex cell
20. Change in a gene
21. Blue eyes are associated with this type of gene in humans

22. Proteins which control chemical reactions
23. Brown eyes occur if this type of gene is present in humans
24. Large molecule which carries genetic information
25. Produced by fusion of sperm and ovum
26. Organisms which can interbreed to produce fertile offspring belong to the same . . .
27. Outward expression of genes
28. Syndrome caused by presence of extra chromosome

GENETICALLY SPEAKING

WHAT ARE THE CLEANING INSTRUCTIONS FOR CHROMOSOMES ?

Find 19 genetic terms in the word search and fill in the answers on the grid.

F	R	E	H	O	R	M	O	N	E	K	C	L
B	W	I	E	H	A	J	F	V	D	M	Q	D
T	D	G	S	B	E	X	O	N	O	P	T	E
D	S	C	A	V	L	L	S	E	A	H	N	E
I	U	A	E	Z	U	Y	S	I	N	V	A	R
R	M	K	S	T	C	J	I	F	I	G	L	B
B	S	Q	I	L	E	L	L	R	M	O	P	T
Y	O	O	D	S	L	R	O	V	A	R	U	Y
H	N	N	P	E	O	N	W	N	L	G	B	A
O	L	I	D	L	M	X	C	O	E	A	C	D
N	H	E	D	E	T	I	R	E	H	N	I	A
O	F	J	N	C	K	M	E	A	N	I	T	R
M	U	T	A	T	I	O	N	S	T	S	E	W
G	C	X	Y	E	U	R	E	V	R	M	N	I
G	E	Z	A	O	B	W	G	L	S	V	E	N
D	J	I	F	N	K	H	M	O	N	P	O	T

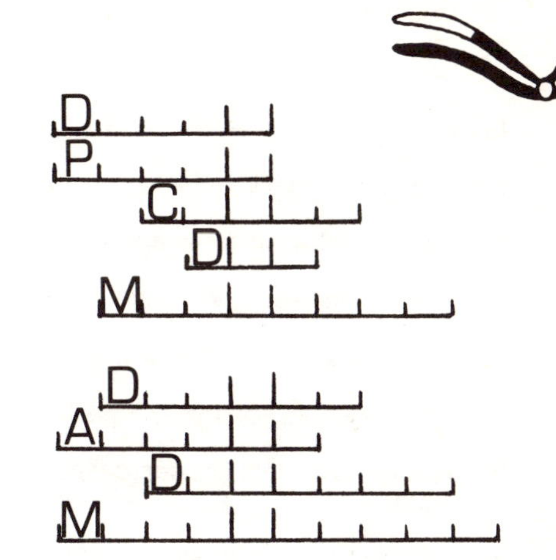

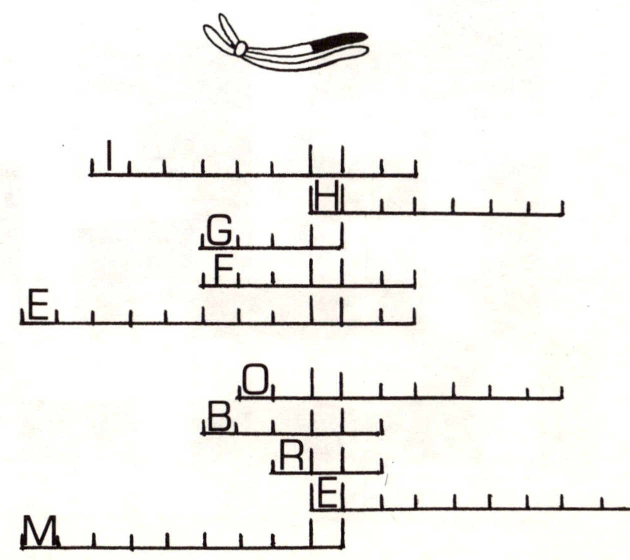

IT'S A WATERY WORLD

ACROSS

1. The amount of water vapour in the air
3. Sudden increase in algal growth which may be caused by pollution
8. Underground water
9. Sediment deposited when a river flows into a lake
11. Excess use may cause No. 3
12. Must be treated in order to prevent water pollution
14. Used for filtration in sewage works
15. Insecticide used to kill mosquito larvae in water
17. Fertile sediment built up where a river reaches the sea
19. Dissolved gas needed by aquatic organisms
22. Removal of vegetation increases .... of soil by water
23. Energy from the sea which can be used to generate electricity
24. This goes down the deeper you go in the ocean

DOWN

2. Useful for cleaning because makes water wetter, but may cause pollution problems
4. North sea pollution
5. Heavy-metal water pollutant that gets into the food chain
6. Process by which solutes spread through still water
7. Increase of the salt concentration of soil by over-use of irrigation
10. Dangerous condition caused by coming up too fast after a dive
13. Water eroded gully in North Africa
16. Number of oxygen atoms in a water molecule
18. Fine sediment carried by water
20. Longest river in the world
21. State in which most of the earth's fresh water exists

DIRTY WORDS

ACROSS

1. Can be added to soil to make it more alkaline
2. To dissolve minerals from the soil
5. Soil layer with most organic matter
6. Organic matter in the soil
7. Important decomposers in soil
8. Fine particles of soil in rivers
10. Fertile wind-blown soil
12. Measure of soil acidity
13. Inorganic components of soil
15. Charged particles in soil solution
16. Limiting factor for plant growth in many soils
17. Type of root well adapted to reach sub-surface water
18. Loss of soil by wind or water
20. To work the soil
22. Gas which must be present in soil for plant growth
23. Texture of soil with good drainage
24. Addition of organic matter to a soil
25. Volcanic rock which weathers to give a fertile soil

DOWN

3. Where soil meets sky
4. An essential for plant growth
9. A fertile soil
11. Soils suffer this near coasts
14. Essential element for protein production by plants
19. A heavy soil
21. Useful animal for aerating soil
23. Soil layer in which minerals accumulate in a wet climate

THE WORLD'S RESOURCES

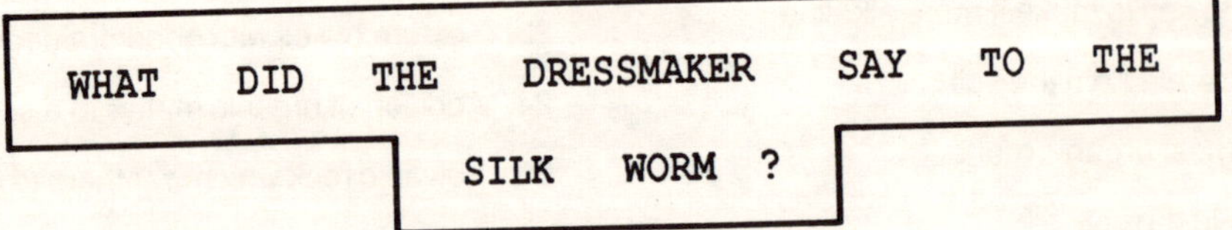

WHAT DID THE DRESSMAKER SAY TO THE
SILK WORM ?

Find 21 of the world's resources in this word search and fill in the answers on the chart.

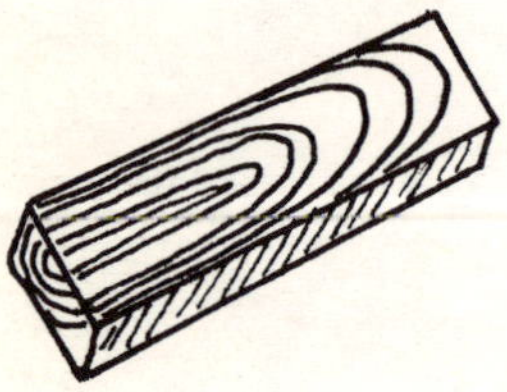

A
M
L
S
T

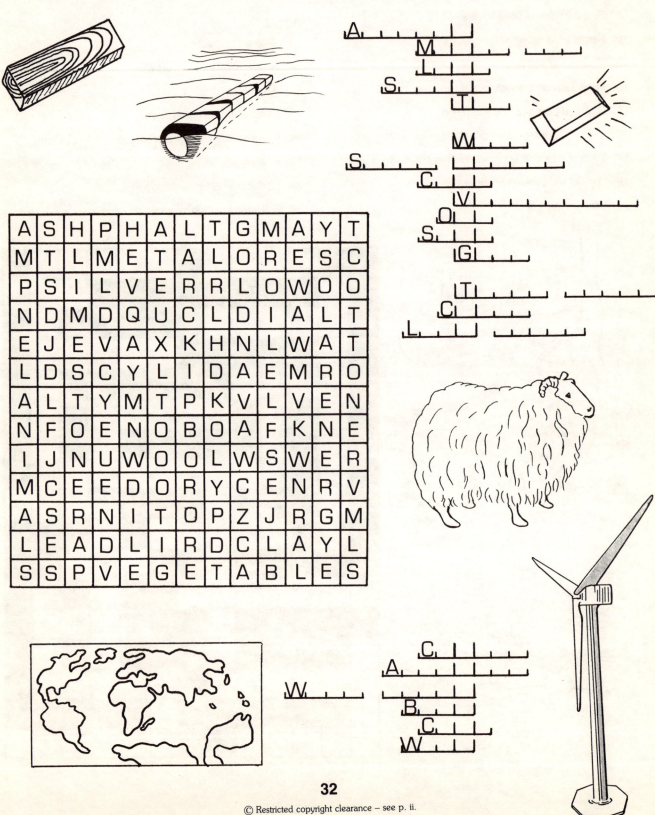

W
S
C
V
O
S
G

T
C
L

A	S	H	P	H	A	L	T	G	M	A	Y	T
M	T	L	M	E	T	A	L	O	R	E	S	C
P	S	I	L	V	E	R	R	L	O	W	O	O
N	D	M	D	Q	U	C	L	D	I	A	L	T
E	J	E	V	A	X	K	H	N	L	W	A	T
L	D	S	C	Y	L	I	D	A	E	M	R	O
A	L	T	Y	M	T	P	K	V	L	V	E	N
N	F	O	E	N	O	B	O	A	F	K	N	E
I	J	N	U	W	O	O	L	W	S	W	E	R
M	C	E	E	D	O	R	Y	C	E	N	R	V
A	S	R	N	I	T	O	P	Z	J	R	G	M
L	E	A	D	L	I	R	D	C	L	A	Y	L
S	S	P	V	E	G	E	T	A	B	L	E	S

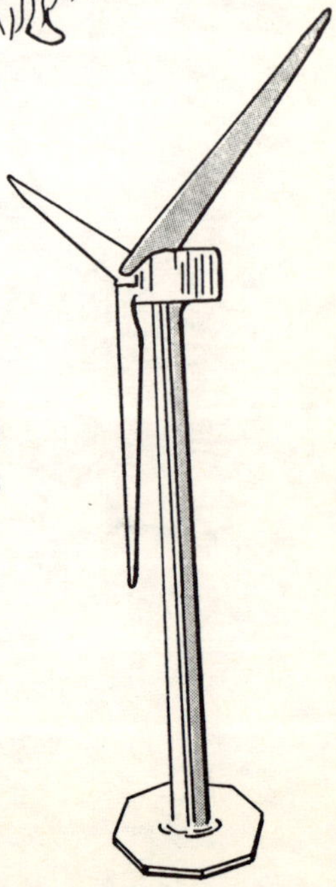

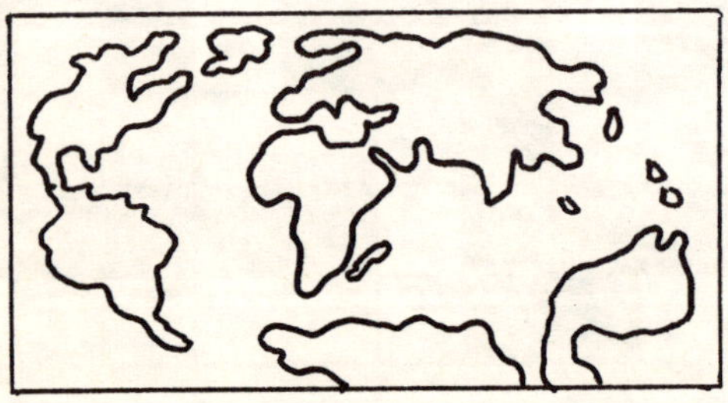

C
A
W
B
C
W

IT'S ELEMENTARY

■	■	1.	2.		3.			■	4.	■
5.	■	■	■	■		■	■	■	6.	
7.							8.	■		■
	■	■	■	■		■		■	9.	
10.		11.						■		■
	■		■	■	■	12.				■
	■	13.	14.		■	■		■	■	■
	■		■	■	15.	■	16.		17.	
	■	18.				19.		■		■
■	■	20.	■	■	21.	■		■	22.	
■	■	23.		■	24.		■	■		■

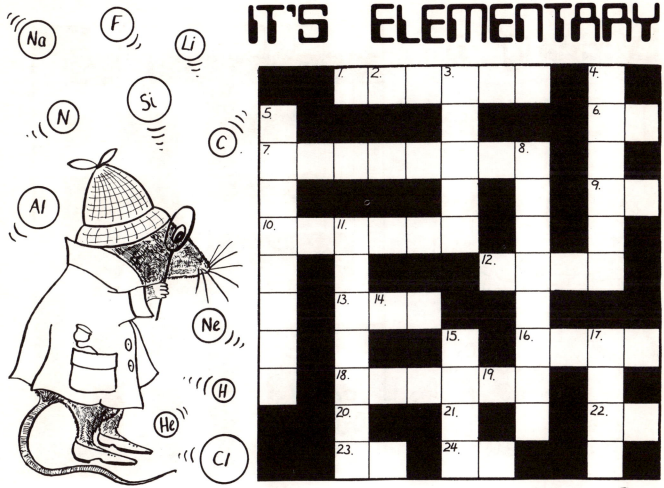

Find the elements which fit these descriptions.
You may use the same element more than once.

ACROSS

1. Metal found in some blue pigments, alloys and catalysts
6. Precious metal – excellent conductor of electricity (symbol)
7. Lightest gas known – explosive with air – caused Hindenburg disaster
9. Salt of this metal used when taking X-rays of digestive system (symbol)
10. Gas needed by most living things
12. The most used metal
13. Alloyed with lead in pewter
16. Unreactive precious metal
18. Needed for functioning of the thyroid gland
20. Fuel for nuclear reactors (symbol)
22. Extracted from bauxite (symbol)
23. Reactive silvery metal (symbol)
24. Alloyed with tin in bronze – used in electric wiring (symbol)

DOWN

1. Exists as diamond, graphite and soot (symbol)
2. Gas produced in photosynthesis (symbol)
3. Inert gas used in welding
4. Found in all organic compounds
5. Poisonous gas used as a bleach
8. Important for plant growth
11. The element that begins with 'Y'!
14. Seaweed a good source of this element (symbol)
15. Used for galvanising iron
17. Metal used in car batteries
19. Gas which makes up 79% of the atmosphere (symbol)

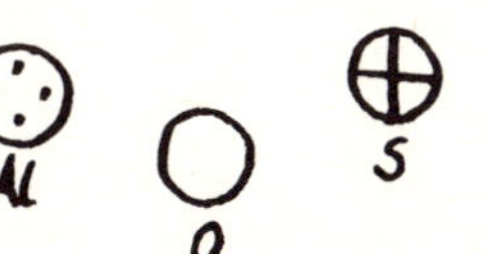

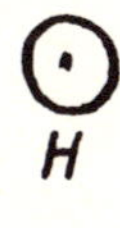

Seeking a Solution

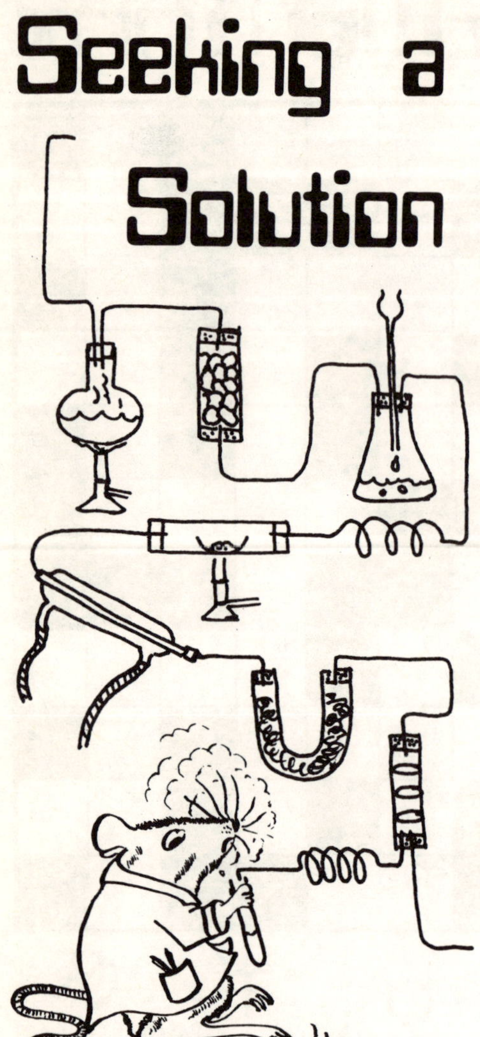

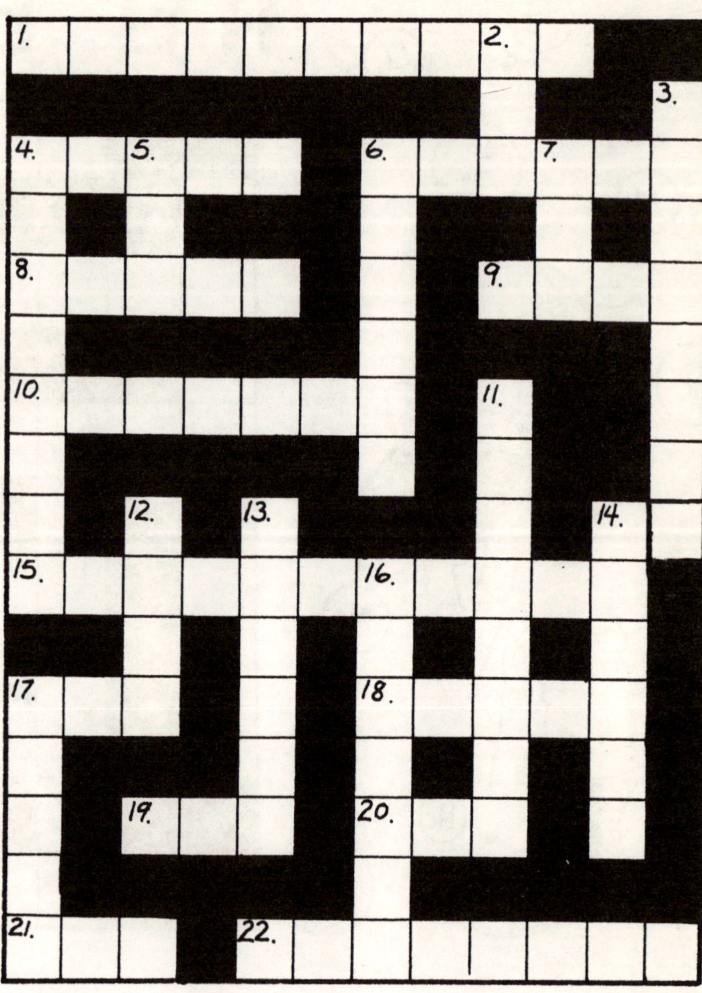

ACROSS

1. Cloudy mixture
4. Sweet solute
6. +6 Down Used for filtration in the laboratory (2 words)
8. Not safe to do this to laboratory solutions
9. Charged particles in solution
10. Solid left behind after filtration
15. Change from a liquid to a gas
17. Detergent increases the ability of water to do this
18. Appearance of a solution compared to a suspension
19. Number of oxygen atoms in a water molecule
20. Thermal state of water which will dissolve most solute
21. Useful for stirring in the laboratory
22. Solute + solvent = ...

DOWN

2. A liquid which is immiscible with water
3. Often obtained from a solution as the solvent evaporates
4. To add so much solute that no more will dissolve
5. Class of substances whose solubility decreases with temperature
6. See 6 Across
7. Number of hydrogen atoms in a water molecule
11. Insoluble material that has settled to the bottom
12. Savoury solute
13. A substance which dissolves
14. Required to pull apart particles
16. An organic solvent
17. Most important solvent on Earth

A Rapid Reaction

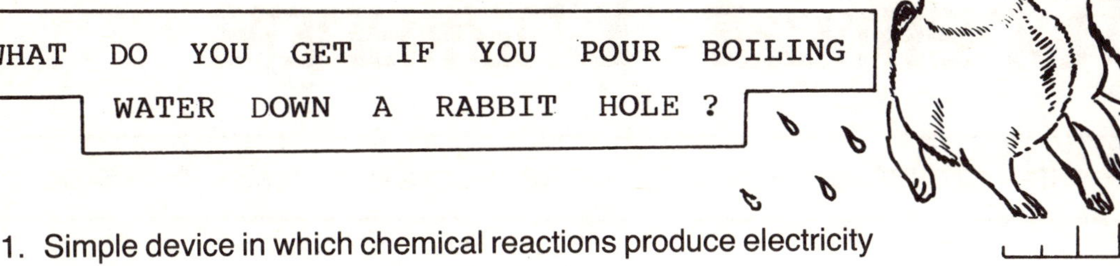

WHAT DO YOU GET IF YOU POUR BOILING WATER DOWN A RABBIT HOLE ?

1. Simple device in which chemical reactions produce electricity
2. Liquid which will conduct an electric current
3. Point at which electrons enter or leave a cell
4. Charged particles

5. Positive electrode in a torch battery
6. Gas obtained by electrolysis of molten sodium fluoride

7. Negative electrode
8. Gas produced at the anode during electrolysis of water
9. Particles with a negative charge

10. Describes compounds made up of charged particles
11. Metal which is purified by electrolysis
12. Positively charged electrode
13. Charge on a hydrogen ion
14. Metal obtained by electrolysis of molten salt

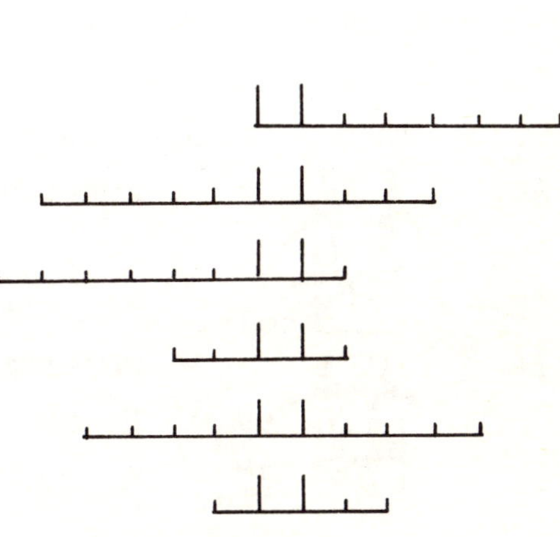

15. Converts chemical energy into electrical energy
16. Acid used in car batteries
17. Released from anode during electrolysis of molten salt
18. Metal used to prevent corrosion
19. Extracted from bauxite by electrolysis
20. Used for car battery electrodes
21. Unprotected iron suffers this

Chemical Challenge

WHAT WAS THE LIGHTEST METAL BEFORE LITHIUM WAS DISCOVERED?

Next to each of the following statements write **T** if it is true and **F** if it is false. Each group of three codes for a letter from the key list. Write the letters in the numbered boxes.

The Reactivity Series

Na ↑ Highest tendency to lose electrons
Ca
Mg
Al
Zn
Fe
Pb
H
Cu
Ag ↓ Increasing tendency to gain electrons

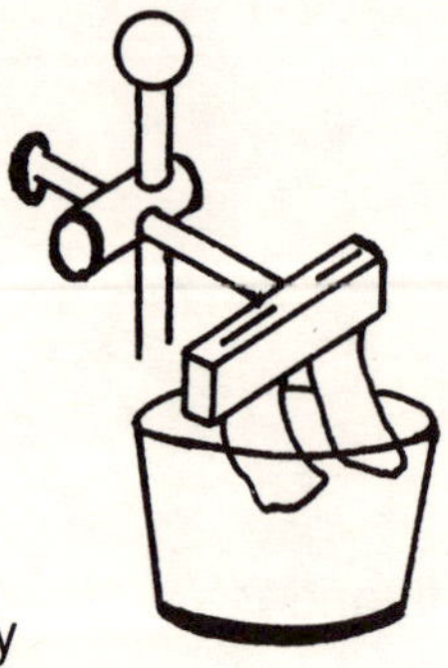

KEY LIST

H.	TTT	O.	FFF
I.	TTF	R.	FFT
L.	TFT	T.	FTF
M.	TFF	U.	FTT

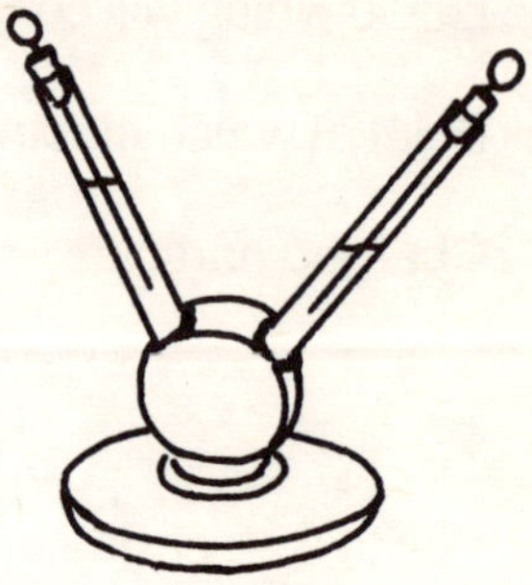

1	2	3	4	5	6	7

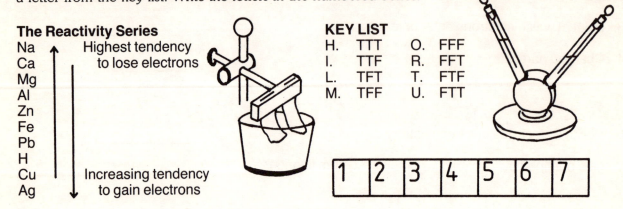

1A. Mg has a greater tendency to lose electrons than Zn has.
1B. Cu has less tendency to lose electrons than has Ag. } ... ...
1C. An iron nail put in $CuSO_4$ solution will become plated with Cu.

2A. Zn will react with hydrochloric acid to give off hydrogen.
2B. Zinc is more reactive than lead. } ... ...
2C. Pb has a greater tendency to gain electrons than has Ag.

3A. A zinc nail in $Mg(NO_3)_2$ solution will become coated with Mg.
3B. Iron has less tendency to lose electrons than has calcium. } ... ...
3C. Copper will react with sulphuric acid to give off hydrogen.

4A. A strip of Al in $AgNO_3$ solution will become coated with Ag.
4B. Na^+ ions will go to the cathode in electrolysis of molten NaCl. } ... ...
4C. Sodium is more reactive than aluminium.

5A. Na metal will react with water to give Na^+ ions.
5B. F^- ions will go to the anode in electrolysis of molten CaF_2. } ... ...
5C. A Cu strip in $Ca(NO_3)_2$ solution will become plated with Ca.

6A. In the experiment shown, Na metal will plate out on the Zn electrode
6B. $Zn(s) \rightarrow Zn^{2+}(aq) + 2e^-$ } ... ...
6C. An electric current will flow.

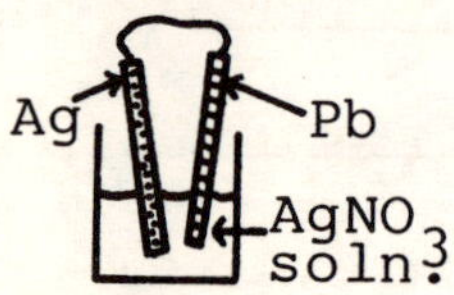

7A. In the experiment shown, the Pb electrode will become coated with Ag.
7B. Electrons will travel from the Ag to the Pb. } ... ...
7C. Ag(s) will go into solution as Ag^+.

A Basic Problem

WHAT DO YOU GET WHEN YOU CROSS A JUMBO JET WITH A KANGAROO ?

1. Substances which give hydrogen ions in solution
2. This metal does not react with dilute acids
3. Soluble base
4. Changes colour in acid or alkaline solutions
5. Gas which dissolves in water to give an alkaline solution
6. Dilute ethanoic acid is sold as this
7. Acid produced when milk sours
8. Measure of acidity
9. Neutral liquid
10. Alkaline taste
11. Body organ which produces hydrochloric acid
12. Acids which make up protein molecules
13. Describes acids which give a low concentration of hydrogen ions
14. Body organ which produced sodium hydrogencarbonate
15. These react with acids to give a salt and water
16. Indicator which turns blue in alkaline solutions
17. Acid used in car batteries
18. Ion which combines with hydrogen ions to give water
19. Acid which gives off a brown gas when reacts with metals
20. Acid found in oranges and lemons
21. Reacts with acids to give off carbon dioxide
22. Gas produced when metals react with dilute hydrochloric acid
23. Colour of phenolphthalein in acid solutions
24. Produced when an acid reacts with an alkali

The Acid Test

WHO RIDES A CAMEL AND CARRIES A LAMP ?

Complete each equation by filling in the missing formula and balancing the equation. Find the corresponding letter from the key list and write it next to the number of the equation. Read down the letters to get the answer.

1.	$NaOH$	+	HCl	$\longrightarrow$	$NaCl$	+	☐			
2.	$Ca(OH)_2$	+	$2HCl$	$\longrightarrow$	$CaCl_2$	+	☐			
3.	Zn	+	H_2SO_4	$\longrightarrow$	$ZnSO_4$	+	☐			
4.	CuO	+	☐	$\longrightarrow$	$Cu(NO_3)_2$	+	H_2O			
5.	☐	+	H_2SO_4	$\longrightarrow$	K_2SO_4	+	$2H_2O$			
6.	$2Fe$	+	☐	$\longrightarrow$	$2FeCl_3$	+	$3H_2$			
7.	☐	+	$CaCO_3$	$\longrightarrow$	H_2O	+	CO_2	+	$CaSO_4$	
8.	MgO	+	☐	$\longrightarrow$	$MgCl_2$	+	H_2O			
9.	☐	+	NH_4OH	$\longrightarrow$	NH_4NO_3	+	H_2O			
10.	☐	+	H_2SO_4	$\longrightarrow$	$ZnSO_4$	+	H_2O			
11.	☐	+	$2HCl$	$\longrightarrow$	CO_2	+	H_2O	+	$2NaCl$	
12.	NH_4OH	+	☐	$\longrightarrow$	NH_4Cl	+	H_2O			
13.	$Fe_2(CO_3)_3$	+	$6HNO_3$	$\longrightarrow$	$2Fe(NO_3)_3$	+	$3H_2O$	+	☐	
14.	Al_2O_3	+	$6HNO_3$	$\longrightarrow$	$2Al(NO_3)_3$	+	☐			
15.	$2Al$	+	$6HCl$	$\longrightarrow$	☐	+	$2AlCl_3$			
16.	$(NH_4)_2CO_3$	+	H_2SO_4	$\longrightarrow$	$(NH_4)_2SO_4$	+	☐	+	H_2O	

KEY LIST

O.	$1H_2$	B.	$3H_2O$	E.	$2HCl$	A.	$1CO$	K.	$1NaHCO_3$
H.	$2H_2$	U.	$4H_2O$	P.	$4HCl$	V.	$2CO_2$	A.	$1Na_2CO_3$
I.	$3H_2$	O.	$1HNO_3$	N.	$6HCl$	A.	$3CO_2$	T.	$2Na_2CO_3$
J.	$4H_2$	R.	$2HNO_3$	C.	$1H_2SO_4$	M.	$1KOH$	F.	$1ZnO$
F.	$1H_2O$	S.	$3HNO_3$	A.	$2H_2SO_4$	E.	$2KOH$	D.	$2ZnO$
L.	$2H_2O$	R.	$1HCl$	W.	$3H_2SO_4$	Y.	$3KOH$	E.	$1Zn(OH)_2$

METAL MASTERY

HOW CAN YOU AVOID GETTING A SHARP PAIN IN YOUR EYE WHEN YOU DRINK CHOCOLATE MILK SHAKE ?

1. Able to be drawn out into a wire
2. Metal used in car batteries
3. Metal used in making coins
4. Able to be beaten into shape

Mg

5. Number of positive charges on a zinc ion
6. Electrode at which aluminium is deposited during electrolysis of alumina
7. Compounds of metals with oxygen

8. An alloy of copper and zinc
9. Alloyed with tin to produce bronze
10. Gas produced when magnesium reacts with hydrochloric acid
11. Silvery metal which reacts vigorously with water
12. A most important metal

13. Number of positive charges on a sodium ion
14. Only metal which is liquid at room temperature
15. Metal used to make Concorde

16. Minerals from which metals are extracted
17. Process of purifying a metal

Al

18. Sodium compound used for making explosives
19. Number of charges on an aluminium ion
20. Metal used in flash bulbs and flares

21. Inert precious metal
22. Metal mixtures
23. First radioactive metal to be discovered
24. Alloy of iron and carbon
25. 'Shininess' of a metal

PETROLEUM PUZZLE

WHAT IS THE FIRST THING THAT A SCIENTIST LEARNS ABOUT PETROLEUM ?

1. Gaseous hydrocarbon used in bunsen burners
2. Petrol additive that is harmful
3. Hydrocarbon with eight carbon atoms
4. Element contained in all organic compounds
5. Oxide of carbon produced during complete combustion of hydrocarbons
6. Process by which oil is separated into its components
7. Solid hydrocarbons used for waterproofing and candles
8. Problem caused by No. 2 and poor combustion of fuels
9. Type of rock in which oil is found

10. State of petrol as it enters the engine cylinder
11. Process used to increase amount of petrol obtained from crude oil
12. Liquid hydrocarbon used for jet engines
13. Oil straight from the ground
14. Solid hydrocarbons used for road-making
15. Compounds containing carbon and hydrogen only
16. Type of geologic formation in which oil may be found
17. Survey done to locate oil-bearing deposits

18. Liquid hydrocarbon obtained from pine trees used as a paint solvent, now replaced by white spirit
19. Hydrocarbons used as lubricants
20. Lightest hydrocarbon – 'Marsh gas'
21. Mixture of sem-solid hydrocarbons that keeps moving things going smoothly

Clued up on Carbon

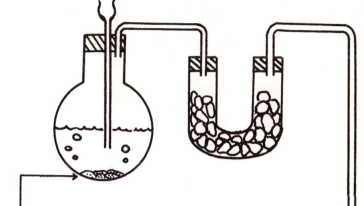

ACROSS

2. Carboniferous fossil fuel
5. Hard allotrope of carbon
7. Metal which is alloyed with carbon in steel
8. Class of compound which gives off CO_2 when mixed with an acid
9. Hydrocarbon used for candles
10. Form of calcium carbonate
11. Useful suspension of carbon particles in water
12. Liberates CO_2 from hydrogencarbonates
13. See 5 Down
17. Number of hydrogen atoms in a methane molecule
18. Slippery allotrope of carbon
19. Form of calcium carbonate used for sculptures

DOWN

1. Valency of carbon
3. Used to test for CO_2
4. Poisonous oxide of carbon
5. +13 Across Solid CO_2
6. Oxide of carbon needed by plants
8. Form of carbon obtained by wood-burning
10. Formula of 4 Down
14. Form of carbon used in iron smelting
15. Information about fossils which can be determined using radioactive carbon
16. Atomic number of carbon

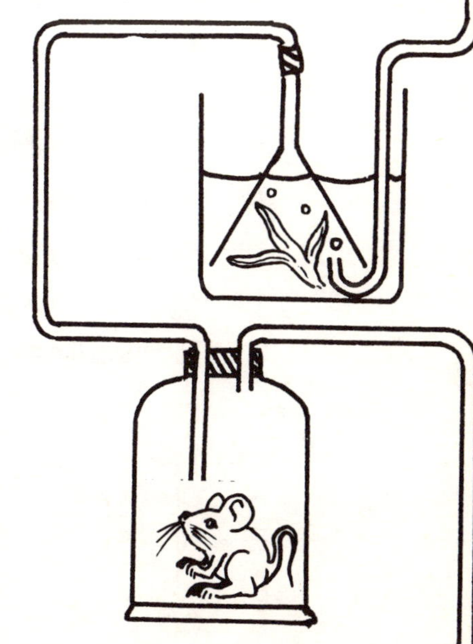

COMPOUND CONUNDRUM

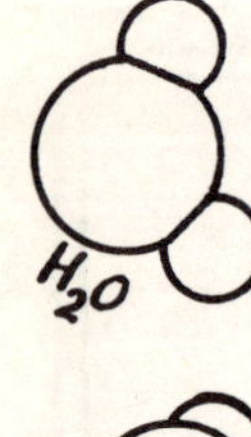

WHAT HAPPENED TO THE MAN WHO COULDN'T TELL THE DIFFERENCE BETWEEN PUTTY AND PORRIDGE?

Find the formula of the chemical compound which best fits each description below. For each one, write the corresponding letter from the key list next to the formula. Read down the page.

1. Blue copper compound – used to kill algae ....
2. Strong alkali – used for cleaning drains ....
3. Simple sugar which we use for energy ....
4. Rotten egg gas given out by volcanos ....
5. Baking powder – gives off CO_2 with acids ....
6. Strong bleach – rocket propellant ....
7. Common table salt ....
8. Potassium salt used in fertilisers and explosives ....
9. Strong acid – gives off brown gas with metals ....
10. Gas used in bunsen burners ....
11. Slaked lime ....
12. Ammonium salt used as a fertiliser ....
13. Brilliant purple potassium salt ....
14. Weak organic acid – vinegar ....
15. Strong acid used in car batteries ....
16. Chalk – limestone – marble ....
17. Black oxide – reacts with H_2SO_4 to give No. 1 ....
18. Gas used by green plants in photosynthesis ....
19. Highly soluble gas with a pungent smell – solution used for cleaning ....
20. Red metallic oxide – source of man's most important metal ....

KEY LIST

F.	CH_3COOH	S.	$C_6H_{12}O_6$	T.	Fe_2O_3	E.	H_2SO_4	L.	NH_4NO_3
E.	CH_3OH	L.	$CaCO_3$	S.	HCl	L.	$KMnO_4$	D.	NaCl
A.	CH_4	R.	CaO	W.	HNO_3	O.	KNO_3	I.	$NaHCO_3$
B.	CO	A.	$Ca(OH)_2$	P.	H_2O	S.	$MgCl_2$	M.	$NaNO_3$
O.	CO_2	L.	CuO	N.	H_2O_2	N.	$MgSO_4$	I.	NaOH
S.	C_3H_8	H.	$CuSO_4$	W.	H_2S	U.	NH_3	F.	Na_2CO_3

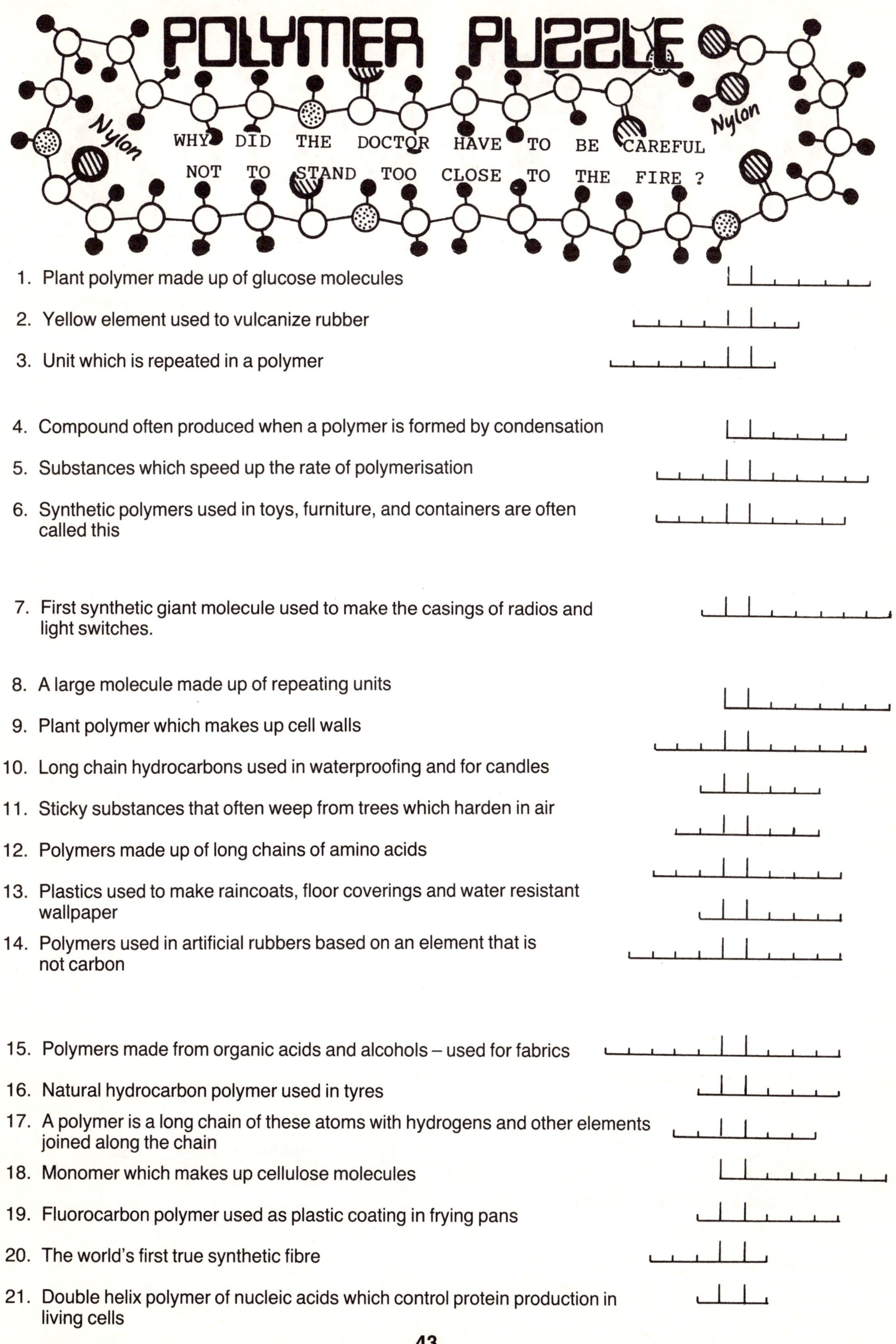

POLYMER PUZZLE
Nylon
Nylon
WHY DID THE DOCTOR HAVE TO BE CAREFUL NOT TO STAND TOO CLOSE TO THE FIRE ?

1. Plant polymer made up of glucose molecules
2. Yellow element used to vulcanize rubber
3. Unit which is repeated in a polymer
4. Compound often produced when a polymer is formed by condensation
5. Substances which speed up the rate of polymerisation
6. Synthetic polymers used in toys, furniture, and containers are often called this
7. First synthetic giant molecule used to make the casings of radios and light switches.
8. A large molecule made up of repeating units
9. Plant polymer which makes up cell walls
10. Long chain hydrocarbons used in waterproofing and for candles
11. Sticky substances that often weep from trees which harden in air
12. Polymers made up of long chains of amino acids
13. Plastics used to make raincoats, floor coverings and water resistant wallpaper
14. Polymers used in artificial rubbers based on an element that is not carbon
15. Polymers made from organic acids and alcohols – used for fabrics
16. Natural hydrocarbon polymer used in tyres
17. A polymer is a long chain of these atoms with hydrogens and other elements joined along the chain
18. Monomer which makes up cellulose molecules
19. Fluorocarbon polymer used as plastic coating in frying pans
20. The world's first true synthetic fibre
21. Double helix polymer of nucleic acids which control protein production in living cells

IT'S A GAS !
WHAT KIND OF INDIANS DOES DRACULA LIKE ?

Draw a line connecting each gas with its correct description. Circle any letters through which the lines pass. Read down the circled letters to find the answer to the riddle. Number 1 is done for you.

1. Needed by plants for photosynthesis. Used as 'dry ice' in solid state
2. Second lightest gas known – inert. Used in balloons and by divers
3. Makes up to 79% of atmosphere. Used in ammonia production
4. Deadly poisonous because it combines with haemoglobin
5. 'Rotten egg' gas given off by volcanoes
6. 'Fire damp' – hydrocarbon which is a hazard in mines
7. Chlorinated hydrocarbon – one of first anaesthetics
8. Lightest gas known – reactivity caused the 'Hindenburg' disaster
9. Pungent smell – highly soluble. Used to produce fertilisers
10. Light anaesthetic used in dentistry and childbirth
11. Greenish-yellow – used as a poison gas in World War I
12. Short-chain hydrocarbon used as a fuel
13. Reddish-brown gas – formed by lightning
14. Needed by most living organisms for respiration
15. Most corrosive gas known but compounds important in dental care

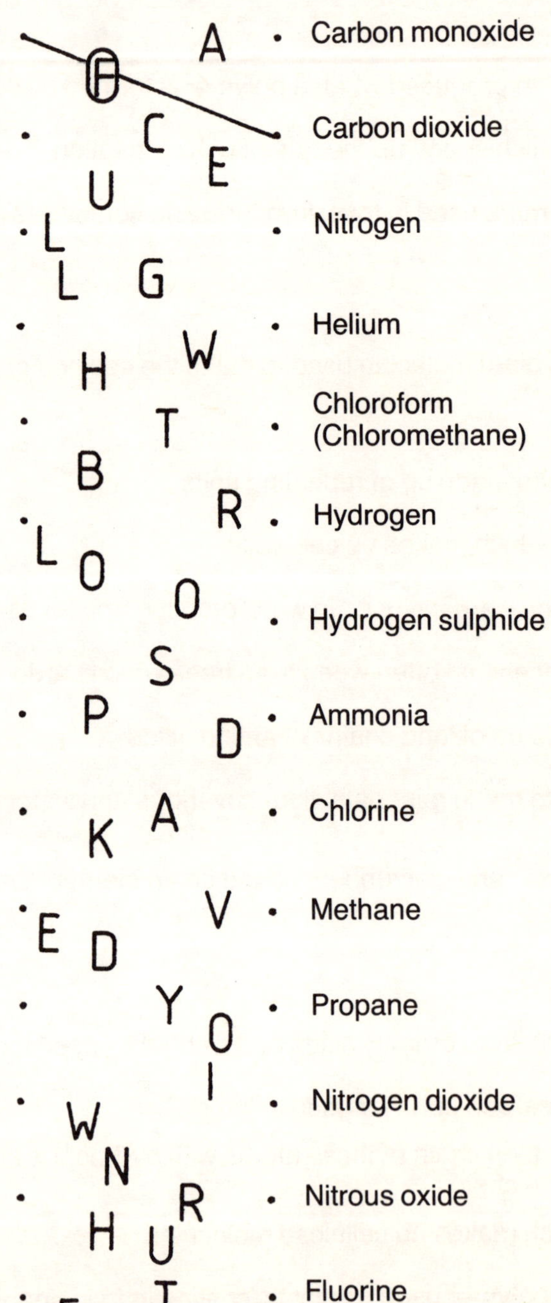

Metals and Man

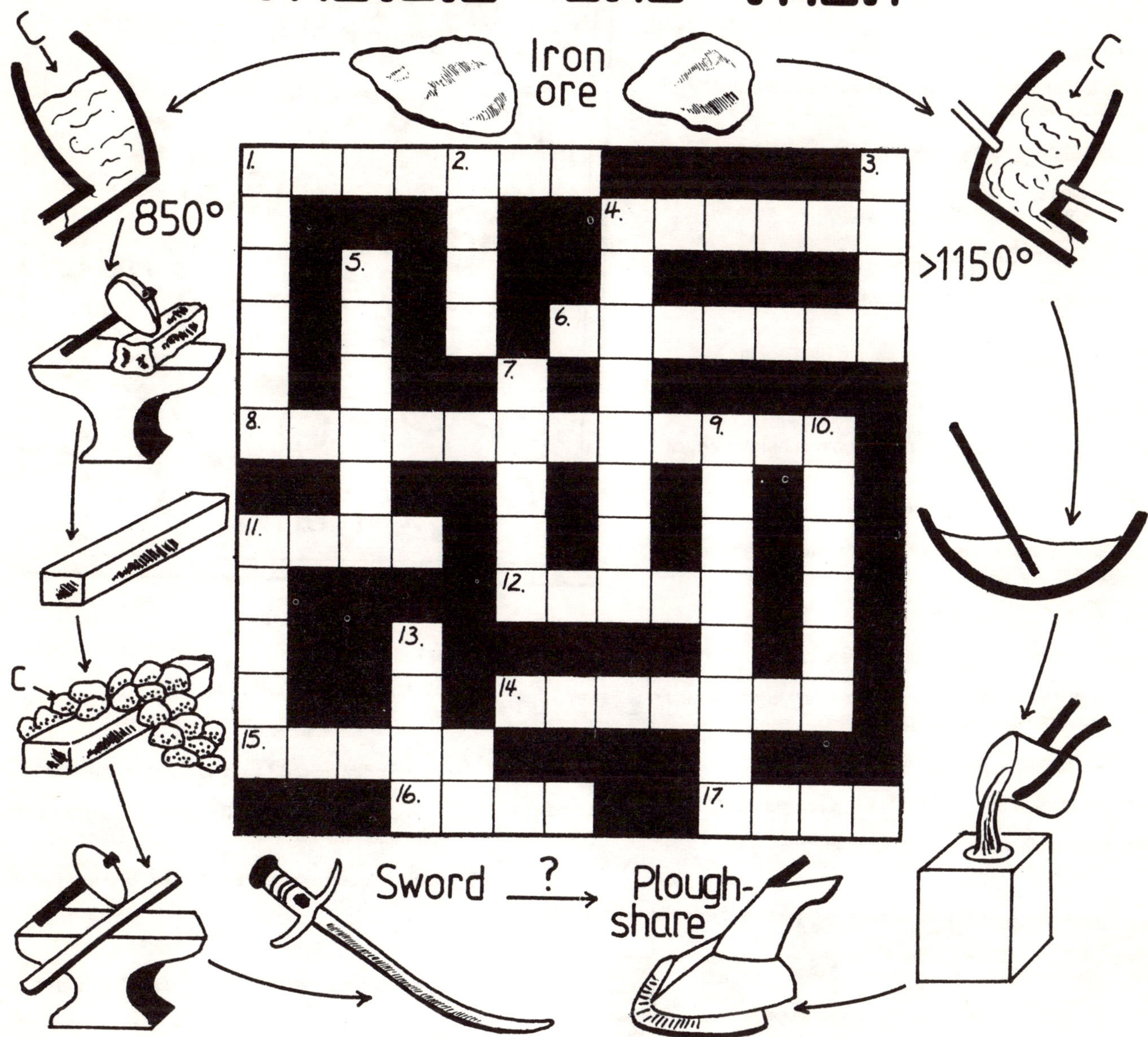

ACROSS

1. Aluminium ore
4. Metal used for electrical wiring and heating elements
6. Copper ore – 'Fool's gold'
8. Process by which sodium is obtained from sodium chloride
11. Dull-grey unreactive metal formerly used in plumbing
12. Iron alloy used in cars, bridges, construction work etc.
14. Radioactive metal used in nuclear reactors
15. See 11 Down
16. Reducing agent used for smelting iron
17. Precious metal used in jewelry and coins

DOWN

1. Alloy of copper and tin formerly used for making weapons
2. Our most important metal
3. Substances from which metals are extracted
4. Used to lower the melting point of alumina in electrolysis process
5. Lead ore
7. Decorative alloy of copper and zinc
9. Extraction of metals by heat
10. Used as a coolant in a few nuclear reactors
11. +15 Across: Used with 16 Across in iron smelting process
13. Used to prevent corrosion of mild steel

ACROSS

2. Inert gas produced by potassium decay – useful for dating rocks
7. Least penetrating type of nuclear radiation
9. Radioactive isotope of this element used as a tracer to study thyroid function (symbol)
10. Fuel for nuclear reactors
12. Electromagnetic radiation which may be produced during nuclear changes
14. Becomes polluted following a nuclear explosion
15. Yellowcake is uranium ....
17. Member of solar system producing energy by nuclear fusion
18. First atom bomb fell here
20. Radioactive isotope which gets into milk after nuclear explosions (sym.)
22. Intensive light beam machine
25. Most dangerous part of a nuclear reactor
26. Protective layer of atmosphere likely to be seriously damaged by nuclear war
28. Number of protons in hydrogen nucleus
29. Metal used as a coolant in a few nuclear reactors
30. Radioactive isotope of hydrogen

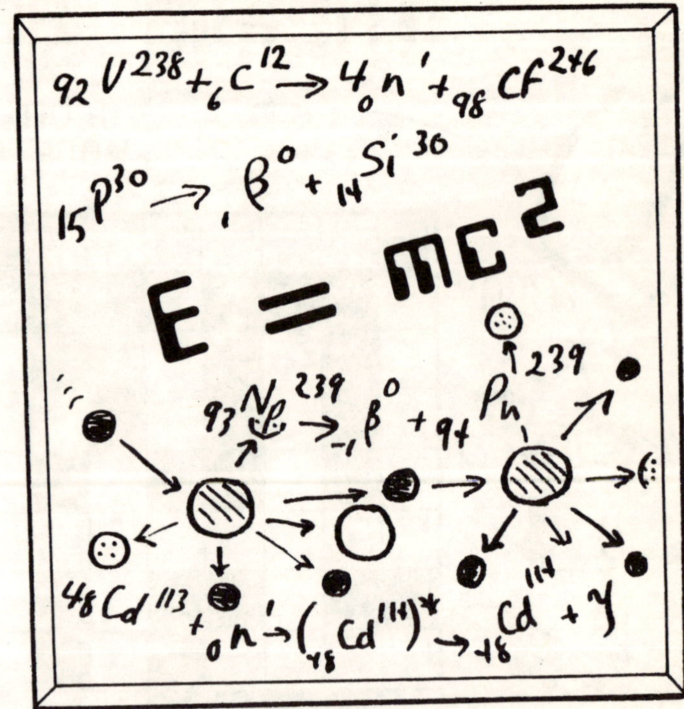

DOWN

1. Unit for measuring radiation
2. Symbol for 2 Across
3. Lethal radiation produced by nuclear explosions
4. Radioactive isotope of this element useful for studying respiration (sym.)
5. Particle which maintains chain reaction in a nuclear reactor
6. Radioactive waste at uranium mines
8. By-product in nuclear reactors used for weapons
11. Some scientists predict increased amounts of this state of water following nuclear war
13. This state of matter is very dangerous if radioactive
16. Atoms of an element with different atomic masses
19. Produced by nuclear fusion of hydrogen in stars
21. Particle with a positive charge
23. Beds of this substance may be used for storage of nuclear waste
24. First radioactive element discovered
25. First scientist to isolate 24 Down
27. Number of neutrons in a deuterium nucleus

State Secrets

WHY WAS THE SCIENTIST SO FRIGHTENED BY THE SMOOTH, YELLOW SUBSTANCE WHICH HE DISCOVERED ?

1. State of matter with a fixed volume but not shape
2. General name for anything which takes up space
3. Liquid which boils at 100 °C
4. To change from a liquid to a gas below the boiling point
5. Gases, liquids and solids are the three ...... of matter
6. State of matter in which the particles are far apart
7. A solid, but not a liquid or a gas, has a definite ......
8. Building blocks of all matter
9. A gas, but not a liquid or a solid, can be ......
10. Energy of movement
11. To purify by boiling and condensing
12. To change from a gas to a liquid
13. To change from a liquid to a solid
14. Smallest particles of a compound which can normally exist
15. Exerted by gases because of molecular movement
16. Irish chemist who first put forward the modern atomic theory
17. Kinetic is one form, potential is another
18. State of matter with definite volume and shape
19. Has a regular arrangement of particles
20. Solids and liquids, but not gases have a definite ......
21. Describes distances between particles in a solid
22. Change from a solid to a liquid
23. Describes distances between particles in a gas
24. Lightest gas known
25. Liquids and gases are known as ......

IN THE BALANCE

WHAT DO STUDENTS FIND THE HARDEST THING TO BELIEVE ABOUT CHEMISTRY ?

Balance these equations. Write in all the numbers, including '1'. For each equation, find the sequence of number in the key list and write the corresponding letter next to the equation. Read down the letters to find the answer to the riddle.

1. $Ba(NO_3)_2$ + K_2SO_4 ⟶ KNO_3 + $BaSO_4$
2. CH_4 + O_2 ⟶ H_2O + CO_2
3. CuO + HNO_3 ⟶ $Cu(NO_3)_2$ + H_2O
4. Fe + Al_2O_3 ⟶ Fe_2O_3 + Al
5. HCl + CaO ⟶ $CaCl_2$ + H_2O
6. Al_2O_3 + C ⟶ CO + Al
7. $FeCl_3$ + $AgNO_3$ ⟶ $Fe(NO_3)_3$ + $AgCl$
8. $NaOH$ + H_3PO_4 ⟶ Na_3PO_4 + H_2O
9. Fe_2O_3 + C ⟶ Fe + CO
10. $Pb(NO_3)_2$ + Na_2SO_4 ⟶ $NaNO_3$ + $PbSO_4$
11. $NaOH$ + HCl ⟶ $NaCl$ + H_2O
12. Na + H_2O ⟶ H_2 + $NaOH$
13. H_2SO_4 + $Cu(OH)_2$ ⟶ $CuSO_4$ + H_2O
14. BaO + HNO_3 ⟶ $Ba(NO_3)_2$ + H_2O
15. $Pb(NO_3)_2$ + KCl ⟶ $PbCl_2$ + KNO_3
16. $Al(OH)_3$ + HNO_3 ⟶ H_2O + $Al(NO_3)_3$
17. H_2O + K ⟶ H_2 + KOH

KEY LIST

A.	1, 1 1, 1	F.	1, 2 1, 2	U.	1, 3 3, 1	W.	2, 1 2, 1
B.	1, 1 1, 2	H.	1, 2 2, 1	S.	1, 3 3, 2	N.	2, 2 1, 2
C.	1, 1 2, 1	T.	1, 3 1, 3	I.	2, 1 1, 1	G.	3, 1 1, 2
E.	1, 2 1, 1	Y.	1, 3 2, 3	M.	2, 1 1, 2	R.	3, 1 1, 3

DISPLACEMENTS

WHAT HAPPENS AT THE POLICE STATION AT CLOSING TIME ?

Complete each equation by using one formula from the key list. The corresponding letters will give you the answer.

1.	$CuSO_4$	+	Fe	$\longrightarrow$	$FeSO_4$	+	
2.	H_2SO_4	+	Zn	$\longrightarrow$	$ZnSO_4$	+	
3.		+	Zn	$\longrightarrow$	$Zn(NO_3)_2$	+	2Ag
4.	2KI	+	Cl_2	$\longrightarrow$		+	2KCl
5.		+	Mg	$\longrightarrow$	$MgSO_4$	+	Cu
6.	Ca	+	$ZnCl_2$	$\longrightarrow$	$CaCl_2$	+	
7.	Mg	+	$2AgNO_3$	$\longrightarrow$	$Mg(NO_3)_2$	+	
8.	$CuCl_2$	+		$\longrightarrow$	$MgCl_2$	+	Cu
9.	2NaI	+	Br_2	$\longrightarrow$	I_2	+	
10.		+	$FeCl_2$	$\longrightarrow$	$CaCl_2$	+	Fe
11.	Mg	+		$\longrightarrow$	$MgSO_4$	+	Fe
12.	$Cu(NO_3)_2$	+	Ca	$\longrightarrow$		+	Cu
13.	Ca	+	$CuCl_2$	$\longrightarrow$		+	Cu
14.		+	Mg	$\longrightarrow$	$MgCl_2$	+	H_2
15.	$Pb(NO_3)_2$	+	Fe	$\longrightarrow$		+	Pb
16.	2NaBr	+		$\longrightarrow$	Br_2	+	2NaCl
17.	$Pb(NO_3)_2$	+	Zn	$\longrightarrow$	$Zn(NO_3)_2$	+	

KEY LIST

S.	Mg	C.	Cu	R.	Zn	U.	Ca
I.	2Ag	P.	I_2	A.	$AgNO_3$	S.	$FeSO_4$
E.	$CuSO_4$	U.	Cl_2	P.	$2AgNO_3$	P.	2NaBr
T.	Pb	O.	H_2	E.	$CaCl_2$	D.	2HCl
F.	2Zn	J.	$FeNO_3$	O.	$Fe(NO_3)_2$	H.	$Ca(NO_3)_2$

GETTING PHYSICAL

Next to each change described below, write **P** if it is physical only, **C** if it is physical and chemical, and **N** if it is nuclear. To check if you got them right, colour in the spaces with the numbers of the questions in the mystery picture. Those that you labelled **P**, colour light green; the ones labelled **C**, colour dark green; and those labelled **N**, colour brown. The picture will show you an animal renowned as a quick-change artist.

1. David uses some petrol as a solvent to get a grease stain out of his shirt (not recommended!)
2. Janet leaves the top off a drum of petrol in the garage. The vapour fills the garage.
3. Simon comes into the garage and lights a match ....
4. A palm tree uses energy from the sun to convert carbon dioxide and water into starch.
5. Towards the end of the Sun's life, the frozen methane on Uranus will melt.
6. John beats an egg white to make meringue.
7. On 6th August 1945 the first atomic bomb to be used in warfare was exploded on Hiroshima.
8. A maize plant takes up water through its roots and then evaporates it through its leaves.
9. In the core of the Sun, hydrogen is changed into helium and huge amounts of energy are released.
10. Susie boils an egg for five minutes.
11. During fermentation, yeast produces alcohol and carbon dioxide from sugar.
12. Sally uses a 2 volt battery to run her model train set.
13. Billy eats and digests a chocolate ice-cream.
14. In a giant star, oxygen, carbon, and eventually iron are produced from other elements.
15. Carbon dioxide is cooled until it turns into 'dry ice' to be used for refrigeration.

Symbol Search

The Prof. thinks she has discovered a miracle cure for headaches but she can't remember in which file she has put the formula. Follow the maze by choosing the path at each junction which has the correct symbol for the element. When you get to a file, check a chemistry book to see if you have found the right formula.

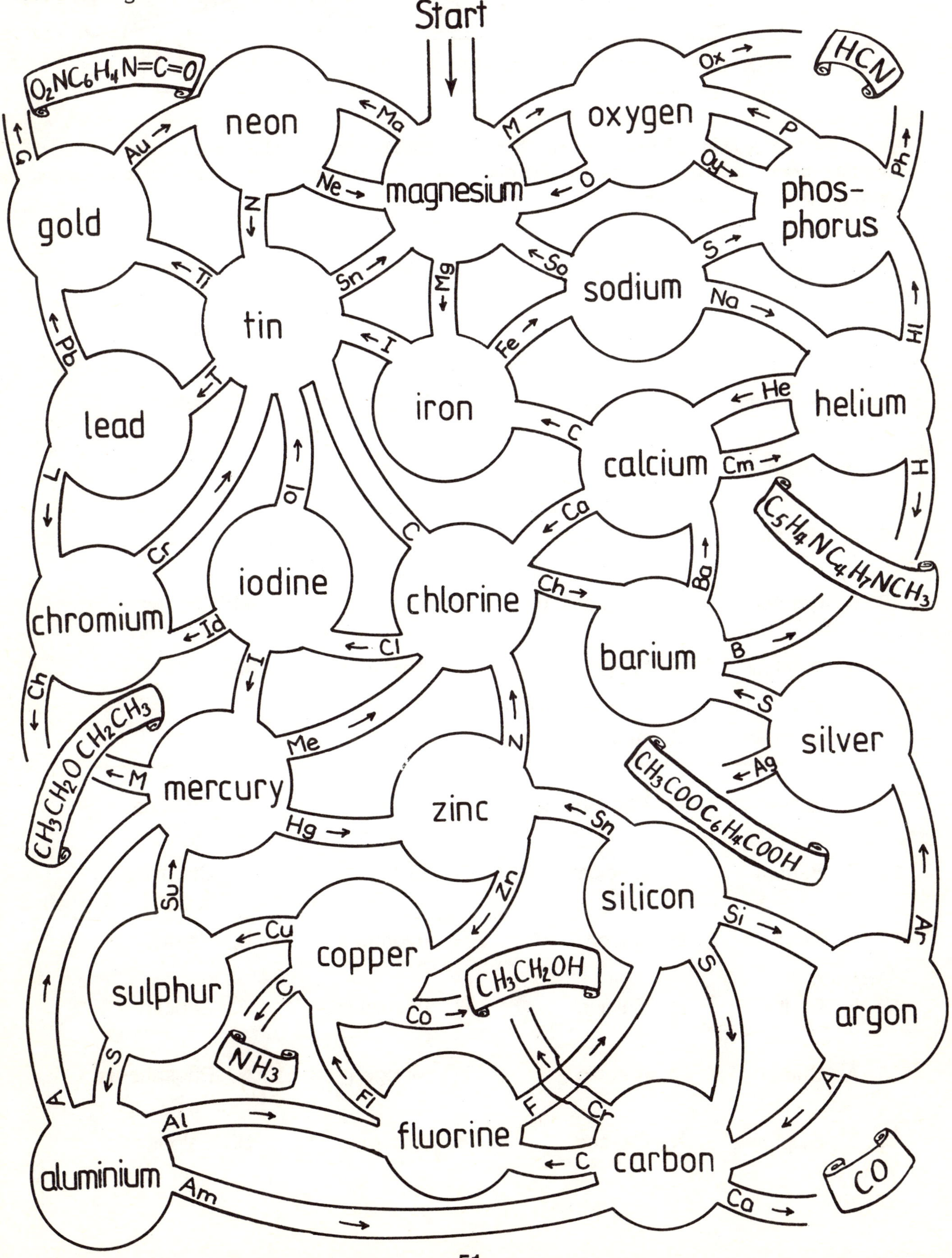

FAMILY FUN

WHEN DO AMERICAN VAMPIRES TAKE A HOLIDAY?

Each set of four elements contains one member which does not belong to the same chemical family as the other three. Circle the letter next to the odd-man-out in each set. Read the circled letters going down the page to find the answer.

1.	F. Iron	P. Sodium	C. Lithium	E. Potassium
2.	D. Neon	A. Nitrogen	R. Helium	J. Argon
3.	X. Strontium	T. Calcium	U. Magnesium	N. Sodium
4.	H. Chlorine	G. Oxygen	O. Fluorine	Z. Bromine
5.	L. Nitrogen	D. Phosphorus	I. Antimony	S. Argon
6.	G. Copper	B. Magnesium	E. Barium	M. Calcium
7.	I. Sulphur	A. Carbon	C. Silicon	K. Tin
8.	O. Bismuth	Q. Antimony	F. Arsenic	V. Lead
9.	G. Iodine	I. Phosphorus	J. Bromine	W. Chlorine
10.	S. Barium	T. Calcium	N. Tin	Y. Strontium
11.	A. Neon	L. Radon	G. Hydrogen	B. Krypton
12.	F. Lithium	D. Calcium	R. Potassium	P. Sodium
13.	A. Carbon	M. Arsenic	L. Nitrogen	N. Phosphorus
14.	T. Sulphur	X. Oxygen	Y. Silicon	B. Selenium

FERRETING OUT FORMULAE

The Prof. has discovered 'Dan-Ban', a miracle cure for dandruff, but as usual she has lost the formula. To help her find it, follow the maze by choosing the path at each junction which has the correct formula for the compound in the circle. When you finish, check to see if you have the right formula for 'Dan-Ban'.

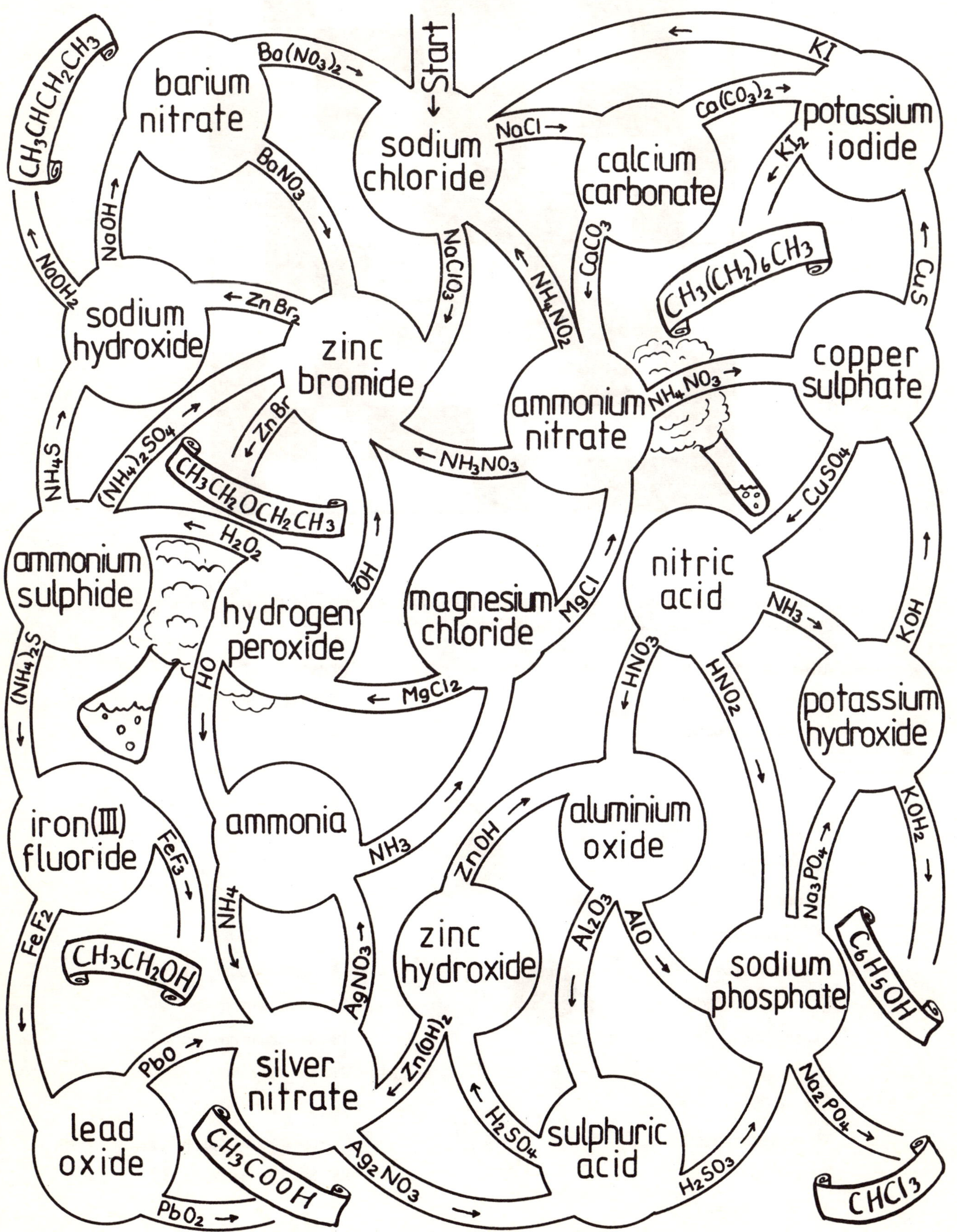

FORMULA FUN

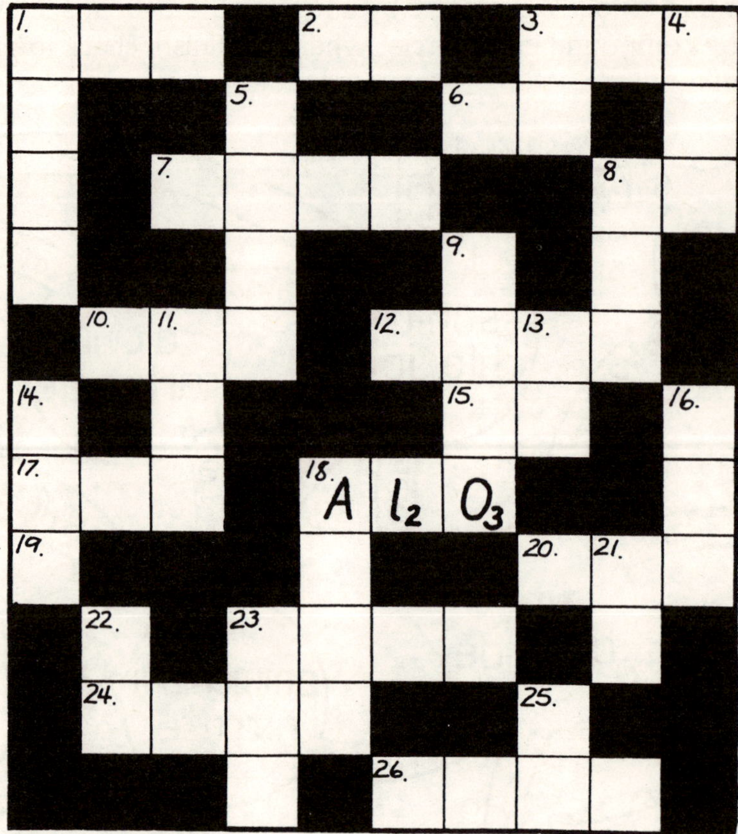

Work out the formulae for these chemical substances and put them into the puzzle. Number 18 Across is done for you as an example.

ACROSS

1. potassium hydroxide
2. hydrogen fluoride
3. lead sulphide
6. ammonia
7. mercury(II) chloride
8. hydrogen peroxide
10. phosphoric acid
12. sodium sulphate
15. carbon dioxide
17. strontium iodide
18. aluminium oxide
19. ozone
20. nitric acid
23. potassium chlorate
24. iron(III) chloride
26. magnesium sulphate

DOWN

1. potassium hydrogencarbonate
3. phosphine
4. silicon dioxide
5. magnesium carbonate
8. sulphuric acid
9. sodium carbonate
11. lead(II) iodide
13. sulphur dioxide
14. sulphuric acid
16. potassium nitrate
18. aluminium chloride
21. nitric(V) oxide
22. potassium fluoride
23. potassium cyanide
25. hydrogen sulphide

The Mole ~ Hole Game

Can you help the lost mole to find his own hole? Follow the maze by taking the path at each intersection which has the correct mass for the specified number of moles of the chemical compound in the circle. When you have finished, check to see if you got to the right mole hole.

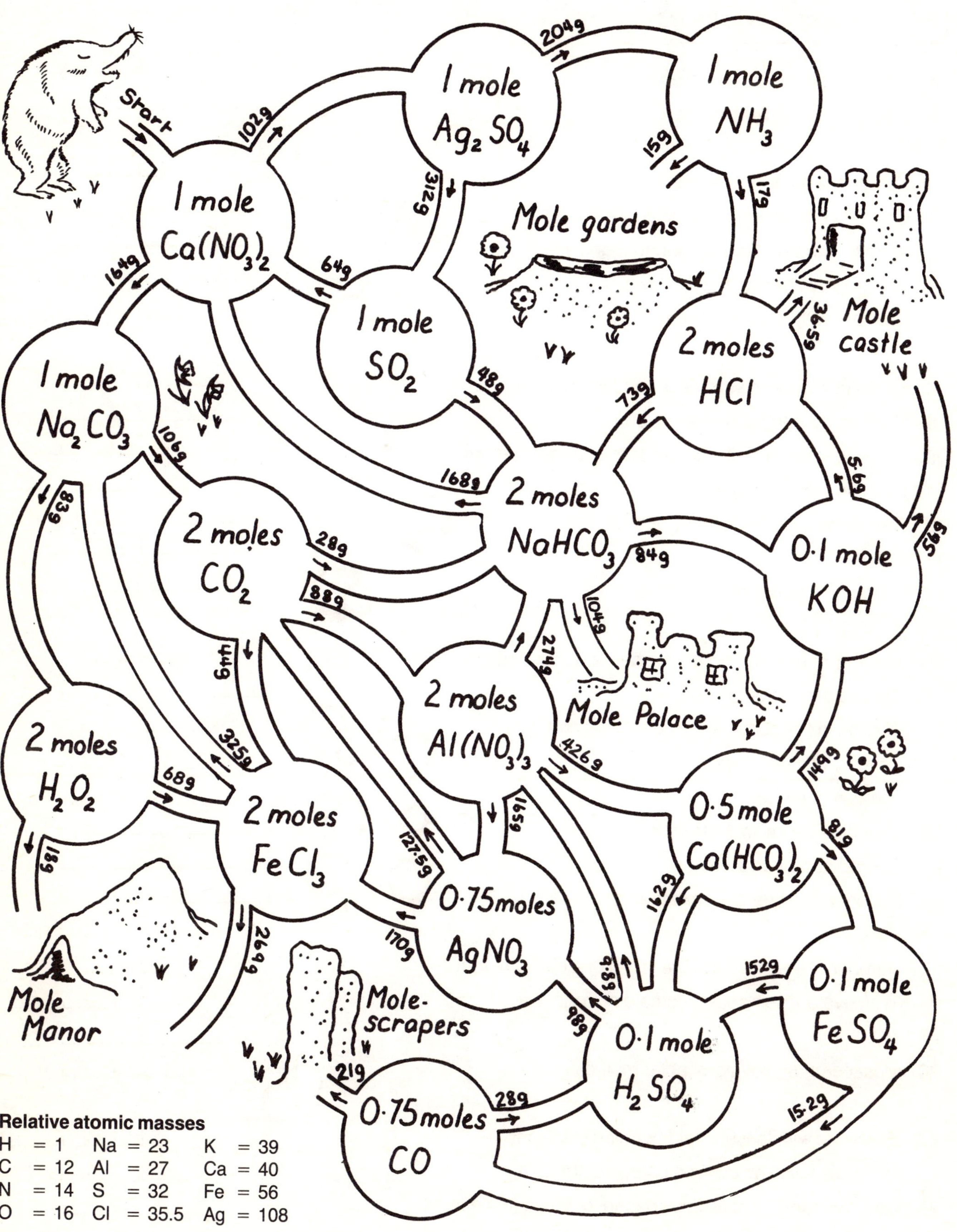

Relative atomic masses

H	= 1	Na	= 23	K	= 39
C	= 12	Al	= 27	Ca	= 40
N	= 14	S	= 32	Fe	= 56
O	= 16	Cl	= 35.5	Ag	= 108

Chemical Conundrum

IF A HIPPOPOTAMUS BREATHES OXYGEN DURING THE DAY,
WHAT DOES IT BREATHE AT NIGHT ?

1. Charged atom or group of atoms
2. Charge on a sodium ion

3. Number of protons in a helium nucleus
4. Consists of elements combined together
5. A small number of atoms joined together
6. Bonding by sharing of electrons
7. Element with atomic number of 11

8. Element with six electrons around the nucleus
9. Uncharged particle in the nucleus
10. Made up of atoms all with the same atomic number
11. Building blocks of matter
12. Part of the atom with a negative charge
13. SO_4^{2-}
14. Combining power of an atom or ion

15. Number of electrons in outer shell of a lithium atom
16. Charge on a chloride ion
17. Particle in the nucleus with a positive charge
18. Valency of aluminium
19. Valency of carbon
20. Explosive gas with a valency of 1
21. Central part of an atom
22. Founder of modern atomic theory

23. Number of electrons in outer shell of a calcium atom
24. In a covalent compound some electrons are ....
25. NO_3^-
26. Most common covalent, polar molecule

27. Elements with loosely held bonding electrons
28. Molecules with an uneven charge distribution
29. Usually made up of widely spaced, covalent molecules
30. Describes the reactivity of the 'noble' gases

!!

TOGETHERNESS

WHAT IS COUNT DRACULA'S FAVOURITE DRINK?

Next to each of the following statements write **T** if the statement is always true, **F** if it is always false, and **S** if it is sometimes true and sometimes false. Each group of three questions codes for one letter in the alphabet. Check the code list and write the letters in the numbered boxes to answer the riddle.

1	2	3	4	5	6	7	8	9	10	11

1A. Protons have a positive charge.
1B. Electrons are much smaller than protons.
1C. Chemical bonds involve attraction between opposite charges. ... ...

2A. HCl gas dissolves in water to give H^+ and Cl^- ions.
2B. Solutions of covalent molecules do not conduct electricity.
2C. Neutrons have a negative charge. ... ...

3A. The formula for magnesium chloride is MgCl.
3B. Ionic solids are crystalline.
3C. Metal ions have a charge of +1. ... ...

4A. A Li^+ ion has the same number of electrons as a H atom.
4B. Hydrogen gas dissolves in water to give hydrogen ions.
4C. Chlorine forms ionic compounds. ... ...

5A. The atomic number is the total number of protons and neutrons.
5B. Electrons can move freely through a crystal of NaCl.
5C. Ionic solids dissolve readily in water. ... ...

6A. Atoms in a glucose molecule are held together by covalent bonds.
6B. The formula for potassium sulphate is KSO_4.
6C. Gas molecules have covalent bonding. ... ...

7A. Iron ions have a charge of +2.
7B. Inert gases have 8 electrons in their outer shell.
7C. The formula for neon is Ne. ... ...

8A. A Mg^{2+} ion has the same number of electrons as a Na atom.
8B. Carbon usually forms ionic bonds with other elements.
8C. The formula for aluminium oxide is Al_2O_3. ... ...

9A. Solutions containing dissolved ions conduct electricity.
9B. Covalent bonds involve sharing of electrons.
9C. Chloride ions have a charge of −1. ... ...

10A. A nitrate ion has the formula for NO_3^{2-}.
10B. A compound containing H and O only has the formula H_2O.
10C. Oxygen forms ionic compounds. ... ...

11A. Carbon conducts electricity.
11B. Metals have very high melting points.
11C. F and Cl have the same number of electrons in their outer shells. ... ...

Code List

A	TTT	J	FTT	S	STT
B	TTF	K	FTF	T	STF
C	TTS	L	FTS	U	STS
D	TFT	M	FFT	V	SFT
E	TFF	N	FFF	W	SFF
F	TFS	O	FFS	X	SFS
G	TST	P	FST	Y	SST
H	TSF	Q	FSF	Z	SSF
I	TSS	R	FSS		

PARTICLE PUZZLE

These words have something to do with atoms and molecules. Unscramble them and fit them into the puzzle. There are clues to help you.

1. Particle with a negative charge	CEELRONT	....
2. Made up of atoms which all have the same atomic number	MELETEN	....
3. Needed for motion	REENGY	....
4. Charged atom or group of atoms	NOI	....
5. Same number of protons – different number of neutrons	TOSIPOE	....
6. Anything which takes up space	TAMRET	....
7. Smallest bit of a substance which can normally exist	ELOMCUEL	....
8. Number of protons in a hydrogen atom	NEO	....
9. Charge on an electron	GEANVITE	....
10. Nuclear particle with no electric charge	TUNENOR	....
11. Central part of the atom	LUNCEUS	....
12. Very small bit of matter	RAPTLIEC	....
13. Charge on a proton	SOIPVIET	....
14. A particle in the nucleus	TORPNO	....

WATERY WORDS

WHY DON'T WHALES EAT TURTLES ?

Unscramble these watery words and their initial letters will spell out the answer to the riddle. There are clues to help you.

	Clue	Scrambled	Answer
1.	Global movements of water caused by gravitational pull of Moon and Sun	DIETS	....
2.	Amount of water vapour in the air	DIMUHITY	....
3.	Change from liquid to a gas	PAVEROTIONA	....
4.	Small two-masted sailing vessel	WAYL	....
5.	Change from water vapour to liquid water	DONCENSE	....
6.	Underground water	RATESIAN	....
7.	World's longest river	LIEN	....
8.	Cyclone of west Pacific ocean	POONTHY	....
9.	River of ice	LACIERG	....
10.	Huge ocean current which affects Earth's weather patterns	LE NOIN	....
11.	The sea goes up and down each day	DIET	....
12.	Physical factor of water which decreases with depth	PEMTREATURE	....
13.	Pellets of falling ice	LIAH	....
14.	Removal of weathered material, often by water	SORIONE	....
15.	Dry river channel in the desert	DIAW	....
16.	Bending of light as it passes through water	FERCARTION	....
17.	Largest river in the southern hemisphere	MAZOAN	....
18.	Places where most of the earth's fresh water is found	LOEPS	....
19.	Physical factor of water which increases with depth	SSUREERP	....
20.	Water with a crystalline structure	ECI	....
21.	Small tidal change	EPAN	....
22.	Gushing steam and water from below Earth's surface	YEGRES	....
23.	Essential gas for living things which dissolves in water	NEOGXY	....
24.	Change from liquid water to ice	ZEEREF	....
25.	Sediment built up where a river flows into a lake	NAF	....

ATMOSPHERICS

ACROSS

1. And 3: Makes up 0.03% of atmosphere – needed by plants for photosynthesis (2 words)
6. Inert gas which makes up 0.9% of the atmosphere
9. Layer of the atmosphere with most ozone
11. Soluble oxide of nitrogen produced in the upper atmosphere (formula)
12. Number of atoms in a nitrogen molecule
13. Radioactive isotope of this gas may be a dangerous pollutant if released into the atmosphere (symbol)
14. And 17 down: Pollutant produced by sulphur dioxide from coal-burning power stations (2 words)
16. Electromagnetic radiation which cannot readily escape from the Earth's atmosphere (abbrev.)
18. And 19: Belts of charged particles trapped in the atmosphere by the Earth's magnetic field (2 words)
21. Short wavelength radiation absorbed by the ozone layer (abbrev.)
23. Poisonous oxide of carbon produced by cars (formula)
24. Oxide of nitrogen produced by lightning in the upper atmosphere (formula)
25. Pungent gas found in Jupiter's atmosphere but not in Earth's, thankfully
26. Mixture of 79% nitrogen, 21% oxygen and 0.9% argon
27. A metal atmospheric pollutant more common in cities

DOWN

1. The cause of winds in the atmosphere
2. Colour of light least strongly refracted by the atmosphere
4. Charged atom or group of atoms
5. Inert gas (symbol)
6. Shimmering lights in the polar atmosphere
7. Form of oxygen which absorbs radiant energy in the stratosphere
8. Inventor of the mercury barometer for measuring atmospheric pressure
9. Fog + man-made pollutants trapped by a temperature inversion
10. Air pollutant, a by-product of burning coal (formula)
15. Scientist who showed in 1648 that air pressure decreases with altitude
20. Unit for measuring radiation
22. Indicates wind direction
25. Symbol for 0.9% of the atmosphere

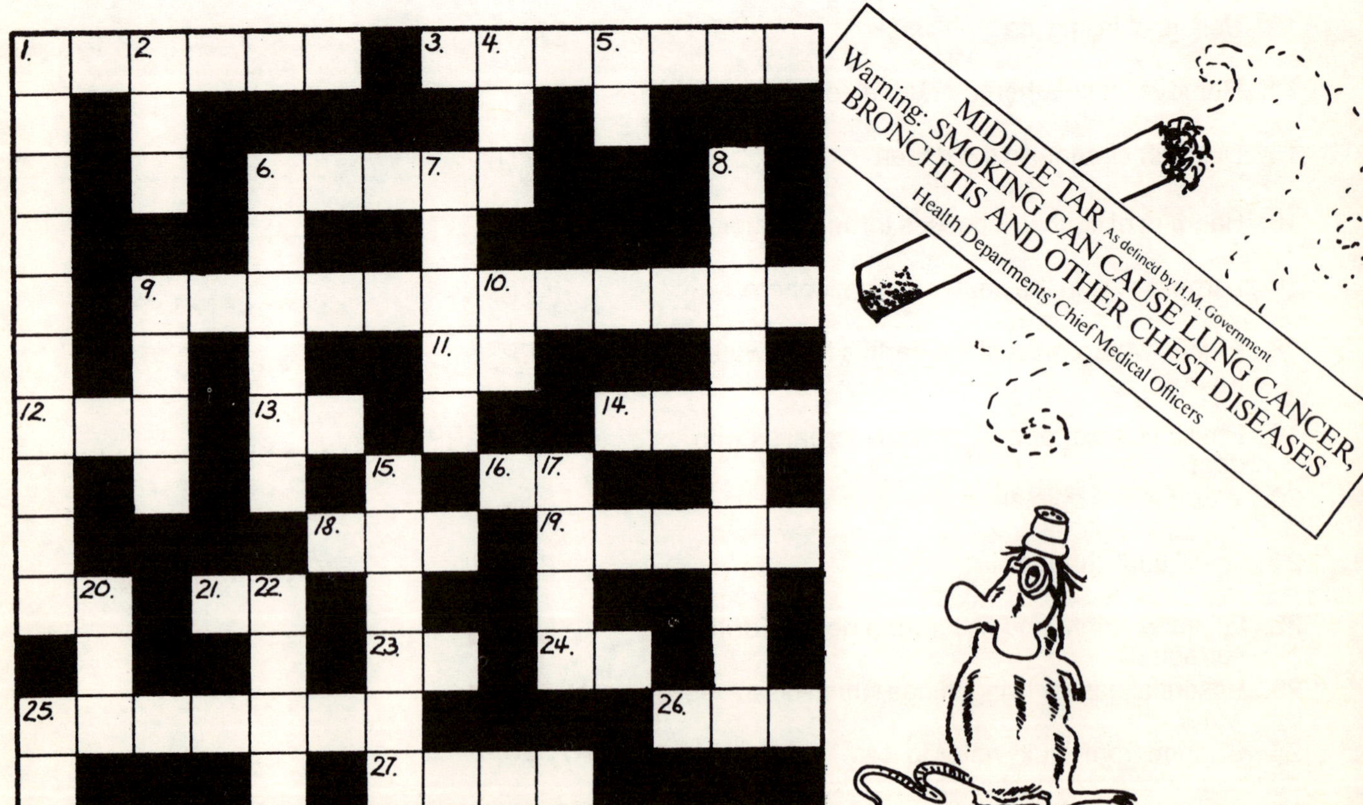

FORECASTING FUN

WHAT'S WORSE THAN BEING OUT WHEN IT'S RAINING CATS AND DOGS ?

1. Lines on a weather map showing equal pressure
2. Instrument for measuring humidity
3. Whispy clouds made up of tiny ice crystals
4. Season of heavy rainfall in tropics
5. Fog + pollution trapped by a temperature inversion

6. Instrument for measuring wind speed
7. Billowy, dome-shaped clouds with flat bases
8. Main way in which heat is circulated through the atmosphere

9. Point at which the atmosphere is saturated with water vapour and condenses on surfaces (2 words)
10. Envelope of gas surrounding the Earth
11. Instrument for measuring air pressure
12. Boundary between masses of warm and cold air

13. Units in which rainfall is measured
14. Clouds in layers or broad sheets
15. Change from a gas to a liquid by cooling

16. Frozen rain
17. Instrument which can track storms
18. Units in which atmospheric pressure is measured
19. High intensity wind system spinning around a centre of low pressure
20. Effect which causes winds to blow east or west because of the Earth's spin
21. Form of oxygen in upper atmosphere which absorbs UV
22. Low-level condensation of water on invisible particles in the air

23. Force 10 on the Beaufort scale
24. Persistent global winds blowing over oceans
25. Very high energy radiation found in the outer atmosphere
26. Measure of the amount of water vapour in the atmosphere
27. Region of Earth's atmosphere mainly responsible for the weather

WHAT IS THE BEST WAY
TO MAKE AN APPLE PUFF ?

1. Densest part of the atmosphere
2. Instrument for measuring wind speed
3. Inert gas found in the atmosphere
4. Metallic air pollutant

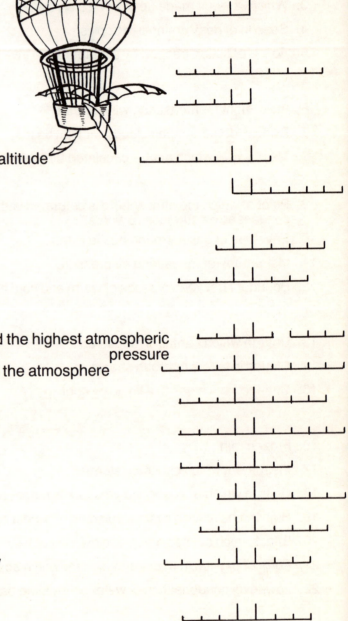

5. Amount of water vapour in the air
6. Small particles of dirt in the air

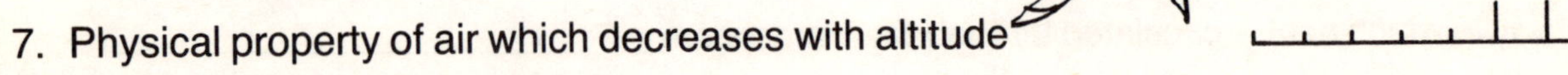

7. Physical property of air which decreases with altitude
8. Gas needed by most living organisms

9. Complete absence of air
10. Chemical reaction which needs oxygen

11. Place on Earth where you would expect to find the highest atmospheric pressure
12. Main process by which heat is passed around the atmosphere

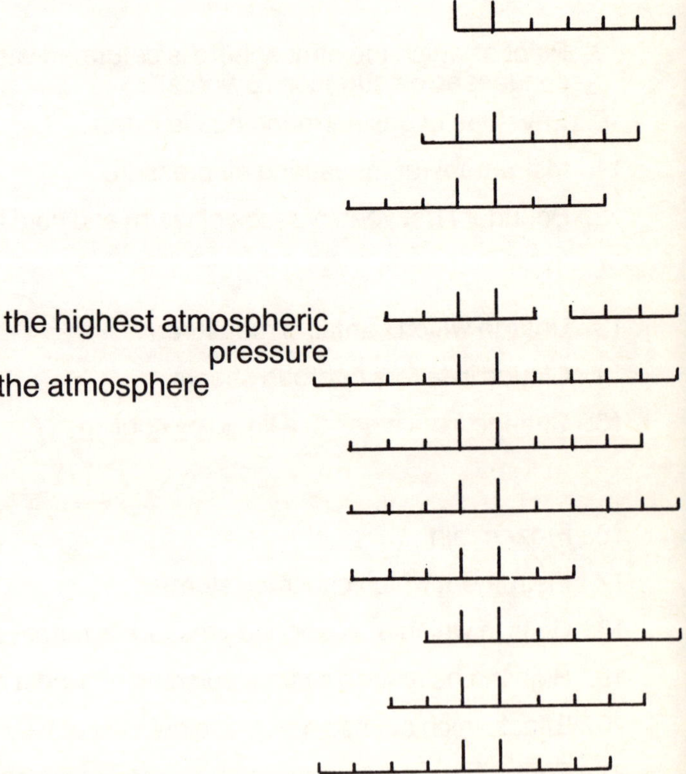

13. Most abundant gas in our atmosphere
14. Instrument for measuring air pressure
15. Main component of soot
16. Oxide needed by green plants
17. Intense low pressure system
18. Winds are caused by variation in this property

19. Natural source of massive air pollution
20. Inert gas used by divers
21. Rising current of hot air
22. Atmospheric layer which contains most ozone
23. Chemist who discovered oxygen

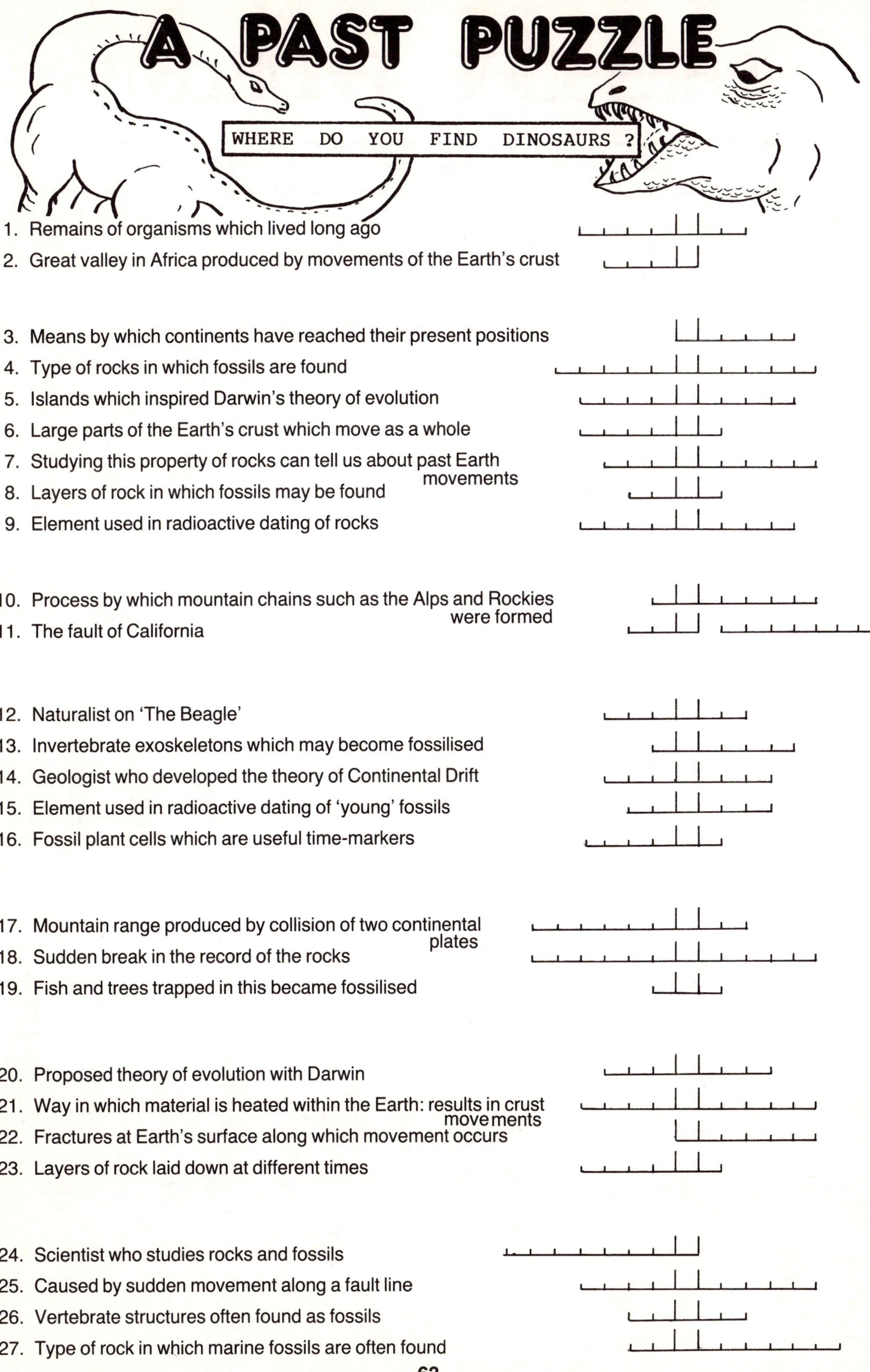

A PAST PUZZLE

WHERE DO YOU FIND DINOSAURS ?

1. Remains of organisms which lived long ago
2. Great valley in Africa produced by movements of the Earth's crust

3. Means by which continents have reached their present positions
4. Type of rocks in which fossils are found
5. Islands which inspired Darwin's theory of evolution
6. Large parts of the Earth's crust which move as a whole
7. Studying this property of rocks can tell us about past Earth movements
8. Layers of rock in which fossils may be found
9. Element used in radioactive dating of rocks

10. Process by which mountain chains such as the Alps and Rockies were formed
11. The fault of California

12. Naturalist on 'The Beagle'
13. Invertebrate exoskeletons which may become fossilised
14. Geologist who developed the theory of Continental Drift
15. Element used in radioactive dating of 'young' fossils
16. Fossil plant cells which are useful time-markers

17. Mountain range produced by collision of two continental plates
18. Sudden break in the record of the rocks
19. Fish and trees trapped in this became fossilised

20. Proposed theory of evolution with Darwin
21. Way in which material is heated within the Earth: results in crust movements
22. Fractures at Earth's surface along which movement occurs
23. Layers of rock laid down at different times

24. Scientist who studies rocks and fossils
25. Caused by sudden movement along a fault line
26. Vertebrate structures often found as fossils
27. Type of rock in which marine fossils are often found

PRESSURE PROBLEMS

WHAT LIES AT THE BOTTOM OF THE SEA AND SHIVERS ?

Fill in the missing quantities next to the diagrams below. Find the numerical value of each answer in the key list and write the corresponding letter in the box with the number of the question.

1	2	3	4	5	6	7	8	9	10	11	12	13

Useful information
$1\ m^2 = 10\,000\ cm^2$
9.8 N = 1 kg-wt
1 Pa = 1 N/m^2

Mass of elephant = 6400 kg
Total surface area of feet = $0.4\ m^2$

1. Force elephant exerts on ground = ... N
2. Pressure elephant exerts on ground = ... Pa

Mass of dancer = 50 kg
Area of foot in contact with ground = $5\ cm^2$

3. Force dancer exerts on ground = ... N
4. Pressure dancer exerts on ground = ... Pa

Density of granite = $2640\ kg/m^3$

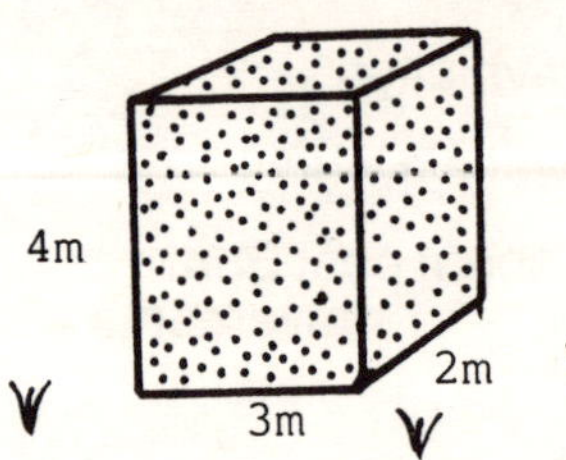

5. Total mass of block = ... kg-wt
6. Pressure of block on ground = ... Pa

Area of top of head = $200\ cm^2$
Air pressure = 98 000 Pa

7. Total force acting down on head due to air = ... N

Density of water = $1000\ kg/m^3$
Density of concrete = $2160\ kg/m^3$

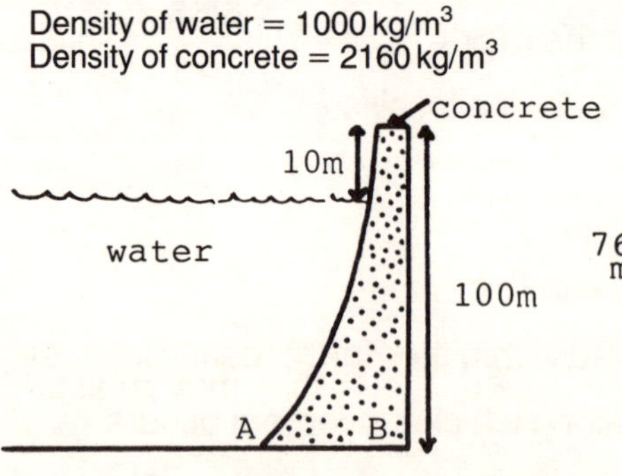

8. Mass of water above $1\ m^2$ of bottom at A = ... kg
9. Mass of concrete above $1\ m^2$ of base at B5 = ... kg

Density of sea water = $1020\ kg/m^3$
Depth of diver = 50 m
Area of upper surface of body = $0.9\ m^2$

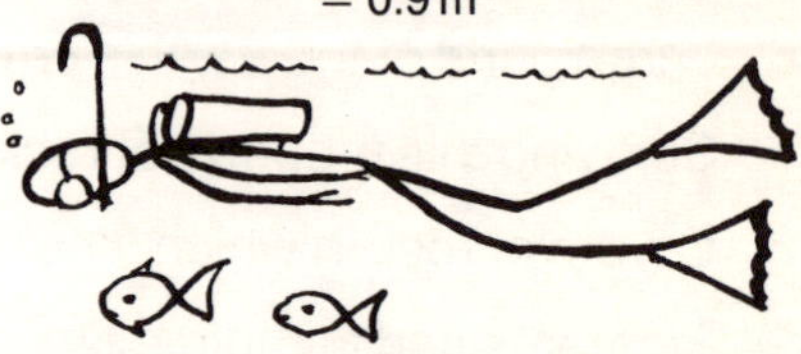

10. Mass of water above $1\ m^2$ at 50 m depth = ... kg
11. Mass of water above diver's body = ... kg

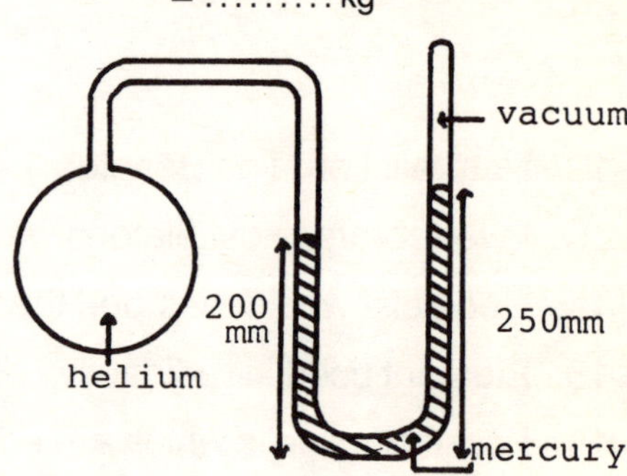

12. Pressure of helium = ... mmHg

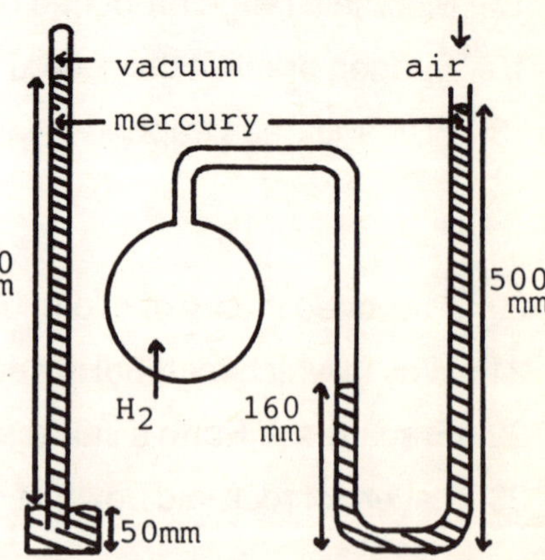

13. Pressure of hydrogen = ... mmHg

KEY LIST

C.	50	I.	340	M.	2640	R.	51 000	L.	100 000
G.	98	E.	490	D.	6400	A.	62 720	N.	156 800
F.	200	K.	1100	O.	103 488	V.	63 360	W.	216 000
T.	250	U.	1960	E.	45 900	S.	90 000	R.	980 000

FINDING FORCES

Work out these problems. If your answers are correct they will fit into the puzzle below. (1 tonne = 1000 kg. The value of g, the acceleration due to gravity = 9.8 m/s^2. (Mass of 1 dm^3 of water = 1 kg). Find the force needed:

ACROSS

1. To give a 1.5 kg discus an acceleration of 20 m/s^2. .... N
2. For a 50 kg woman on a 20 kg bicycle travelling at 6 m/s to come to a halt in 2 seconds. .... N
5. To accelerate a 10 kg mass from 5 m/s to 10 m/s in 1.25 s. .... N
6. For a pump to raise 60 dm^3 of water. .... N
8. To bring a 37.5 tonne engine travelling at 20 m/s to a halt in 10 seconds. .... N
10. To give a mass of 25 kg an acceleration of 18 m/s^2. .... N
11. To give a 100 000 kg rocket an acceleration of 15 m/s^2 in outer space .... N

DOWN

1. To shoot a 55 kg human cannonball out of a cannon with an acceleration of 7 m/s^2. .... N
2. To lift a bullock with a mass of 250 kg. .... N
3. For a bowler to give a 150 g cricket ball enough acceleration for it to reach a velocity of 60 km/h in 0.25 s. .... N
4. To accelerate a 1500 kg space probe from 54 000 to 54 900 km/h in 20 seconds. .... N
7. To increase the velocity of 1000 kg car from 10 m/s to 20 m/s in 5 seconds. .... N
9. To decrease the velocity of a 250 kg motor-bike from 20 m/s to 12 m/s in 4 seconds. .... N

WHERE ON HIS TRAVELS DID MAD MIKE SEE MUMMIES SWIMMING?

To find the answer, first of all you must solve these problems. Find the numerical value of each answer in the key list and write the corresponding letter next to your answer, then read down.

Useful formulae for coping with Mad Mike

$$\text{Speed or velocity} = \frac{\text{distance travelled}}{\text{time taken}}$$

$$\text{Acceleration} = \frac{\text{velocity change}}{\text{time taken}}$$

Acceleration due to gravity = 9.8 m/s^2

1. Mad Mike is one of those super-fit types. He sets off to run non-stop from Paris to Berlin at an average speed of 5 km/h. He takes exactly eight days to reach Berlin. How far has he travelled?

   .... km
2. He now sets off to Bombay by motor-bike. It takes him 25 days to cover the 6000 kilometres. What was his average speed?

   .... km/h
3. It's another 2000 km to Calcutta and Mike does the trip at an average speed of 25 km/h. How long does it take him?

   .... hs
4. Mike sets off to Kathmandu by bullock cart. He travels at an average speed of 2.5 km/h, and arrives 22 bone-shattering days later. How far did he travel?

   .... km
5. Overcome by the mountain air, the bullock breaks into a trot and increases its velocity from 1 m/s to 3 m/s in 4 seconds. What is its acceleration?

   .... m/s^2
6. Mike decides to take a sight-seeing flight to Mount Everest. The plane hurtles down the runway, and is airborne ten seconds after it starts moving. If it accelerates at 5 m/s^2, what is its take-off velocity?

   .... km/h
7. The plane climbs for four minutes at a vertical speed of 3.5 m/s. How much height does it gain?

   .... m
8. Panic! The engines fail. Neglecting air resistance, how fast is the plane falling at the end of 10 seconds?

   .... m/s
9. How much height has the plane lost?

   .... m
10. The engines start again! Once the plane is climbing at a rate of 2.5 m/s how long will it take to regain the height lost (in No. 9)?

    .... s

KEY LIST

E. 0.5	H. 10	E. 80	A. 196	J. 528	B. 980
R. 0.75	L. 40	S. 98	W. 240	D. 840	U. 1225
I. 4	P. 50	A. 180	E. 490	T. 960	D. 1320

Mad Mike 2

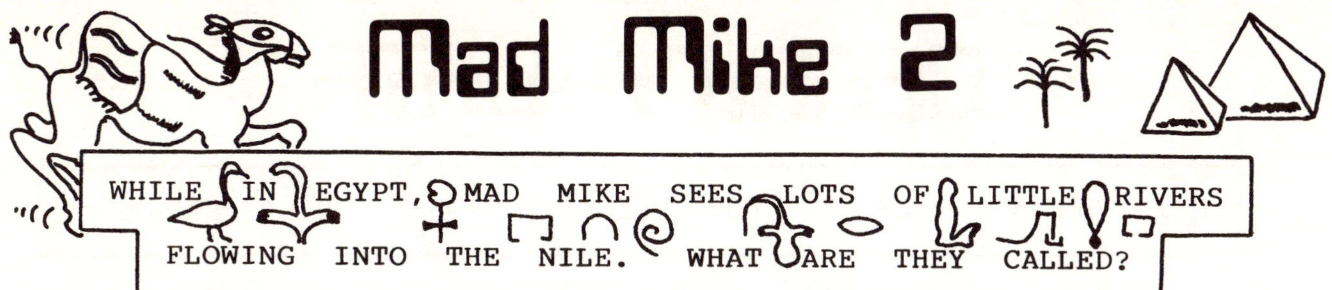

WHILE IN EGYPT, MAD MIKE SEES LOTS OF LITTLE RIVERS FLOWING INTO THE NILE. WHAT ARE THEY CALLED?

To find out, first of all you must solve these problems. Find the numerical value of each answer in the key list and write the corresponding letter next to your answer. Read down the page.

$$\text{Work done} = \text{force used} \times \text{distance moved}$$

$$\text{Power} = \frac{\text{work done}}{\text{time taken}}$$

$$\text{Force} = \text{mass} \times \text{acceleration}$$

$$\text{Acceleration due to gravity} = 9.8\ \text{m/s}^2$$

1. Mad Mike takes off from Peking airport in a 747 with a mass of 350 tonnes. What force will be needed to lift the plane off the runway?
   .... N
2. Mad Mike plans to go to Egypt but catches a plane to Moscow by mistake. The 5800 km flight takes six hours. Four hours later he takes off for Cairo. The 2750 km trip takes him five hours. What was his overall average speed from Peking to Cairo?
   .... km/h
3. The direct distance from Peking to Cairo is 7500 km. What was Mad Mike's average velocity between Peking and Cairo?
   .... km/h
4. Mad Mike heads west across the Sahara by camel. The camel (Cedric) makes a great effort and from a standing start reaches a velocity of 8 m/s in 5 seconds. This requires a muscular force of 1200 N. What is Cedric's mass? (Neglect friction.)
   .... kg
5. Many days later Mike reaches Casablanca where he and Cedric stop for a long, cool drink. Mike lifts a 500 g mug of beer to a height of 0.5 m. How much work does he do?
   .... J
6. Cedric (being a camel) has further to lift his 1 kg mug of beer, but manages to raise it to a height of 2.5 m in 5 seconds. What power (rate of doing work) does he develop?
   .... watts (J/s)
7. Mike and Cedric take a ship for Rome. The ship has a mass of 4500 tonnes and the engine provides a thrust (force) of 90 000 N. What is the shortest time in which the ship can accelerate from 10 to 28 km/h?
   .... s
8. The ship reaches Rome but disaster is in store for Mad Mike. The captain forgets to put on the brakes and hits the wharf with a dreadful crash while travelling at 9 km/h. Five seconds later the ship shudders to a halt. What was the deceleration?
   .... m/s^2
9. All this messing around fair gives Cedric the hump and he decides to leave. Hanging on grimly, Mike does 1700 J of work in order to stop him. If Mike was pulling on the halter with a force of 500 N, how far did Cedric get before he was stopped?
   .... m

KEY LIST

A.	0.25	R.	1.8	I.	4.9	B.	30	V.	500	O.	1500
C.	0.3	N.	2.45	P.	5	D.	50	U.	570	M.	3500
E.	0.5	S.	3.4	L.	25	I.	250	E.	750	F.	350 000
								T.	780	J.	3430 000

DENSITY DATA

WHAT DO YOU GET IF YOU TEACH A YOUNG SHEEP KARATE ?

Solve these problems on density. For each one, find the letter in the key list corresponding to the numerical value of your answer and write it next to the number of the question. Read the letters down the page to get the answer to the riddle.

Table of densities

battery acid	1.4 g/cm^3
carbon dioxide at 1 atmosphere pressure	2.0 g/cm^3
glass	2.7 g/cm^3
glycerol	1.26 g/cm^3
lead	11.4 g/cm^3
mercury	13.6 g/cm^3
rock	3.9 g/cm^3
water	1.0 g/cm^3

1. Find the density of a sample of seawater if 15 dm^3 has a mass of 15.30 kg. .... kg/dm^3
2. What will be the mass of a bar of lead which measures 3 cm × 2 cm × 5 cm? .... g
3. By how much is 250 cm^3 of glycerol heavier than 250 cm^3 of water? .... g
4. What is the volume of a vessel which contains 100 g of carbon dioxide at atmospheric pressure? .... dm^3
5. A 40 dm^3 drum has a mass of 5 kg. When filled with petrol it has a total mass of 32.6 kg. What is the density of the petrol? .... kg/dm^3
6. A student has a beam balance with 10 cm^3 of mercury in one pan. What volume of water will he need in the other pan to balance the mercury? .... cm^3
7. A measuring cylinder contains 35 cm^3 of water. When a piece of rock is dropped into the water the level rises to 60 cm^3. What is the mass of the rock? .... g
8. 500 cm^3 of water are added to 500 cm^3 of battery acid. What is the density of the mixture? .... g/cm^3
9. A glass cube has a mass of 21.6 g. How long is the edge of the cube? .... cm

KEY LIST

C.	0.69	P.	1.2	D.	5	M.	65	B.	200
W.	0.815	S.	2	E.	6.9	O.	97.5	G.	234
R.	0.98	J.	2.4	K.	8	H.	136	I.	315
L.	1.02	E.	2.63	B.	50	F.	126	A.	342

PUSH 'N PULL

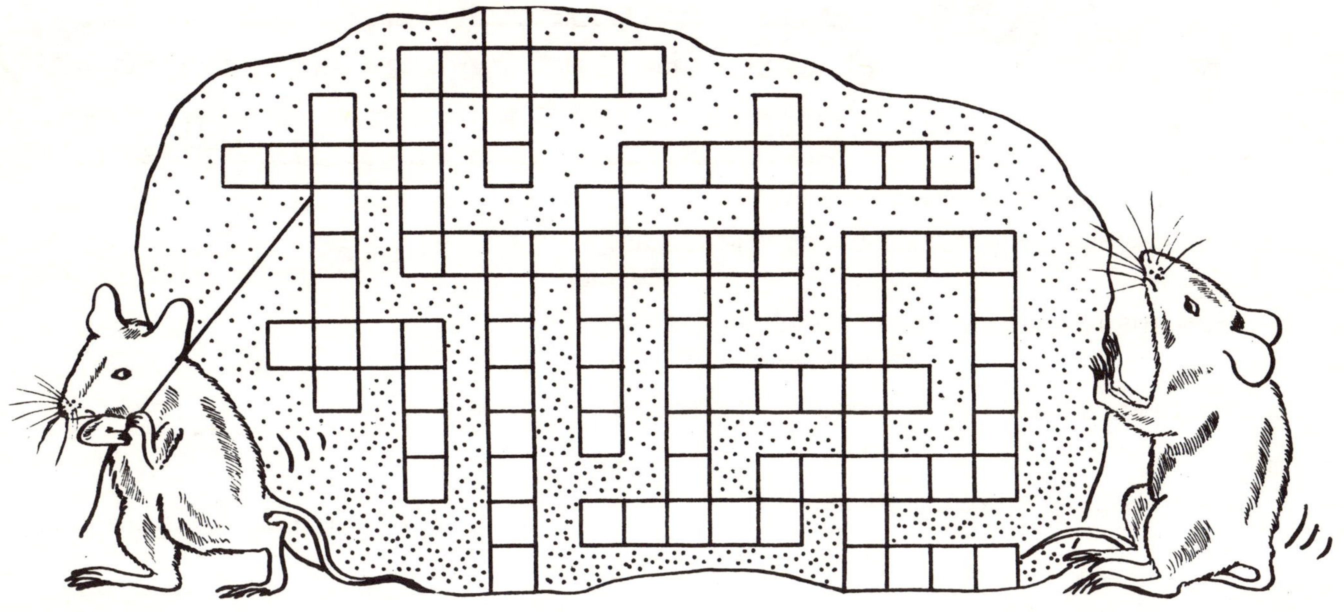

All these words are connected with forces. Unscramble them and fit them into the puzzle. There are clues to help you.

	Clue	Scrambled	Answer
1.	To start to do this needs a force	VOEM	....
2.	A force can make an object move faster or . . .	WOLSER	....
3.	. . . can be changed by a force	EPESD	....
4.	Force which pulls you towards the centre of the Earth	VARGITY	....
5.	Large unit of mass	NOTEN	....
6.	Can change the way in which an object moves	CEROF	....
7.	Measure of speed in a particular direction	COELVITY	....
8.	} Whenever a force acts these are equal and opposite	TACOIN	....
9.		ERTACOIN	....
10.	A force is needed to change this	RIDCETION	....
11.	Has force of gravity ⅙ that of Earth	NOMO	....
12.	} Two kinds of change in motion which both require a force	POST	....
13.		TRAST	....
14.	This must reach escape velocity if it is to escape into space	CORTEK	....
15.	Tendency to resist changes in movement	RIENIAT	....
16.	If you increase this it takes more force to get it moving	SAMS	....
17.	Unit of force	WETNON	....
18.	A force can be a push or a . . .	LUPL	....
19.	The result of mass times velocity	NEMOMTUM	....
20.	Something moving is said to be in . . .	TOMION	....

A Weighty Problem

WHAT TIME IS IT WHEN AN ELEPHANT SITS ON A FENCE ?

1. Force which attracts objects together
2. Tendency of a body to resist changes in its state of motion
3. 16th century scientist who studied the motion of pendulums and planets
4. Kind of force between two magnetic north poles
5. Force between charged particles
6. Force which keeps an object moving in a circle
7. Mass times velocity
8. Force field produced by the Earth
9. Kind of force between a negative and a positive charge
10. Speed in a definite direction
11. Force with which an object is pulled towards the centre of the Earth
12. Arrow showing direction of a force
13. Force between two surfaces in contact
14. Quantity of matter in an object
15. Describes the effect of two forces which produce no change in motion
16. Velocity required to overcome Earth's gravitational pull
17. Unit of force
18. Needed to change the state of motion
19. Planet with largest force of gravity
20. Maximum velocity reached by an object falling through air
21. An opposite and opposing force
22. A force can change the speed or .... of a moving object

Directional Dilemma

WHAT IS LONG, YELLOW AND ESSENTIAL FOR MONKEYS LOST IN THE DESERT ?

Next to each of the following statements write **T** if the statement is always true, **F** if it is always false, and **S** if it is sometimes true and sometimes false. Each pair of questions codes for one letter in the alphabet. Check the code list and write the letters in the numbered boxes to answer the riddle.

CODE LIST

A	TT	E	FT	M	ST
B	TF	G	FF	N	SF
C	TS	I	FS	T	SS

1.	2.	3.	4.	5.	6.	7.	8.	9.	10.	11.	12.	13.	14.	15.

1A. The quantity of matter in an object is its mass.
1B. An object in outer space has mass but no weight. } ......

2A. More force is needed to stop a truck than a car.
2B. The gravitational attraction between two objects depends on their masses. } ......

3A. A centripetal force tends to keep an object moving in a circle.
3B. Whenever a force acts there is an equal force in the opposite direction. } ......

4A. There is no gravity on the moon.
4B. There is a force of attraction between positive electric charges. } ......

5A. If a force acts on an object the object will go faster.
5B. A man would weigh more on the Earth than he would on Jupiter. } ......

6A. The momentum of an object depends on its size.
6B. Friction opposes motion. } ......

7A. Acceleration involves a change in direction.
7B. A magnet has a force of attraction for a metal. } ......

8A. There can be no gravity in a vacuum.
8B. Forces are measured in newtons. } ......

9A. If an object is changing direction the forces acting on it must be unbalanced.
9B. A moving bus has more momentum than a moving car. } ......

10A. All objects in the solar system are attracted to the Earth.
10B. There is a force of repulsion between unlike magnetic poles. } ......

11A. If the distance between two objects is doubled, the force of attraction is reduced by ¾.
11B. A force is needed to change the direction in which an object is moving. } ......

12A. Change in velocity means an increase in speed.
12B. There is a force of repulsion between negative electric charges. } ......

13A. The inertia of an object is its tendency to resist changes in its state of motion.
13B. A force has magnitude and direction. } ......

14A. When a force acts on an object there is a change of motion.
14B. When a rocket reaches escape velocity it is no longer pulled towards the earth. } ......

15A. Objects of different masses fall at the same rate in a vacuum.
15B. The forces acting on an object at constant velocity are balanced. } ......

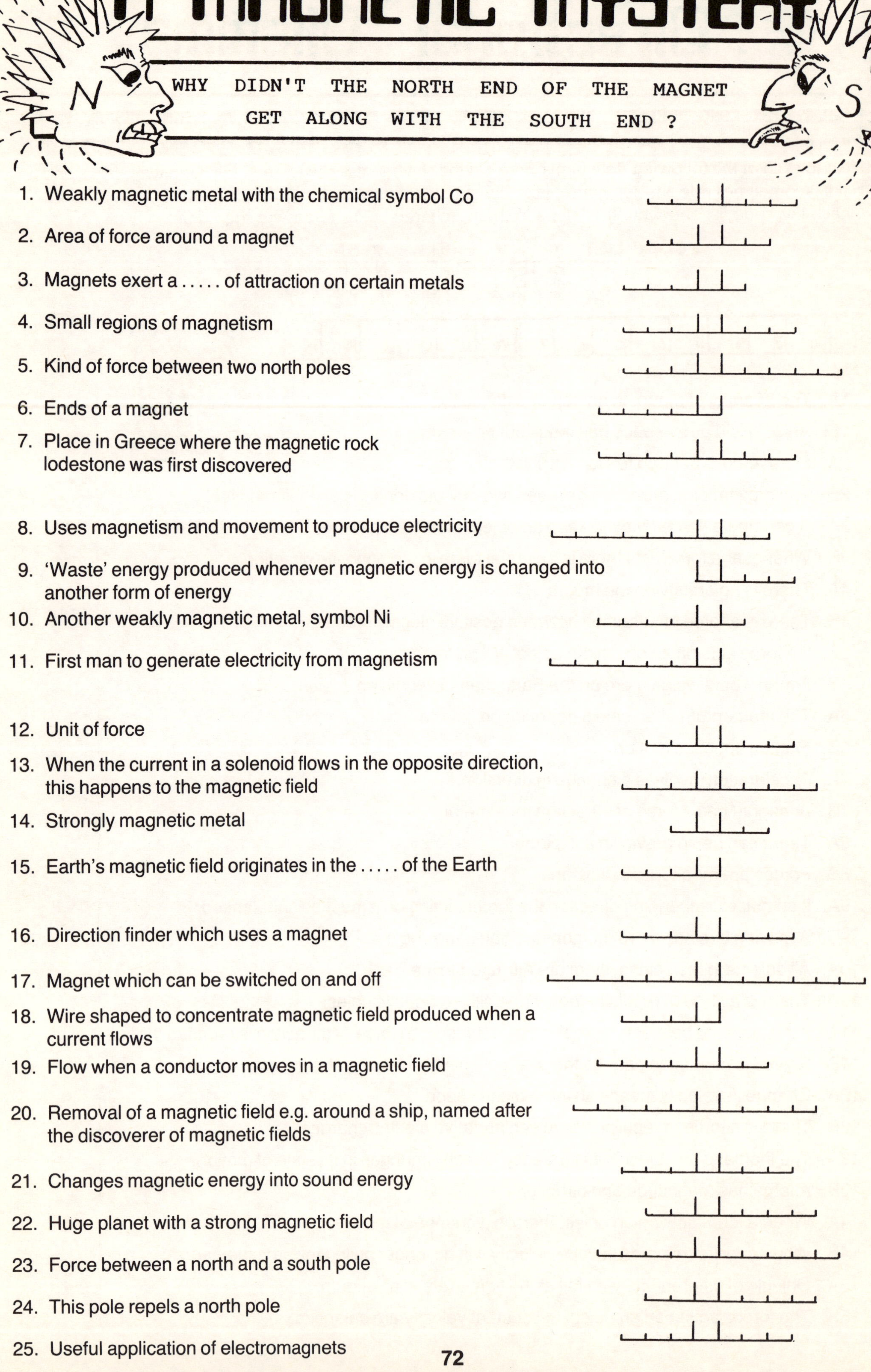

A MAGNETIC MYSTERY

WHY DIDN'T THE NORTH END OF THE MAGNET GET ALONG WITH THE SOUTH END ?

1. Weakly magnetic metal with the chemical symbol Co
2. Area of force around a magnet
3. Magnets exert a . . . . . of attraction on certain metals
4. Small regions of magnetism
5. Kind of force between two north poles
6. Ends of a magnet
7. Place in Greece where the magnetic rock lodestone was first discovered
8. Uses magnetism and movement to produce electricity
9. 'Waste' energy produced whenever magnetic energy is changed into another form of energy
10. Another weakly magnetic metal, symbol Ni
11. First man to generate electricity from magnetism
12. Unit of force
13. When the current in a solenoid flows in the opposite direction, this happens to the magnetic field
14. Strongly magnetic metal
15. Earth's magnetic field originates in the . . . . . of the Earth
16. Direction finder which uses a magnet
17. Magnet which can be switched on and off
18. Wire shaped to concentrate magnetic field produced when a current flows
19. Flow when a conductor moves in a magnetic field
20. Removal of a magnetic field e.g. around a ship, named after the discoverer of magnetic fields
21. Changes magnetic energy into sound energy
22. Huge planet with a strong magnetic field
23. Force between a north and a south pole
24. This pole repels a north pole
25. Useful application of electromagnets

'Ohm at Last

Omega mouse is on the run from the cat but doesn't know which of his mouseholes is secure. At each intersection he must solve the Ohm's Law problem and then go in the direction of the correct answer. Can you help him to reach safety? When you reach a mouse-hole check to see if you got the right one.

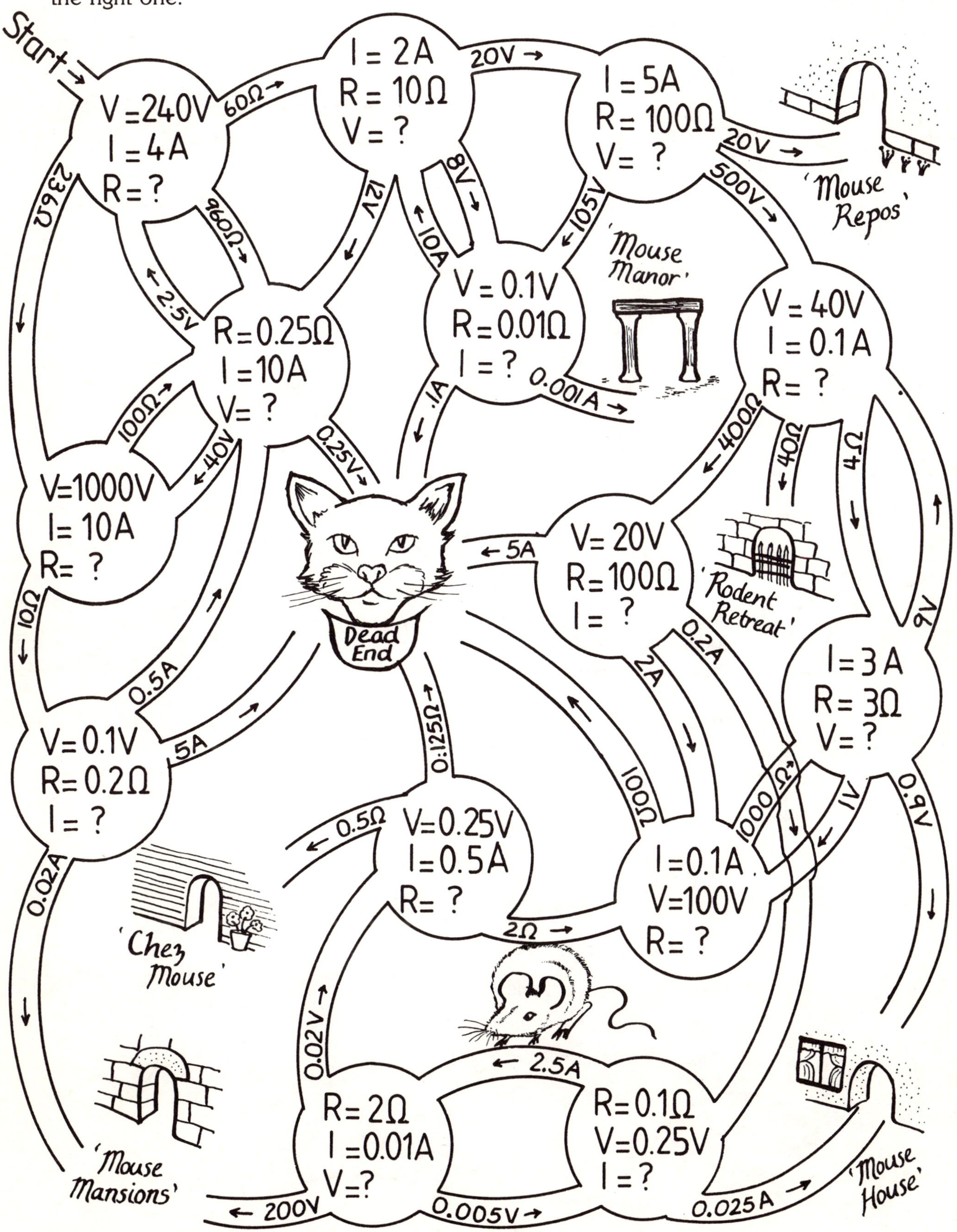

The Electrical Circuit

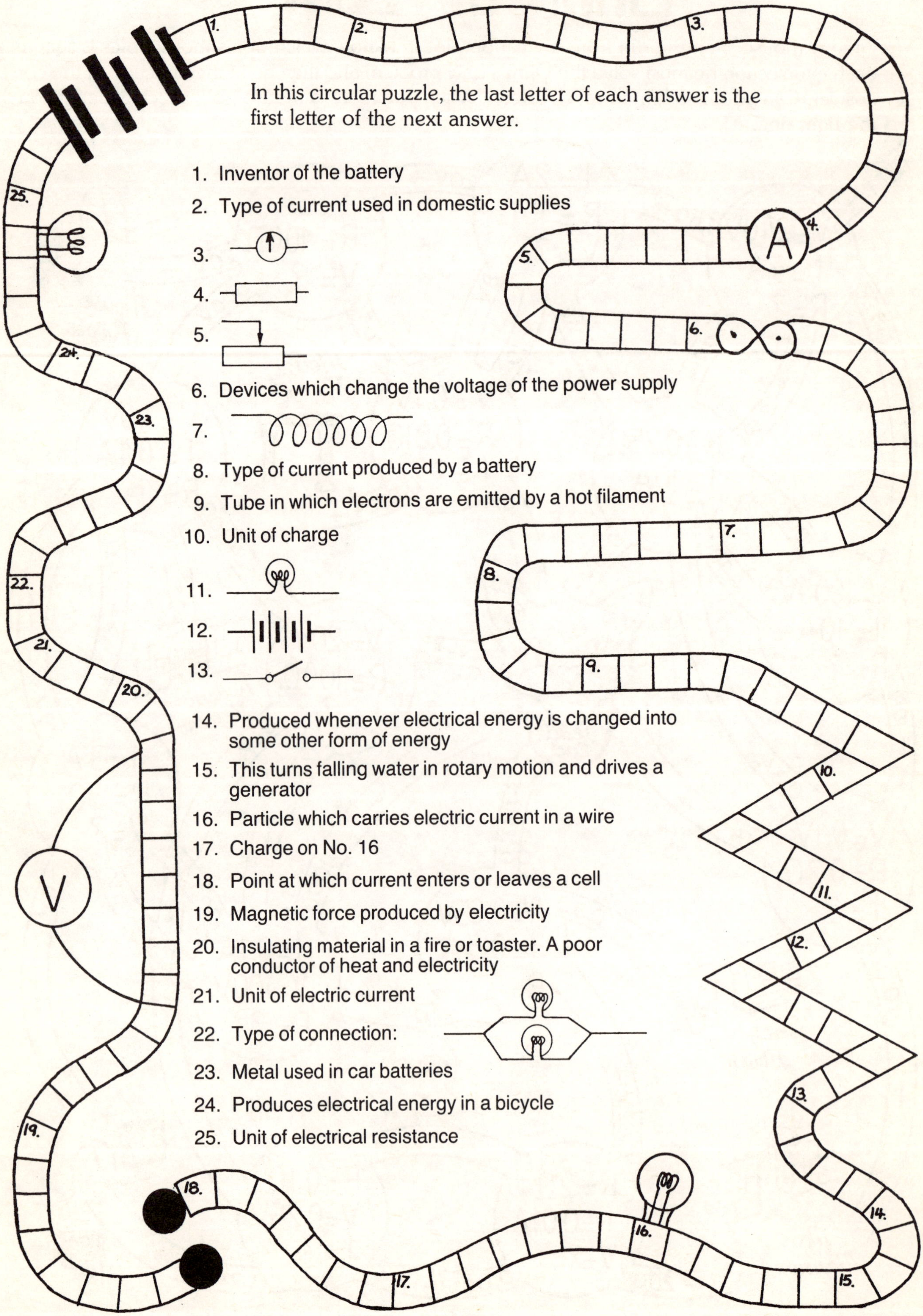

In this circular puzzle, the last letter of each answer is the first letter of the next answer.

1. Inventor of the battery
2. Type of current used in domestic supplies
3.
4.
5.
6. Devices which change the voltage of the power supply
7.
8. Type of current produced by a battery
9. Tube in which electrons are emitted by a hot filament
10. Unit of charge
11.
12.
13.
14. Produced whenever electrical energy is changed into some other form of energy
15. This turns falling water in rotary motion and drives a generator
16. Particle which carries electric current in a wire
17. Charge on No. 16
18. Point at which current enters or leaves a cell
19. Magnetic force produced by electricity
20. Insulating material in a fire or toaster. A poor conductor of heat and electricity
21. Unit of electric current
22. Type of connection:
23. Metal used in car batteries
24. Produces electrical energy in a bicycle
25. Unit of electrical resistance

ReVOLTing Riddles

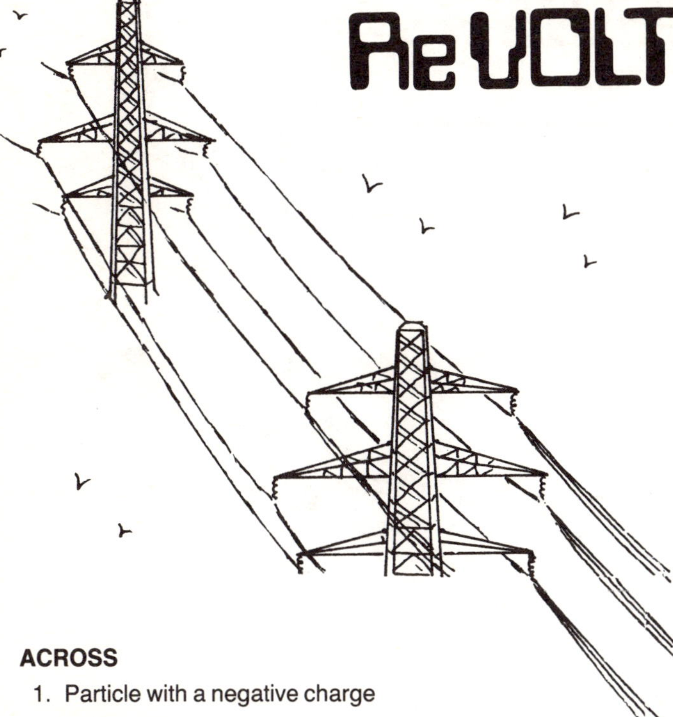

DOWN

2. They turn in a magnetic field within a generator
4. The windings slotted into this drum on the axle of the generator
5. Unit of electric current
6. Induces an electric current when moved near a conductor
7. Type of current used in domestic supplies
9. Charge on an electron
10. Type of current produced by a bicycle dynamo
13. Source of almost all energy on Earth
14. A type of turbine
15. This energy is free, but changing it into electrical energy can be expensive
16. This metal is the negative terminal of a dry cell battery
18. Unit of electrical resistance

ACROSS

1. Particle with a negative charge
3. Discovered the relationship between electricity and magnetism
8. Metal used as a core in a generator
11. Simple device to change chemical energy into electrical energy
12. These use movement and magnetism to produce electricity
17. Used for the brushes in a generator
19. Current-carrying coil of wire which behaves as a magnet
20. Part of a generator which is magnetised even when no current flows
21. This energy is converted into electrical energy by a steam turbine
22. Passes the current from the generator to the electrical circuit

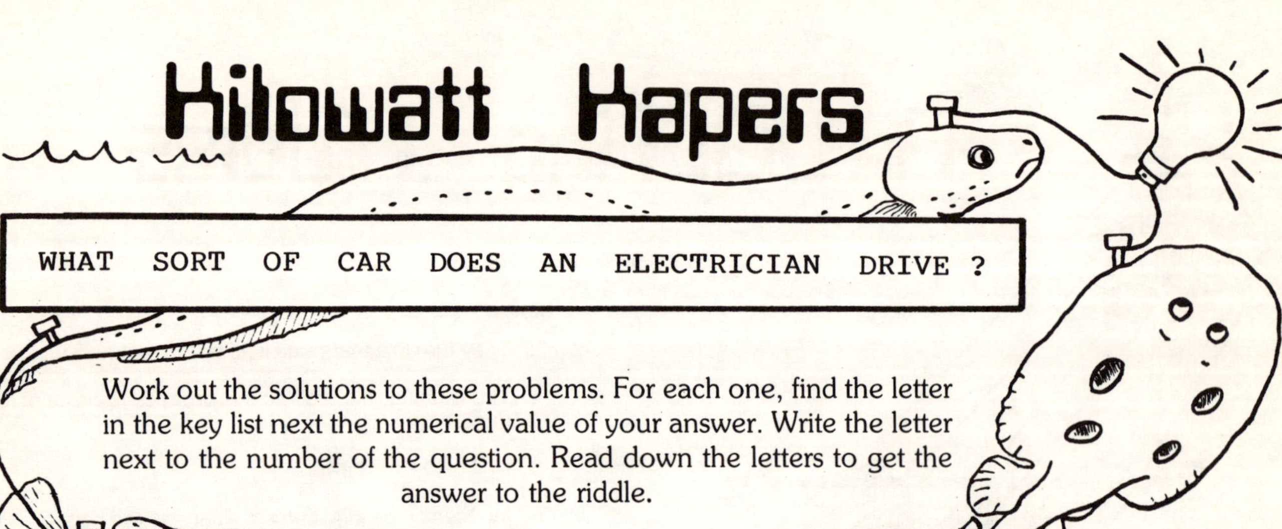

Kilowatt Kapers
WHAT SORT OF CAR DOES AN ELECTRICIAN DRIVE ?
Work out the solutions to these problems. For each one, find the letter in the key list next the numerical value of your answer. Write the letter next to the number of the question. Read down the letters to get the answer to the riddle.

1. A microwave oven is plugged into the 240 volts supply. If it draws a current of 5 amps, what is its resistance? .... ohms
2. An electric blanket has a resistance of 960 ohms. What current would it draw from a 240 volts supply? .... amps
3. A refrigerator has a resistance of 27.5 ohms and draws 4 amps from the power supply. What is the voltage? .... volts
4. What current would be drawn from a 240 volts supply by a 600 watt vacuum cleaner? .... amps
5. A 350 watt floor polisher draws 3 amps. What is the voltage of the supply? .... volts
6. An electric radiator draws 5.5 amps from a 240 volts supply. What is its power rating? .... watts
7. How much electricity is used when a 1200 watt air conditioner is operated for five hours? .... kWh
8. How much electricity is used when a 1500 watt radiator is used for 30 minutes? .... kWh
9. A 1000 watt electric lawn mower uses 0.75 kWh of electricity. For how long was it in use? .... min
10. A hairdryer uses 0.1 kWh when it is operated for 15 minutes. Find its wattage. .... kW
11. An electric toaster draws 4 amps from a 240 volts supply. How much electricity does it use in ten minutes? .... kW

KEY LIST

N.	0.16	L.	2.5	G.	45	T.	120	D.	1080
V.	0.25	E.	4.0	A.	48	R.	240	M.	1200
A.	0.75	W.	6.0	U.	75	O.	400	S.	1320
P.	1.5	J.	9.6	O.	110	C.	720	H.	6000

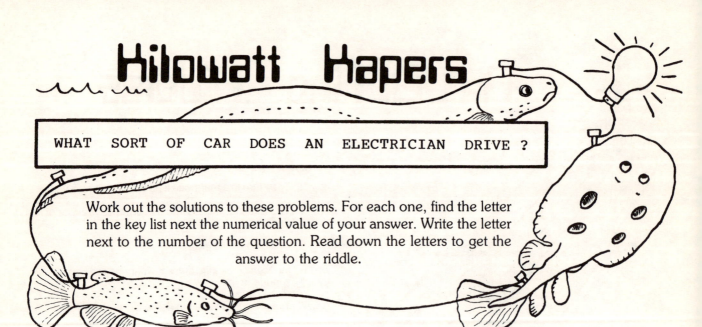

IT'S I.T.

WHAT IS A MICRO'S DIET ?

Find 19 micro-electronics terms in the word search below and fill in the answers on the grid.

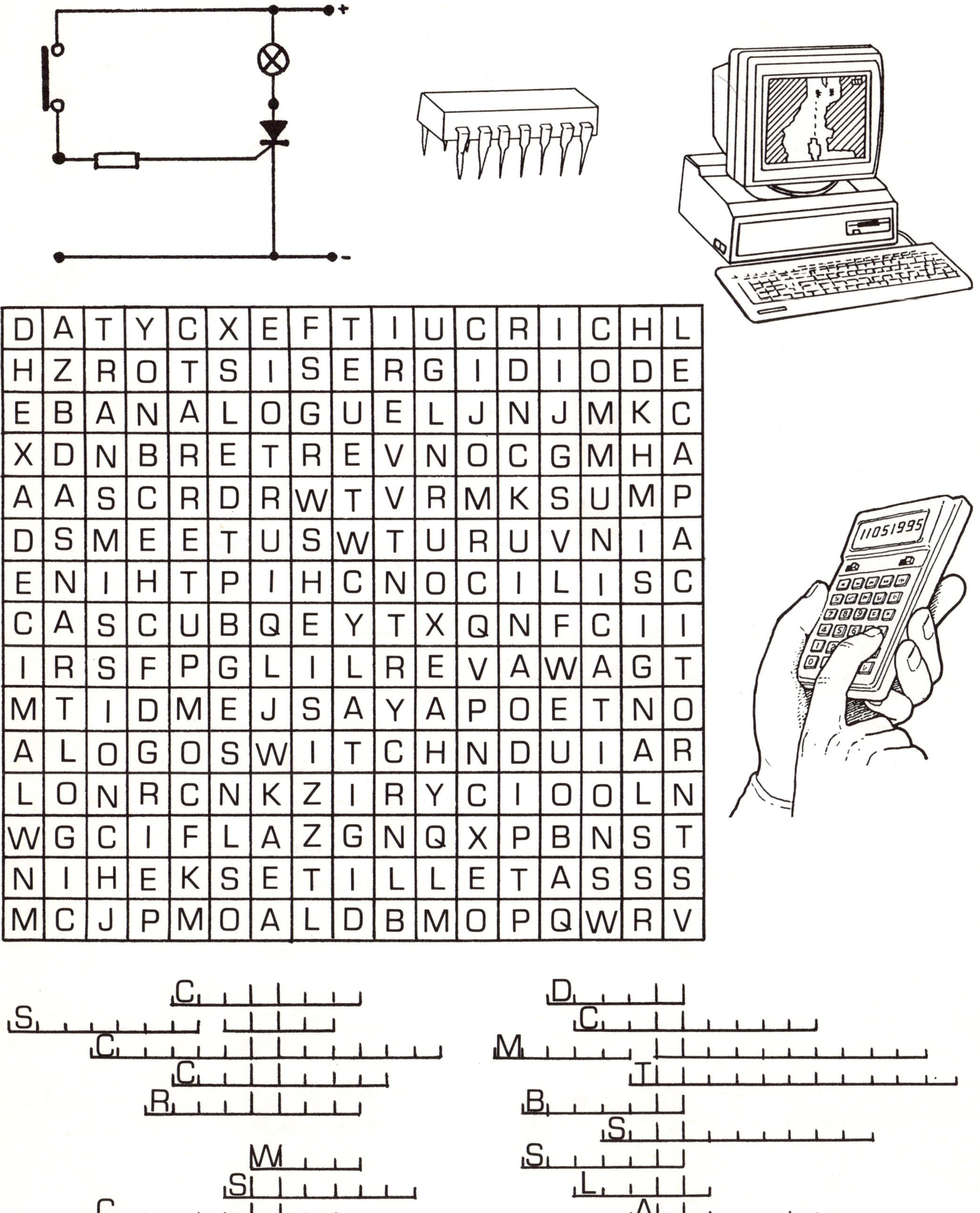

D	A	T	Y	C	X	E	F	T	I	U	C	R	I	C	H	L
H	Z	R	O	T	S	I	S	E	R	G	I	D	I	O	D	E
E	B	A	N	A	L	O	G	U	E	L	J	N	J	M	K	C
X	D	N	B	R	E	T	R	E	V	N	O	C	G	M	H	A
A	A	S	C	R	D	R	W	T	V	R	M	K	S	U	M	P
D	S	M	E	E	T	U	S	W	T	U	R	U	V	N	I	A
E	N	I	H	T	P	I	H	C	N	O	C	I	L	I	S	C
C	A	S	C	U	B	Q	E	Y	T	X	Q	N	F	C	I	I
I	R	S	F	P	G	L	I	L	R	E	V	A	W	A	G	T
M	T	I	D	M	E	J	S	A	Y	A	P	O	E	T	N	O
A	L	O	G	O	S	W	I	T	C	H	N	D	U	I	A	R
L	O	N	R	C	N	K	Z	I	R	Y	C	I	O	O	L	N
W	G	C	I	F	L	A	Z	G	N	Q	X	P	B	N	S	T
N	I	H	E	K	S	E	T	I	L	L	E	T	A	S	S	S
M	C	J	P	M	O	A	L	D	B	M	O	P	Q	W	R	V

CROSS CIRCUIT

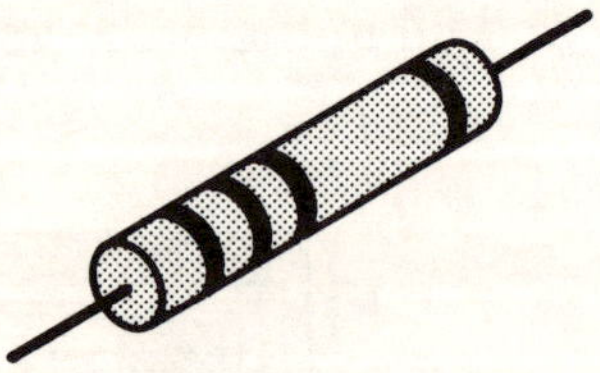

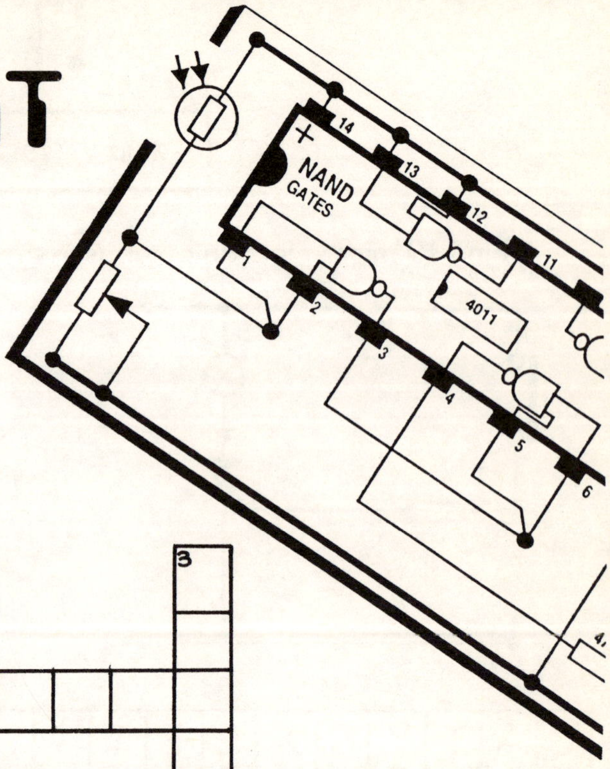

ACROSS

4. Stores charge
7. Computers have good ones. Do you?
8. World-wide communication link
9. On and Off make this system
10. Starts the circuit
13. Ends the circuit
14. Electronic brains do this
15. A baby set of connectors
18. Six decimals
19. Bit of memory

DOWN

1. YES and NOT are both one of these
2. Random memory
3. Floppy stores of information
5. A little piece of silicon
6. Has to be overcome for a current to flow
8. A turn off
11. The sense in a circuit
12. Mono or bi
16. Magnetic switch
17. Random access memory

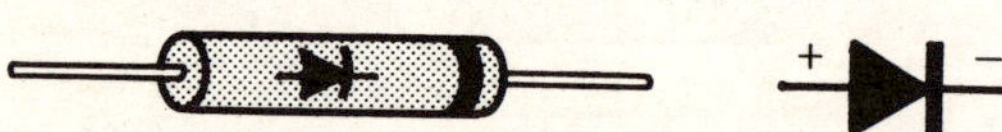

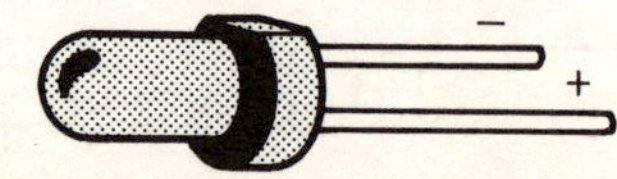

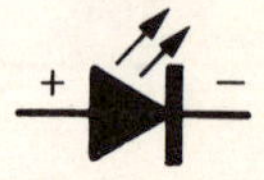

GETTING HOTTER

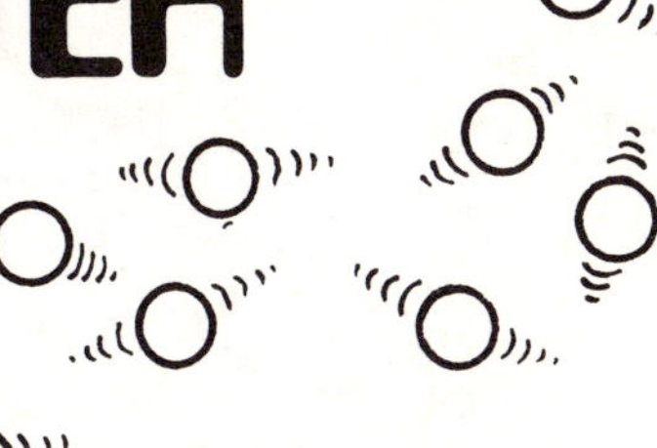

ACROSS

6. Main way in which liquids and gases transfer heat
9. Unit of heat energy
10. Way in which Sun's energy reaches us
11. Large body of water heated by radiation from the Sun
12. Turns into liquid magma when heated by convection currents below the earth's surface
13. Type of surface which strongly absorbs radiant heat
15. Heat flows from a .... body to a cold one
17. Substances through which heat is transferred mainly by conduction
20. Source of most of Earth's heat energy
21. Good insulator for mammals
22. A valuable insulator from tropical trees
23. Symbol of metal used as a coolant in some nuclear reactors
24. Insulates our planet from large variations in temperature
25. Differences in this property within a fluid produce convection currents

DOWN

1. Short wavelength electromagnetic radiation
2. When this forms on a surface of a lake it insulates the water below
3. Substance which is a poor conductor of heat
4. Particles have this energy in hot objects
5. Heat from the Sun
6. Process of heat transfer in metals
7. A state of matter in which heat transfers mainly by convection
8. Enormous convection currents in the atmosphere
14. A hot fluid will ....
16. State of matter in which heat is transferred mainly by convection but also by conduction
18. Type of surface which best reflects radiant heat
19. As a convection current in a liquid cools it ....

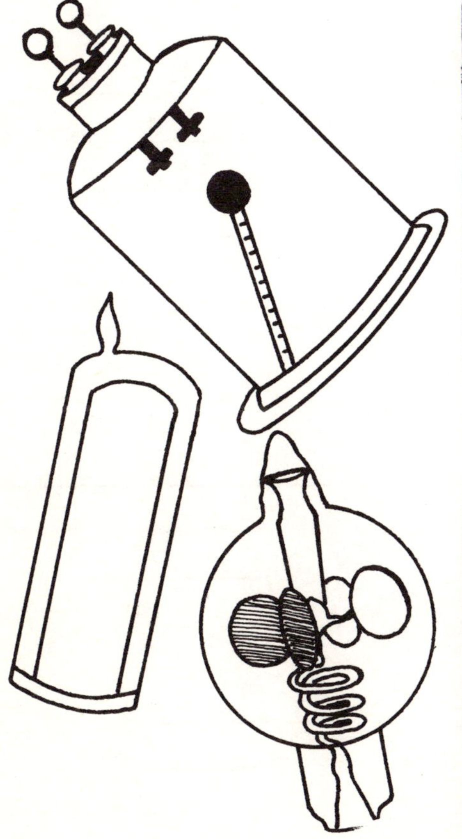

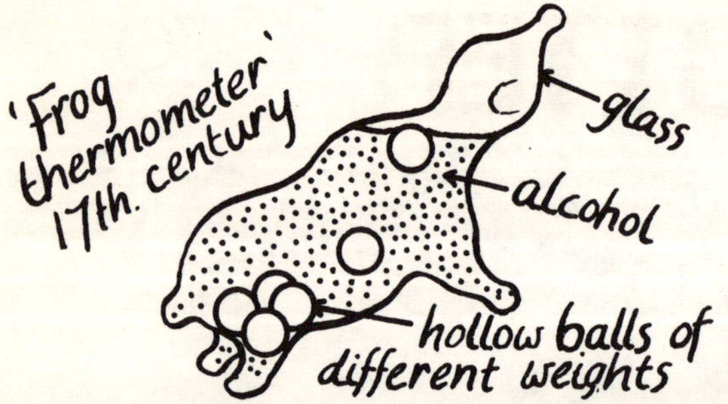

HOT STUFF

WHAT WOULD HAPPEN IF FIREMEN DIDN'T WEAR RED BRACES ?

1. Energy which increases motion of particles
2. Liquid used in thermometers because of its low freezing point
3. Unit of heat energy
4. Thermometer used to measure body temperature
5. Liquid used in most thermometers

6. Electrical property which increases with temperature
7. Measures the degree of hotness
8. Instrument for measuring hotness
9. Rises in gases which increases with temperature
10. May cause problems with railway lines as they get hotter
11. Metric scale of temperature
12. As a liquid is heated its volume ....
13. State of matter most affected by temperature changes

14. .... and dry bulb thermometers are used to measure humidity
15. Describes the 'runniness' of a liquid
16. Mercury thermometers depend on changes in this quantity
17. The .... of a star depends upon its temperature
18. Type of surface which best absorbs heat energy

19. Useful in electrical circuits because it melts when overheated
20. This strip of two metals is used as a thermostat
21. Change from solid to liquid caused by heating
22. Reservoir for liquid in a thermometer

23. State of matter with smallest coefficient of expansion
24. Metal used for electrical wiring
25. Liquid which expands on cooling from 4 °C to 0 °C
26. Most substances .... when cooled

A Specific Solution

WHAT DO YOU GET IF YOU CROSS A CENTIPEDE WITH A PARROT ?

Solve these problems on quantities of heat. For each one, find the letter corresponding to the numerical value of your answer in the key list and write it next to the number of the question. Read the letters down the page to get the answer to the riddle.

Table of specific heats

Alcohol	2680 J/kg/°C	Iron	460 J/kg/°C
Aluminium	920 J/kg/°C	Mercury	130 J/kg/°C
Copper	380 J/kg/°C	Water	4200 J/kg/°C

1. How many joules of heat will raise the temperature of 100 g of copper from 25 °C to 30 °C? .... J
2. How many joules of heat will raise the temperature of 250 g of iron from 15 °C to 50 °C? .... J
3. How much water can be heated from 30 °C to 80 °C by 315 000 J of heat? .... g
4. How much mercury can have its temperature raised from 0 °C to 200 °C by 6500 J of heat? .... g
5. 460 J of heat are used to raise the temperature of some aluminium from 100 °C to 150 °C. What is the mass of the aluminium? .... g
6. What is the specific heat of sand if 197 500 J of heat raise the temperature of 5 kg by 50 °C? .... J/kg/°C
7. How much iron can have its temperature raised from 200 °C to 800 °C by 207 000 J of heat? .... g
8. How many joules of heat are needed to raise the temperature of 200 g of aluminium from −10 °C to 20 °C? .... J
9. What is the specific heat of turpentine if 39 600 J of heat raise the temperature of 500 g by 45 °C? .... J/kg/°C
10. Some water is heated from 5 °C to 50 °C by 4725 J of heat. What is the mass of the water? .... g
11. How much heat is needed to increase the temperature of 5 g of alcohol from 10 °C to 20 °C? .... J
12. 38 000 J of heat are used to heat 2 kg of copper, originally at a temperature of 130 °C. What is the final temperature of the copper? .... °C
13. How much alcohol will have its temperature raised from 50 °C to 70 °C by 5360 J of heat? .... g

KEY LIST

K. 10	E. 100	K. 134	A. 1500	G. 3680
H. 23	I. 180	E. 750	A. 1760	W. 4025
L. 25	A. 190	I. 790	P. 1900	T. 5520
F. 40	L. 250	R. 1340	D. 3250	C. 5750

A COOL QUESTION

HOW CAN YOU TELL IF THERE IS AN ELEPHANT IN THE REFRIGERATOR ?

Calculate the answers to the problems below. For each one, find the corresponding letter from the key list and write it next to the number of the question. Read down the letters to get the answer to the riddle.

Latent Heats (kJ/kg)

Benzene	126 at 5 °C
Ice	336 at 0 °C
Lead	21 at 327 °C
Mercury	126 at −39 °C
Silver	92.4 at 960 °C
Alcohol	865 at 78 °C
Benzene	403 at 80 °C
Ether	348 at 35 °C
Mercury	285 at 358 °C
Water	2268 at 100 °C

Specific Heat Capacities (kJ/kg/°C)

Alcohol (l)	2.680
Benzene (l)	1.680
Benzene (g)	1.050
Lead (s)	0.134
Mercury (l)	0.130
Water (s)	2.100
Water (l)	4.200
Water (g)	2.100

Find the quantity of heat in kilojoules required to:

1. Melt 2 kg of ice at 0 °C ....
2. Melt 100 g of benzene at 5 °C ....
3. Melt 250 g of mercury at −39 °C ....
4. Melt 2 kg of lead at 327 °C ....
5. Boil 500 g of alcohol at 78 °C ....
6. Boil 900 g of ether at 35 °C ....
7. Boil 0.5 kg of benzene at 80 °C ....
8. Boil 100 g of mercury at 358 °C ....
9. Boil 250 g of silver at 960 °C ....
10. Heat 500 g of alcohol from −22 °C until it has all boiled at 78 °C ....
11. Heat 50 kg of lead from 300 °C until it has all melted at 327 °C ....
12. Boil 100 g of benzene at 80 °C and then heat it to 180 °C ....
13. Heat 800 g of water from 50 °C to 150 °C ....
14. Melt 900 g of benzene at 5 °C and then raise its temperature to 100 °C ....
15. Heat 750 g of water from −20 °C to +120 °C ....

KEY LIST

H. 12.6	E. 31.5	F. 57.1	O. 432.5	T. 672.0
C. 21.6	A. 40.3	B. 71.3	G. 537.6	T. 1230.9
O. 23.1	D. 42.0	R. 201.5	N. 566.5	H. 2066.4
W. 28.5	S. 50.8	O. 313.2	U. 608.4	T. 2331.0

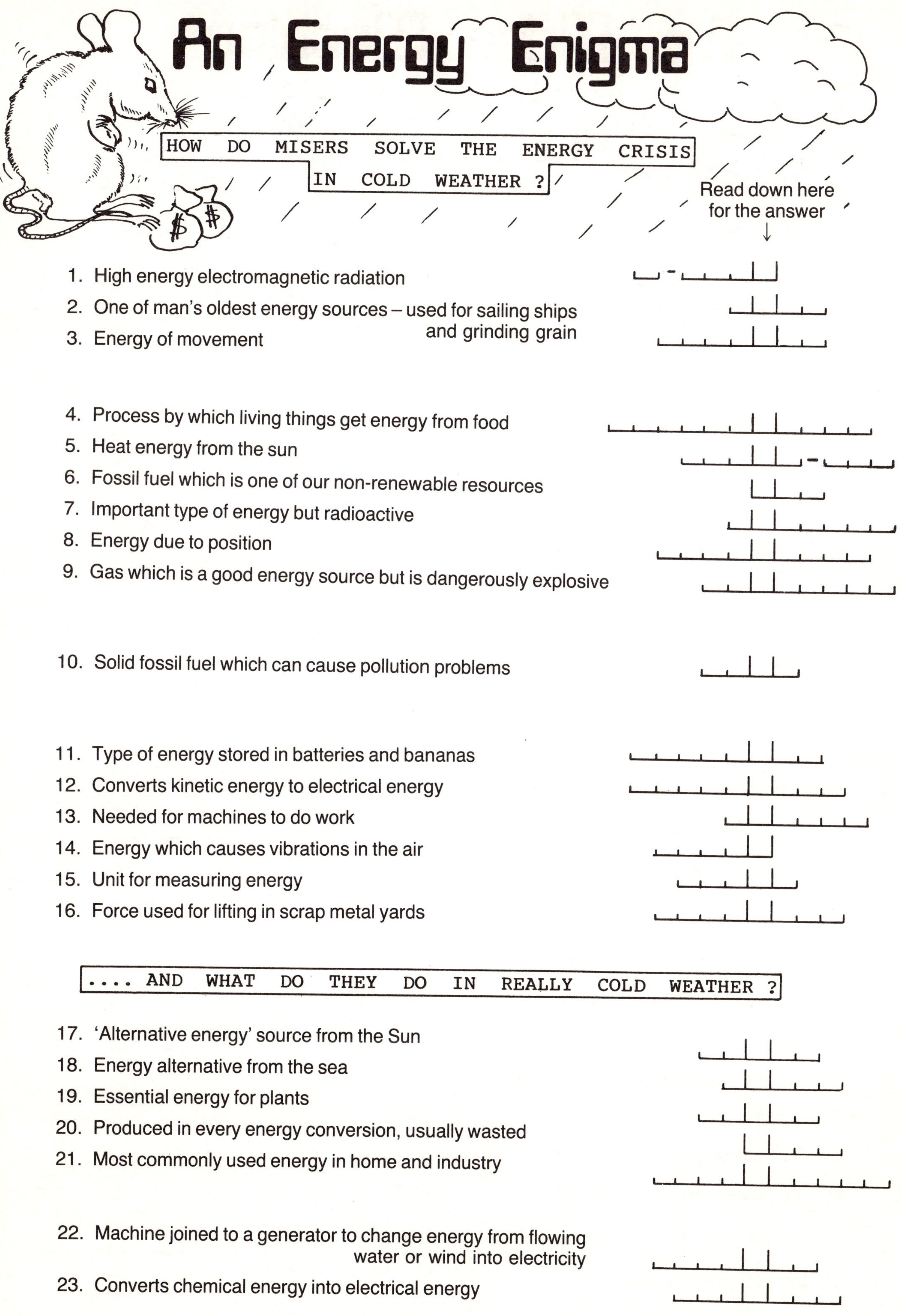

An Energy Enigma
HOW DO MISERS SOLVE THE ENERGY CRISIS IN COLD WEATHER ?
Read down here for the answer

1. High energy electromagnetic radiation
2. One of man's oldest energy sources – used for sailing ships and grinding grain
3. Energy of movement

4. Process by which living things get energy from food
5. Heat energy from the sun
6. Fossil fuel which is one of our non-renewable resources
7. Important type of energy but radioactive
8. Energy due to position
9. Gas which is a good energy source but is dangerously explosive

10. Solid fossil fuel which can cause pollution problems

11. Type of energy stored in batteries and bananas
12. Converts kinetic energy to electrical energy
13. Needed for machines to do work
14. Energy which causes vibrations in the air
15. Unit for measuring energy
16. Force used for lifting in scrap metal yards

.... AND WHAT DO THEY DO IN REALLY COLD WEATHER ?

17. 'Alternative energy' source from the Sun
18. Energy alternative from the sea
19. Essential energy for plants
20. Produced in every energy conversion, usually wasted
21. Most commonly used energy in home and industry

22. Machine joined to a generator to change energy from flowing water or wind into electricity
23. Converts chemical energy into electrical energy

The Mean Machine

WHAT WOULD HAPPEN IF YOU RAN OVER A CANARY WITH A LAWN-MOWER ?

1. The crankshaft in a car converts up-and-down motion into .... motion
2. A machine changes the size and/or direction of a ....
3. Pivot point of a lever
4. This rotates around an axle
5. Levers used in small boats
6. Machine which makes it easier to lift a heavy weight
7. Centre of wheel
8. The force which must be overcome by a machine
9. Notched wheels which change the speed of rotation
10. Spiral inclined plane that holds wood together
11. The force put into a machine
12. Machine for lifting things on building sites
13. Distance between adjacent threads of a screw
14. Inventor of the dynamo and electric motor
15. Simple machine that pivots around a fulcrum
16. A moving inclined plane or shape of an axehead
17. First man to develop the factory assembly line to make cars
18. Kitchen example of No. 16
19. Inventor of electric light bulb and talking films
20. Must be overcome before a force can do work
21. Unit in which force is measured
22. Using an inclined .... makes it easier to overcome the force of gravity
23. Used for pulling out teeth
24. A machine may change the size or .... of a force

A SOUND SOLUTION

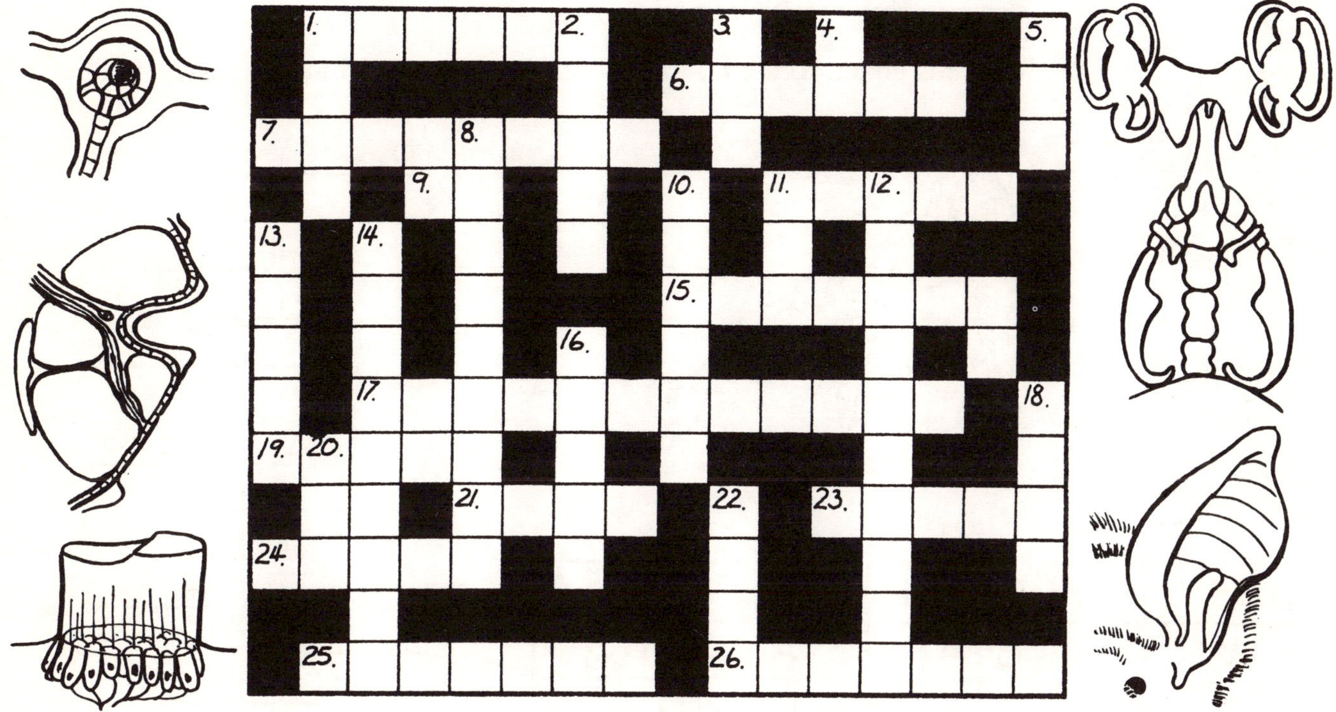

ACROSS

1. Velocity of sound = frequency × wave-......
6. Closest ear-bone to the ear-drum
7. Nerve which carries impulses from the cochlea to the brain
9. Blood group factor which may result in deafness if mother and foetus are incompatible
11. Middle ear bone
15. Unit of sound intensity
17. Type of vibration in sound waves
19. Increasing the frequency of a note will ...... the pitch
21. Sound waves can be described as a number of simple ...... waves
23. Describes how high or low a note is
24. Percussion instruments
25. Increasing the ...... of a string will raise the pitch of the note
26. As the ...... of a medium (eg. air) increases, the velocity of sound will increase

DOWN

1. Describes a sound when there is a large amplitude of vibration
2. Unit of sound frequency
3. Animal which uses high frequency sound for direction-finding
4. Broadcasting uses either AM or ......
5. Organ of hearing
8. If the ...... is increased the pitch of a note produced by a string will be lowered
10. The general name for a material through which sound can be transmitted
11. First three notes of the scale of A Major
12. Things make these when they produce sound
13. Increasing the length of a vibrating column of air will ...... the pitch
14. A note will sound softer if the ...... of vibration is decreased
16. External part of the ear – important in sound location
18. Reflected sound
20. At 15 °C sound travels at 1000 km/h through this medium
22. Causes the sound vibrations in a clarinet

SOUND BOX

WHY IS THE COMPOSER UNHAPPY ?

Find 18 words linked to sound in this wordsearch and fill in the answers below.

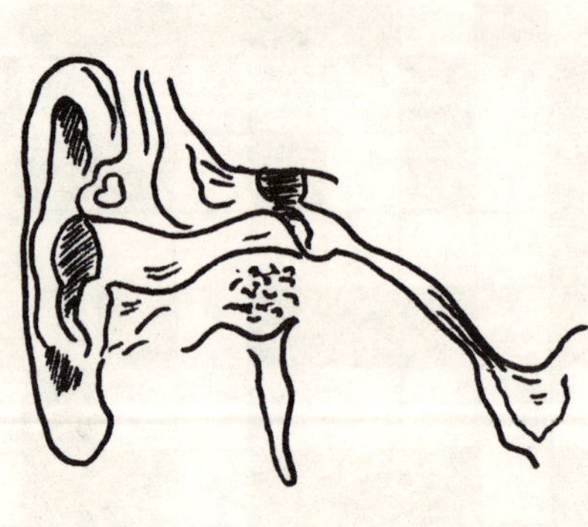

P _ _ _ _

M _ _ _ _ _ _ _ _ _

H _ _ _

E _ _

I _ _ _ _ _ _ _ _ _

T _ _ _ _ _

A _ _ _ _ _ _

L _ _ _ _ _ _ _

N _ _ _ _

A _ _ _ _ _ _ _

Q _ _ _ _

V _ _ _ _

D _ _ _ _ _ _

D	M	I	C	R	O	P	H	O	N	E	B	E	A
S	V	C	Y	B	U	A	H	E	A	R	D	C	M
E	P	X	V	O	C	A	L	X	C	B	O	N	P
T	I	E	Z	Q	T	B	O	S	Z	M	Y	A	Q
A	T	E	E	O	I	Q	U	H	J	I	W	N	N
R	C	W	P	D	G	R	D	P	F	T	R	O	M
B	H	F	U	I	O	V	N	O	I	S	E	S	S
I	G	A	A	D	E	F	E	C	T	S	L	E	E
V	B	L	V	T	K	N	S	K	E	C	S	R	R
C	H	E	U	M	E	U	S	O	I	T	G	W	E
K	A	J	N	S	C	I	T	S	U	O	C	A	A
R	I	L	D	R	M	O	U	J	Q	N	H	V	F
I	N	S	T	R	U	M	E	N	T	I	D	E	E

V _ _ _ _ _ _ _

S _ _ _ _   _ _   _ _ _ _ _

R _ _ _ _ _ _ _ _

W _ _ _

M _ _ _ _

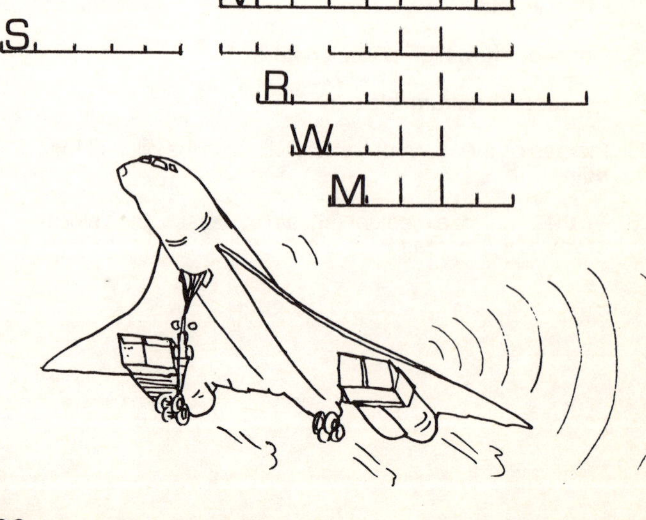

RESOUNDING SUCCESS

WHY DID THE DRUM ROLL ?

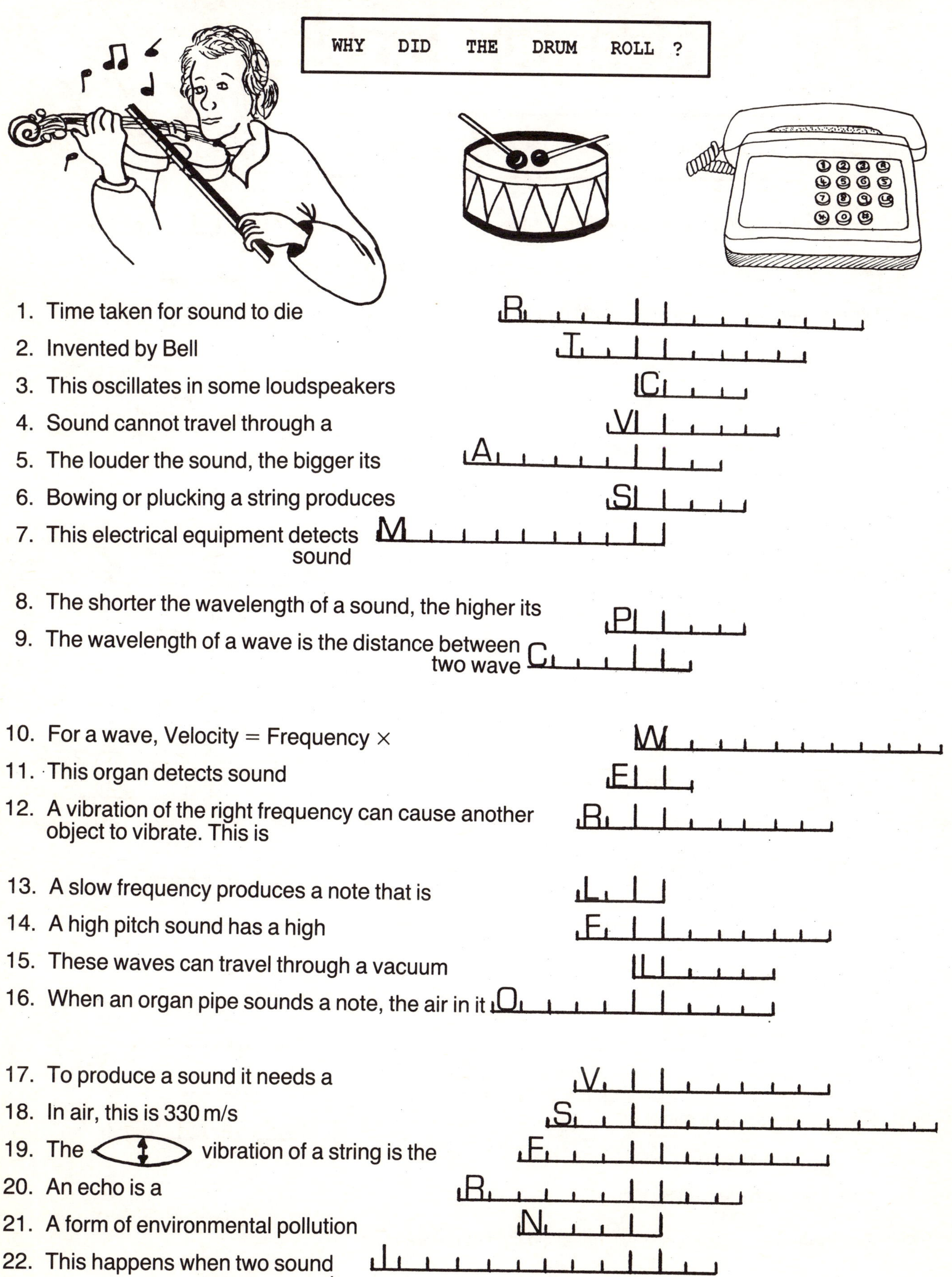

1. Time taken for sound to die R
2. Invented by Bell T
3. This oscillates in some loudspeakers C
4. Sound cannot travel through a V
5. The louder the sound, the bigger its A
6. Bowing or plucking a string produces S
7. This electrical equipment detects sound M
8. The shorter the wavelength of a sound, the higher its P
9. The wavelength of a wave is the distance between two wave C
10. For a wave, Velocity = Frequency × W
11. This organ detects sound E
12. A vibration of the right frequency can cause another object to vibrate. This is R
13. A slow frequency produces a note that is L
14. A high pitch sound has a high F
15. These waves can travel through a vacuum L
16. When an organ pipe sounds a note, the air in it O
17. To produce a sound it needs a V
18. In air, this is 330 m/s S
19. The (⟷) vibration of a string is the F
20. An echo is a R
21. A form of environmental pollution N
22. This happens when two sound waves cancel I

An Incidental Inquiry

WHY DOES BATMAN CARRY WORMS ?

1. Surface which does not reflect visible light
2. Describes image obtained with a concave mirror when the object is outside the focus
3. Type of mirror used as a magnifying mirror
4. Line at right angles to the surface of a mirror
5. Describes image obtained with a plane mirror
6. Point at which image is obtained in No. 7
7. Telescope which collects light with a curved mirror
8. Camera with no lens
9. Type of mirror used at hidden entrances
10. Particle of light energy
11. Type of inversion in a plane mirror
12. Objects in the universe which emit their own light
13. Inventor of reflector telescope
14. Reflective surface with a silvered backing
15. Describes 'spread out' light
16. Way in which light travels
17. Type of mirror which produces an image as far behind the mirror as the object is in front
18. Ray of light striking a mirror
19. Colour of light reflected by plants
20. Describes substance which will not allow light to pass through it
21. 'Bundle' of parallel rays of light
22. What we see when we look into a mirror
23. Objects in the universe which shine by reflected light

FOCUSING FUN

ACROSS

1. Type of lens used in microscopes and telescopes
6. Illusion produced by refraction of light through heated air
7. Transparent material with at least one curved surface
9. Gives a clearer image when using a microscope on high power
10. Triangular piece of glass which splits up white light
15. Bending of light
16. An image which can be projected onto a screen
17. Colour of light which is least strongly refracted
19. This apparatus produces a real, diminished image which is caught on film
20. It has a lens which can be made thinner or thicker
21. Colour between orange and green in a rainbow

DOWN

2. Long filament which uses total internal reflection – used in surgery to shine light in the exact place (2 words)
3. Describes images obtained with a concave lens
4. Controls amount of light entering the eye
5. Glass will do this to light rays
8. Bands of light obtained when light is refracted through a prism
11. Eye defect in which image is focused in front of the retina
12. Describes rays of light, coming from an object at the focus, as they leave a convex lens
13. Point at which the image will be produced by a convex lens when the object is at infinity
14. Lens which always produces an erect, diminished image
17. Narrow beam of light
18. Water droplets on plants often, seen to refract light

SEARCH LIGHT

HOW DID THE SEWER SEE ?

Find 19 words, associated with light, in the word search and fill in the answers on the grid.

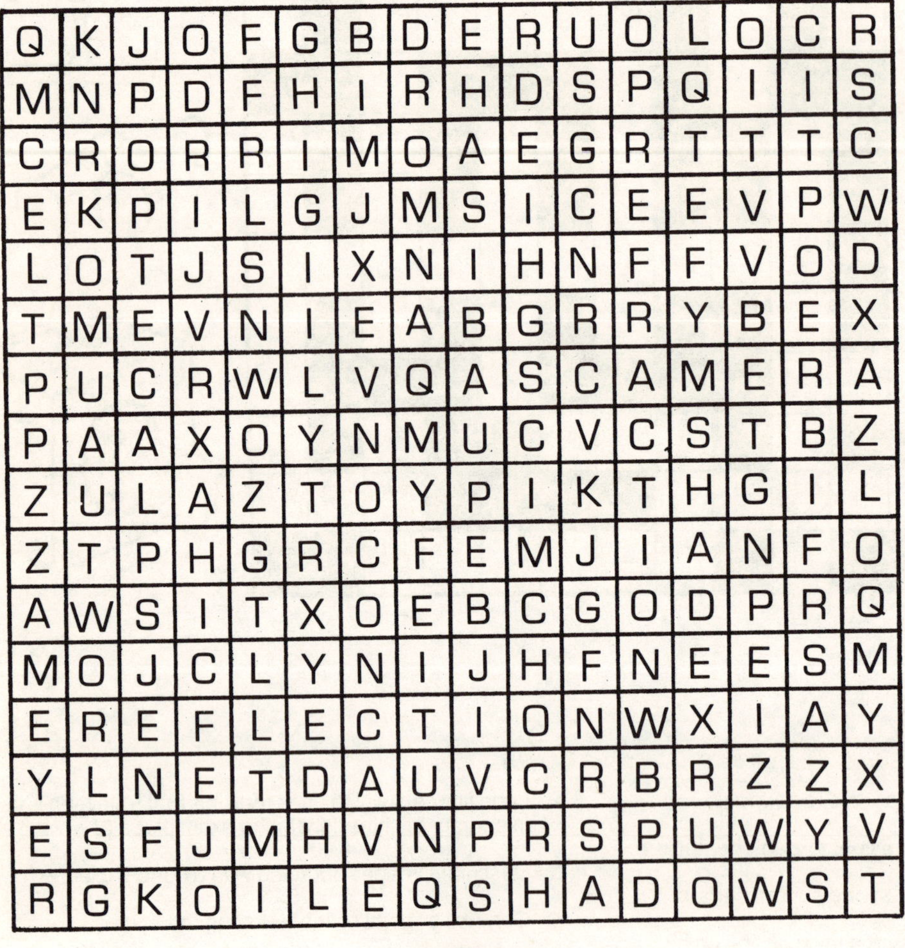

Q	K	J	O	F	G	B	D	E	R	U	O	L	O	C	R
M	N	P	D	F	H	I	R	H	D	S	P	Q	I	I	S
C	R	O	R	R	I	M	O	A	E	G	R	T	T	T	C
E	K	P	I	L	G	J	M	S	I	C	E	E	V	P	W
L	O	T	J	S	I	X	N	I	H	N	F	F	V	O	D
T	M	E	V	N	I	E	A	B	G	R	R	Y	B	E	X
P	U	C	R	W	L	V	Q	A	S	C	A	M	E	R	A
P	A	A	X	O	Y	N	M	U	C	V	C	S	T	B	Z
Z	U	L	A	Z	T	O	Y	P	I	K	T	H	G	I	L
Z	T	P	H	G	R	C	F	E	M	J	I	A	N	F	O
A	W	S	I	T	X	O	E	B	C	G	O	D	P	R	Q
M	O	J	C	L	Y	N	I	J	H	F	N	E	E	S	M
E	R	E	F	L	E	C	T	I	O	N	W	X	I	A	Y
Y	L	N	E	T	D	A	U	V	C	R	B	R	Z	Z	X
E	S	F	J	M	H	V	N	P	R	S	P	U	W	Y	V
R	G	K	O	I	L	E	Q	S	H	A	D	O	W	S	T

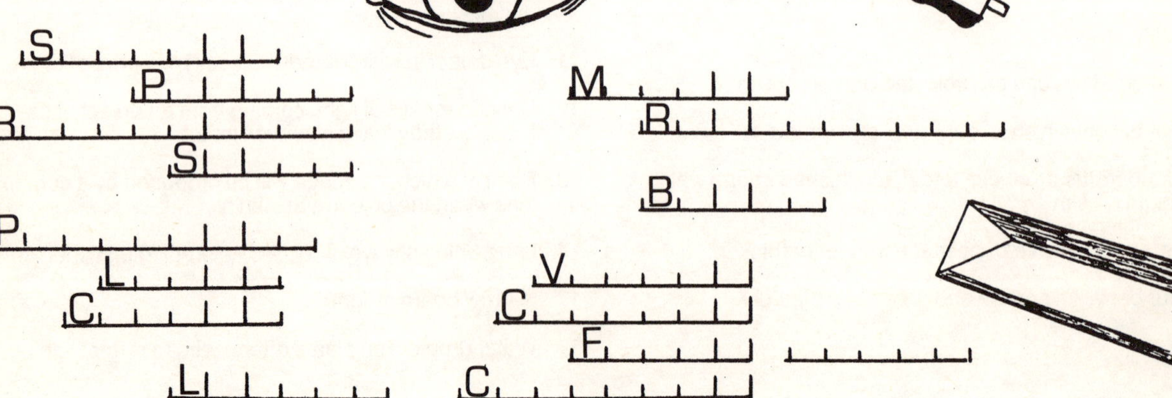

CAN YOU SEE THE LIGHT?

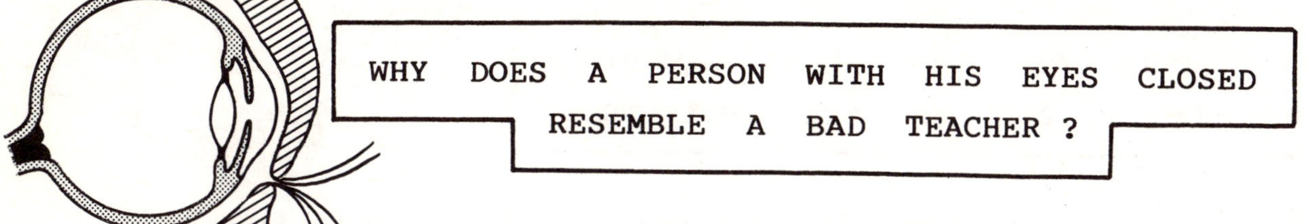

WHY DOES A PERSON WITH HIS EYES CLOSED
RESEMBLE A BAD TEACHER ?

1. Light obtained when all colours of the spectrum are mixed
2. Shape of the lens in the eye

3. Appears blue because of light scattered by gas and dust
4. Colour of light used by plants for photosynthesis
5. Obtained by splitting light into its component colours
6. Used to split light
7. Light/dark receptors in the eye

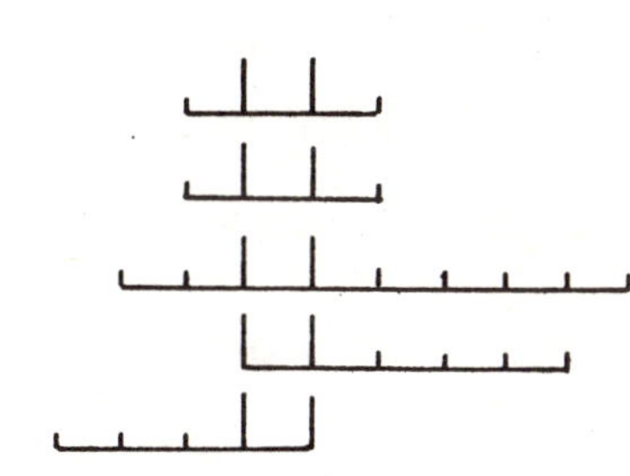

8. Eye infection which may cause blindness
9. Black lining of the eyeball
10. Part of eye important in focusing

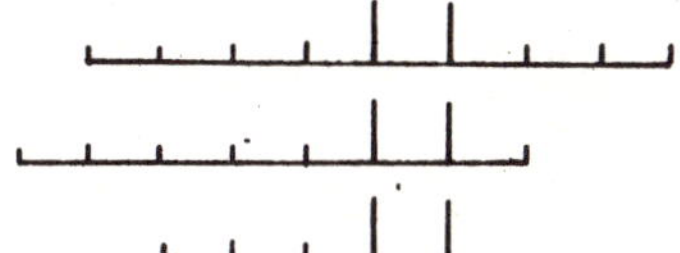

11. Short-sightedness
12. Colour of light between green and indigo in a rainbow
13. Type of eye found in insects
14. Nerve which carries impulses from eye to brain
15. Colour obtained when red and green lights are mixed
16. Colour receptors in the eye

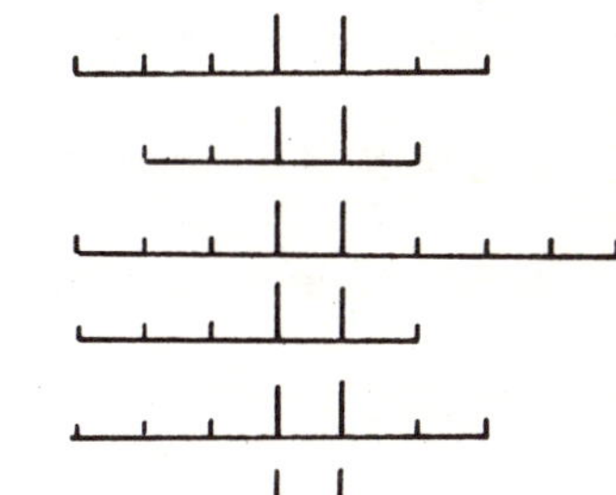

17. Controls the amount of light which can enter the eye
18. Colour of light obtained by mixing green and blue

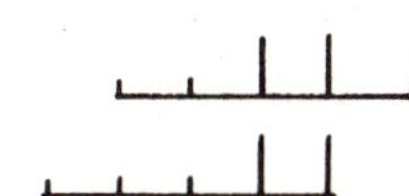

19. Scientist who did important early work with spectra
20. Fluid in the eye, that causes a chuckle
21. Colour of light with shortest wavelength

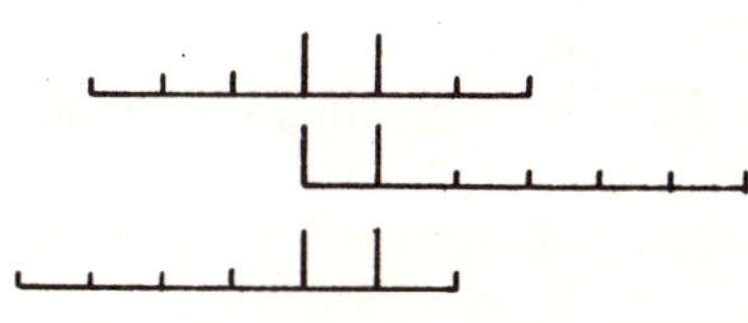

22. Point where optic nerve enters eyeball
23. Bending of light
24. Colour of light reflected by plant leaves
25. Causes the pupil of the eye to open up

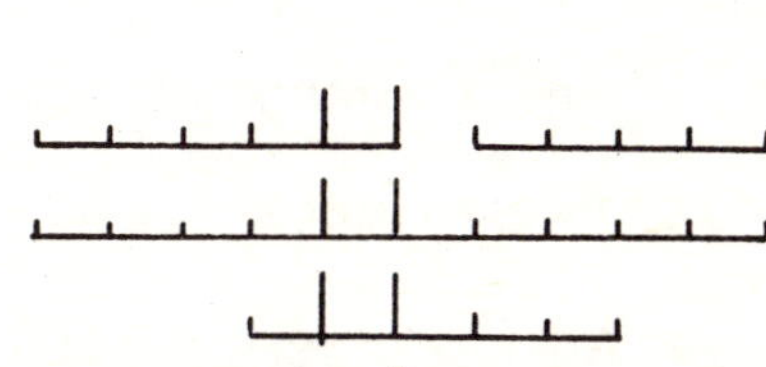

SPACE SECRETS

WHERE WOULD YOU LOOK IN A NEWSPAPER TO FIND A LIST OF DEAD PLANETS ?

Unscramble these astronomical words and their initial letters will spell out the answer to the riddle. There are clues to help you.

	Clue	Scrambled	Answer
1.	One of Jupiter's moons	OI	....
2.	Furthest planet from the Sun at present	PENUNET	....
3.	Instrument for looking at stars	LETESPOCE	....
4.	Most common chemical element in the universe	DYHRGENO	....
5.	Shadow of one celestial body falling on another	CELISPE	....
6.	Shines by reflected light	NALPET	....
7.	Lump of rock in space	RESTOIDA	....
8.	Smallest, coldest planet	TULOP	....
9.	Asteroid which approached close to earth in 1931	ROES	....
10.	Blue giant in constellation of Orion	GIREL	....
11.	Planet with spectacular rings	RATSUN	....
12.	The path of a planet around the Sun	BORTI	....
13.	Type of telescope that does not use light	ARIOD	....
14.	Dead star	KALBC RAWFD	....
15.	Long wavelength radiation given out by stars	RAFIN-DER	....
16.	Largest of Saturn's moons	TANIT	....
17.	Distant planet discovered by Sir William Herschel in 1781	SUNUAR	....
18.	Closest large spiral galaxy to the Milky Way	ADEMORAND	....
19.	Describes an expanding star many times the size of the Sun	DER TIANG	....
20.	Star classification of our Sun	WOLLEY RAWFD	....
21.	Members of the Solar System made up of ice, dust, rocks and gas	MOCETS	....
22.	Constellation of 'The Hunter'	NOIRO	....
23.	Unit of astronomical distance	HIGLT REAY	....
24.	Total of all existing things	VINURESE	....
25.	Planet closest to the Sun	REMRUCY	....
26.	Immense cloud of gas and dust	BENLUA	....

PLANETARY PROBE

Fearless Fred, our interplanetary correspondent, has been sending back reports from the Solar System. But Fred's navigation isn't too good, and he's not sure which planets he landed on. Can you name the planets he visited?

1. The Grand Canyon's got nothing on this place. Here I can see a huge canyon stretching a third of the way round the equator. Mountains, craters, volcanoes, and lots and lots of red dirt.

   ....

2. Bit too close to the Sun for comfort: noon-time temperatures are up round the 350 °C mark. In some ways it's quite like being on the Earth's Moon: lots of craters, and no atmosphere to be seen – or rather breathed.

   ....

3. Not a hope of landing on this planet – nothing solid in sight. We couldn't get too close – the powerful magnetic field would have wrecked our instruments. Took lots of photos of the Great Red Spot – seems to be a huge, whirling storm.

   ....

4. Temperature about 500 °C, carbon dioxide atmosphere, pressure about a hundred times that on Earth. Oh yes, and it rains dilute sulphuric acid! They called this planet after the goddess of love, but it seems a pretty hostile place to me.

   ....

5. Don't know why they called this planet after the god of the sea. There's hydrogen, helium and methane around, but not a drop of water! No wonder it's cold – until 1999 this will be the outermost planet in the Solar System.

   ....

6. Brrr! Brrr! Not only is this the smallest place I've been to, it's also the coldest. It gets dark for 3.2 Earth days at a stretch and they're not even sure that it's a proper planet.

   ....

7. This time it's another big, gassy planet, so no chance for a landing. Spectacular views flying past the icy ring system, but a bit strange seeing all those moons in the sky at the same time.

   ....

8. This planet also has rings, but these are as black as coal dust. It's colder than my last stop – the temperature's down to −210 °C. This interplanetary exploration isn't all that it's cracked up to be. I'm heading for home.

   ....

PLANETARY PROBLEMS

WHAT DID THE MAD ASTRONAUT USE TO HELP HIM ESCAPE THE PULL OF THE EARTH'S GRAVITY ?

Use the table below to calculate the answers to the problems. Shade in the sections of the mystery picture which contain the numerical values of the answers.

PLANETARY INFORMATION

	Mercury	Venus	Earth	Mars	Jupiter	Saturn	Uranus	Neptune	Pluto
Average distance from Sun ($\times 10^6$ km)	57.9	108.2	149.6	227.9	778.3	1427.0	3870	4497	5900
Orbital period	88.0d	224.7d	365.26d	687d	11.86y	29.46y	84.0y	164.8y	247.7y
Rotational period	58.7d	243d	23.9h	24.8h	9.84h	10.66h	23h	22h	6.4d
Equatorial diameter (km)	4880	12 104	12 756	6790	142 800	120 000	51 800	49 500	4000
Average density (water=1)	5.44	5.25	5.515	3.94	1.33	0.71	1.3	1.7	0.5
Gravity (Earth=1)	0.38	0.90	1	0.38	2.64	1.16	1.2	1.2	0.03
Atmospheric pressure (Earth=1)	0	91	1	0.01	–	–	–	–	–

PROBLEMS

1. A woman weighs 50 kg on Earth. How much will she weigh on Uranus? .... kg
2. A man is 59 Earth years old. What would his age be if he had lived on Saturn? .... years
3. Jupiter is the biggest planet but is nearly all gas and liquid. How many times is tiny Mercury denser than Jupiter? ....
4. A spaceship can travel at 50 000 km/h. If it was possible to travel in a straight line from Earth to Neptune (it isn't!) what is the least number of years it would take to get there? .... years
5. How many times is the atmospheric pressure greater on Venus than on Mars? ....
6. If the orbit of Mercury was a circle (it's really an ellipse) what would its velocity be? .... km/h
7. How many times would you see the Sun rise during a year on Jupiter? ....
8. How many times could Pluto fit into Saturn? ....

SOLAR POWER

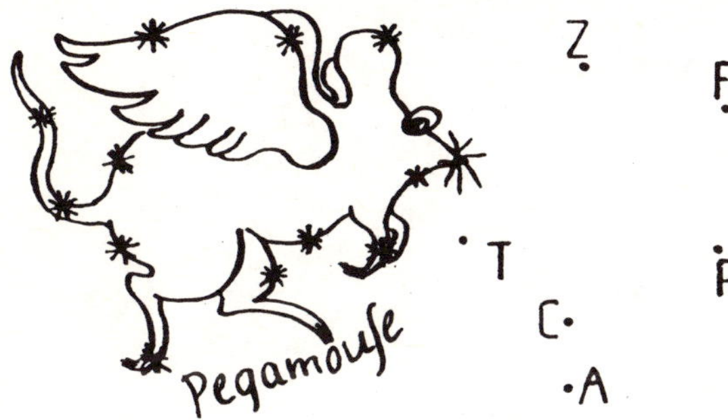

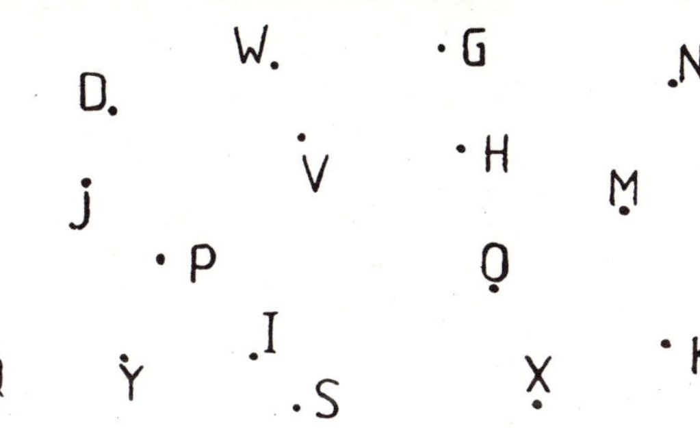

Find the matching word(s) in the key list for each description below. For Q. 1–21, join up in order the dots in the diagram which have the letters in the key list corresponding to your answers. This gives you a picture of the constellation. The key letters for Q. 22–24 spell out its name.

1. 90% of the atoms in the Sun are of this element
2. Sudden eruptions on the solar surface
3. Nearest bright star to the Sun
4. Displays of light at Earth's poles caused by charged particles from the Sun
5. Upper atmosphere of the Sun – 'sphere of colour'
6. Strongly magnetic cooler areas on the Sun's surface
7. Phenomenon observed when the Moon comes between the Sun and the Earth
8. Class of star to which Sun belongs
9. Process by which Sun produces energy
10. High energy radiation from the Sun which can disturb the Earth's ionosphere
11. Seen as a halo of white light around the Moon during a complete eclipse
12. Streams of charged particles from the Sun
13. Different colours obtained by splitting up light from the Sun
14. Region of the Sun's atmosphere where light is absorbed
15. Element produced from hydrogen by nuclear fusion. First discovered on the Sun
16. Galaxy to which the Sun belongs
17. Packets of light energy that travel from the Sun to the Earth
18. Name of the theory about light energy
19. Regions in Earth's atmosphere which traps charged particles from the Sun
20. Central part of the Sun in which energy is produced. It is over 1 000 000 °C
21. Gas in the Earth's upper atmosphere which shields us from the Sun's UV
22. Radiation from the Sun needed by plants for photosynthesis
23. Means of heat transfer in core and photosphere
24. Type of waves given out during periods of high solar activity

KEY LIST

R.	Alpha Centauri	B.	Eclipse	D.	Nuclear fusion	H.	Solar wind
F.	Aurora	C.	Flares	Q.	Ozone	V.	Spectrum
T.	Chromosphere	I.	Helium	Y.	Photons	F.	Sunspots
E.	Convection	A.	Hydrogen	P.	Quantum	P.	Van Allen Belts
R.	Core	L.	Light	O.	Radio waves	W.	X-rays
G.	Corona	S.	Milky Way	P.	Reversing layer	J.	Yellow Dwarf

A SPIRAL SOLUTION

In this spiral puzzle the last letter of each answer is the initial letter of the next answer.

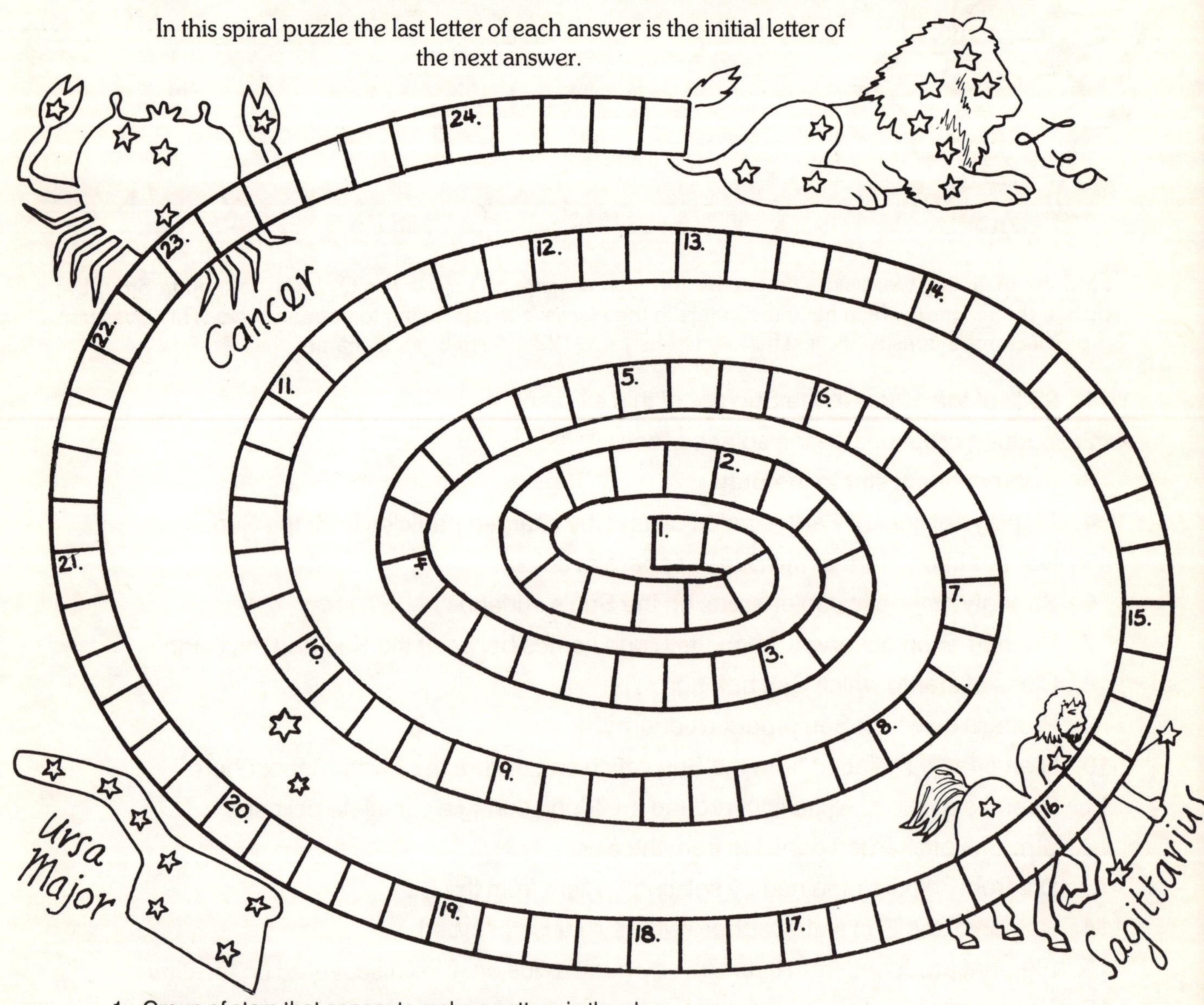

1. Group of stars that appear to make a pattern in the sky
2. Huge cloud of gas and dust
3. 'Nearby' spiral galaxy – two million light years away
4. Hunk of rock in an orbit between Mars and Jupiter
5. Shrunken star near the end of its life
6. Nuclear process by which stars produce energy
7. A star which increases in brightness
8. Red Giant in Taurus
9. He invented the reflecting telescope
10. Collapsed stars are called this
11. Outermost planet in the Solar System
12. The name of a large asteroid
13. Shape of the Milky Way galaxy
14. Astronomical unit of distance (2 words)
15. Telescope which collects long-wavelength radiation
16. Telescope which collects light rays
17. Focuses light rays in a telescope
18. These produce huge amounts of energy by nuclear fusion
19. 'Dog Star'
20. First artificial satellite
21. Astronomer who first stated the laws of planetary motion
22. Colour of a giant expanding star
23. Effect which causes wavelength of radiation to get longer if the source is getting further away
24. Blue supergiant in Orion

A SYSTEMATIC INQUIRY

ACROSS

1. 16th century astronomer who taught that the planets revolved around the Sun
7. Number of moons of Mars
8. Symbol of metallic element found in some meteors
9. Hard planet to observe because of permanent cloud cover
13. Natural satellite of a planet
14. Fragment of rock hurtling through space
17. This is tranquil on the Moon
18. Instrument for analysing light from the Sun
20. Next planet beyond Earth
21. See 4 Down
22. The star in the Solar System

DOWN

2. Fiery clouds in Sun's upper atmosphere
3. To spin on an axis like the Earth does every day
4. And 21 Across: Measuring this radiation tells us about the temperature of the planets (2 words)
5. May not be a true planet
6. Astronomer who first stated the laws of planetary motion
10. Low density collections of gas, dust, rocks and ice orbiting the Sun
11. Rocks in a belt between Mars and Jupiter
12. Moon of Jupiter discovered by Galileo
15. 17th century scientist who showed that planetary motion depends on gravitational forces
16. Path of a planet around the Sun
19. A large asteroid
20. Galaxy to which we belong (initials)

IT'S LUNACY

WHAT DID THE WELL-DRESSED ASTRONAUT WEAR WHEN HE WENT TO THE MOON ?

1. Changing appearance of the Moon
2. Number of known moons of Jupiter

3. Astronomer who first explained tides as result of the Moon's gravitational pull
4. Instrument used to measure 'moonquakes'
5. Dark areas on Moon once thought to be seas
6. Shape of new Moon

7. The name of the first manned lunar landing craft
8. Past geologic activity on the Moon caused these

9. First astronomer to view Moon through a telescope
10. US Moon missions
11. Dense concentrations of mass on the Moon
12. Result of Earth, Moon and Sun being in line
13. Crevasses on the Moon
14. Moon named after the son of Neptune in Greek mythology

15. Largest of Jupiter's moons
16. Water movements on Earth caused by the Moon
17. Crater which is centre of largest ray system on the Moon
18. Soviet space craft which sent back first pictures of far side of Moon
19. Large Moon crater named after 16th century Polish astronomer
20. The Moon goddess of the Romans

21. Planet whose moons were discovered by Galileo
22. Fine particles covering Moon's surface
23. First man to set foot on the Moon
24. Force keeping a Moon in orbit
25. Features of the Moon which could be caused by volcanic activity
26. These damage the Moon

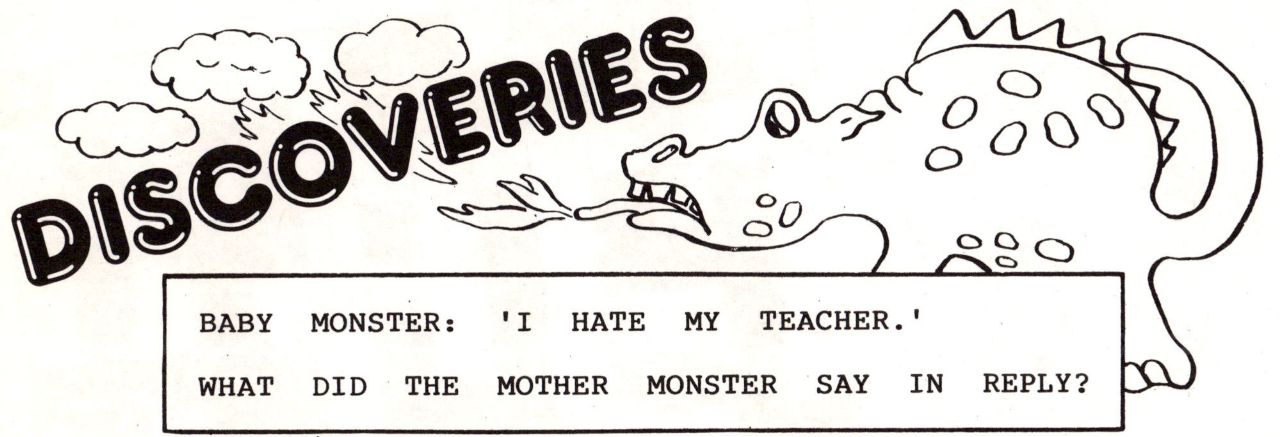

DISCOVERIES
BABY MONSTER: 'I HATE MY TEACHER.'
WHAT DID THE MOTHER MONSTER SAY IN REPLY?

Draw a line connecting the name of each scientist with the discovery with which he or she is most closely associated. Circle the letters through which the lines pass. Read down the circled letters to find the answer. Number 1 is done for you.

	Scientist	Letters	Discovery
1.	BOYLE	T A	RADIUM
2.	CURIE	H C	ATOMS
3.	COPERNICUS	E D	ELECTRICITY
4.	DALTON	N O R	AIR PRESSURE
5.	DARWIN	W J	RELATIVITY
6.	EINSTEIN	U S F	PLANETARY MOTION
7.	FARADAY	B	BLOOD CIRCULATION
8.	FLEMING		EVOLUTION
9.	GALILEO	T E	MOONS OF JUPITER
10.	HARVEY	A	CHEMISTRY OF COMBUSTION
11.	HUBBLE	L G	PENICILLIN
12.	JENNER	Y T I	ANTISEPSIS
13.	WEGENER	N O	CONTINENTAL DRIFT
14.	LAVOISIER	U R	VACCINATION
15.	LISTER	F V	EXPANDING UNIVERSE
16.	MENDEL	S	HEREDITY
17.	NEWTON	C M	DNA
18.	PRIESTLEY	A L	X-RAYS
19.	RÖENTGEN	A E	GRAVITATION
20.	WATSON & CRICK	K D	OXYGEN

Plants and People

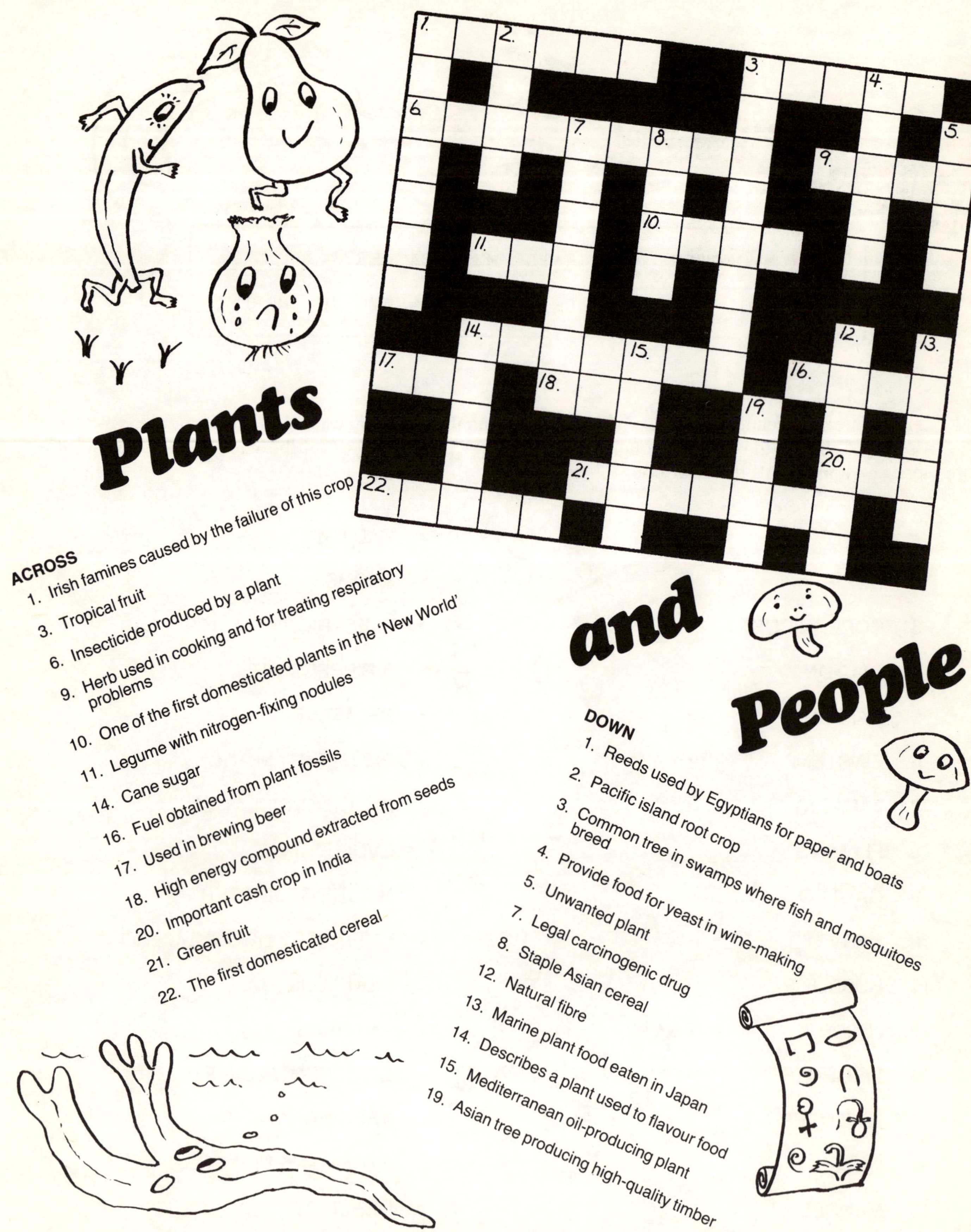

ACROSS

1. Irish famines caused by the failure of this crop
3. Tropical fruit
6. Insecticide produced by a plant
9. Herb used in cooking and for treating respiratory problems
10. One of the first domesticated plants in the 'New World'
11. Legume with nitrogen-fixing nodules
14. Cane sugar
16. Fuel obtained from plant fossils
17. Used in brewing beer
18. High energy compound extracted from seeds
20. Important cash crop in India
21. Green fruit
22. The first domesticated cereal

DOWN

1. Reeds used by Egyptians for paper and boats
2. Pacific island root crop
3. Common tree in swamps where fish and mosquitoes breed
4. Provide food for yeast in wine-making
5. Unwanted plant
7. Legal carcinogenic drug
8. Staple Asian cereal
12. Natural fibre
13. Marine plant food eaten in Japan
14. Describes a plant used to flavour food
15. Mediterranean oil-producing plant
19. Asian tree producing high-quality timber

The words in the lists are the answers to the crossword questions. Use them to help you do the crossword.

algae	oil	tea	sage
avocado	olive	teak	spice
coal	papyrus	tobacco	sucrose
corn	pea	wheat	taro
cotton	potato	weed	
grape	pyrethria		
hop	rice		
mango			
mangrove			

ANSWERS

1. BEAKERS AND BUNSENS

Across		Down	
1	taste	1	test
3	yellow	2	flask
5	shoes	4	water
6	push	7	beaker
7	burns	8	rod
11	sand	9	air
12	tripod	10	collar
14	reagent	13	record
16	blue	15	gauze
18	bunsen	17	amp
19	pipette		
20	acid		

2. UNDERSTANDING UNITS

Correct conversions are:

1	H	17	A	32	W
4	E	19	W	36	E
7	B	20	A	37	R
8	E	22	S	38	E
11	C	24	H	42	W
12	A	26	A	46	O
13	M	28	N	47	L
16	E	29	D	50	F

3. KID'S STUFF

1	5 h	T
2	35 cm	H
3	11 kPa	E
4	10.2 cm^3	I
5	1.1 N	N
6	0.019%	F
7	79 counts/min	A
8	25 flies/h	N
9	0.76	T
10	0.61%	R
11	0.108%	Y

4. FOR WOOLLY THINKERS

THERE ARE MORE OF THEM

5. TOY TIME

1	30.6 °C	H	11	30.5 N	I
2	24.6 °C	E	12	7.5 cm^3	N
3	−6 °C	W	13	12 cm^3	T
4	162 °C	A	14	16 cm^3	H
5	3.3 cm^3	S	15	4.3 cm^3	E
6	0.8 cm^3	A	16	+0.4 A	N
7	0.16 cm^3	P	17	+3.5 A	E
8	1.2 N	A	18	−0.3 A	C
9	7.9 N	I	19	−5.5 A	K
10	4.6 N	N			

6. MEASURING MONSTERS

1	length – metres	T
2	temperature – degrees	H
3	force – newtons	E
4	time – seconds	–
5	electrical resistance – ohms	H
6	volume – litres	O
7	velocity – metres/sec.	R
8	pressure – pascals	R
9	electric current – amps	O
10	power – watts	R
11	energy – joules	–
12	mass – kilograms	S
13	loudness – decibels	C
14	density – grams/cubic centimetre	O
15	frequency – hertz	P
16	electrical potential difference – volts	E

7. TUBULAR TANGLE

1 reagent bottle
2 thistle funnel
3 rubber stopper
4 round-bottomed flask
5 gauze
6 tripod
7 bunsen burner
8 condenser
9 filter funnel
10 conical flask
11 glass tubing
12 crucible
13 burette
14 clamp
15 stirring rod
16 beaker
17 thermometer
18 retort stand

8. DISCOVERING DIFFERENCES

1	stone fish	T
2	bat	H
3	turtle	E
4	platypus	T
5	toad	H
6	Echidna	R
7	Tiger shark	E
8	flying fox	E
9	sting ray	G
10	mud skipper	R
11	bandicoot	O
12	lamprey	U
13	giant earth worm	N
14	penguin	D
15	Archaeopteryx	M
16	Rhesus monkey	I
17	horse	C
18	leopard	E

9. FISH, FEATHERS AND FUR

1	Amphibians	T
2	Cartilaginous fish	H
3	Reptiles	E
4	Monotremes	Y
5	Birds	A
6	True mammals	L
7	True mammals	L
8	Cartilaginous fish	H
9	Birds	A
10	Marsupials	V
11	Reptiles	E
12	Bony fish	F
13	True mammals	L
14	Birds	A
15	Amphibians	T
16	Bony fish	F
17	Reptiles	E
18	Reptiles	E
19	Amphibians	T

10. THE FOOD CHAIN GAME

1	A	5	S	9	T
2	S	6	I	10	0
3	E	7	C	11	U
4	A	8	K	12	R
				13	I
				14	S
				15	T

11. WEB OF WORDS

Across

2 producer
5 oxygen
7 soil
8 hide
10 ant
13 bacteria
14 environment
15 core
16 ET
18 NO_3^-
19 two
20 rats
22 rad
23 mould
25 web
26 water
27 lake

Down

1 erosion
2 pollution
3 one
4 consumer
6 nitrate
8 habitat
9 decomposer
11 carnivore
12 mercury
14 energy
17 tag
21 tick
24 DDT

12. RESEARCHING RELATIONSHIPS

	A	B	C	
1	F	T	T	**J**
2	S	T	S	**U**
3	F	F	T	**M**
4	F	S	T	**P**

	A	B	C	
5	S	T	T	**S**
6	S	T	S	**U**
7	T	S	S	**I**
8	S	T	F	**T**
9	S	T	T	**S**

13. POPULATION

Year	Population	Year	Population
1	110	7	160
2	125	8	156
3	132	9	180
4	133	10	189
5	130	11	171
6	143	12	100

Blood Vessels

14. WHAT AM I?

1 Marsupial
2 Amphibian
3 Bird
4 Shark
5 Reptile
6 Monotreme
7 Bony fish
8 True mammal

15. A TALL STORY

1 LIG**H**T
2 OXYG**E**N
3 GLU**C**OSE
4 OVU**L**ES
5 IOD**I**NE
6 STO**M**ATA
7 EM**B**RYO
8 **S**PORES
9 CELL**U**LOSE
10 PHOS**P**HORUS
11 ST**A**RCH
12 A**N**THER
13 GU**A**RD
14 **C**ARBON
15 DI**O**XIDE
16 CHLO**R**OPHYLL
17 VEI**N**S
18 W**A**LLS
19 POLLE**N**
20 EPI**D**ERMIS
21 LIME**W**ATER
22 LE**A**VES
23 TENDR**I**L
24 FRUC**T**OSE
25 ROOT**S**

16. FLOWER POWER

1	vein	A
2	leaf blade	N
3	petiole	E
4	bud	L
5	stigma	E
6	style	P
7	anther	H
8	filament	A
9	stamen	N
10	ovary	T
11	sepal	W
12	petal	I
13	embryo	T
14	cotyledon	H
15	ovules	A
16	cell wall	W
17	membrane	E
18	chloroplast	T
19	vacuole	S
20	nucleus	N
21	cambium	E
22	phloem	A
23	xylem	K
24	pith	E
25	epidermis	R

17. VERTEBRATE VIBES

	A	**B**	**C**			**A**	**B**	**C**	
1	F	F	F	**N**	6	S	T	T	**S**
2	F	F	S	**O**	7	T	S	F	**H**
3	T	T	T	**A**	8	T	T	T	**A**
4	T	S	F	**H**	9	F	S	S	**R**
5	S	T	T	**S**	10	F	T	F	**K**

18. CAMEL CAPERS

1 **B**IRDS
2 INS**E**CTS
3 CA**C**TUS
4 SWE**A**TING
5 **U**REA
6 DINO**S**AURS
7 INT**E**RNAL
8 **H**AIR
9 CONIF**E**RS
10 EVAPOR**A**TION
11 SKE**L**ETON
12 **W**ATER
13 MAMM**A**LS
14 SHIN**Y**
15 LUNG**S**
16 S**H**ELL
17 TEMPER**A**TURE
18 **S**EEDS
19 FEAT**H**ERS
20 GRAV**I**TY
21 ROOT**S**
22 AMPHI**B**IANS
23 STOM**A**TA
24 ATA**C**AMA
25 S**K**IN
26 NOCT**U**RNAL
27 **P**OLLEN

19. IT'S CYTOLOGICAL

1 CELL
2 CELLULOSE
3 CHLOROPHYLL
4 CARBON DIOXIDE
5 CYTOPLASM
6 ENERGY
7 FATS
8 MEMBRANE
9 OIL
10 WATER
11 NUCLEUS
12 GLUCOSE
13 VACUOLE
14 CLOT
15 STARCH
16 PROTEIN
17 RESPIRATION
18 OXYGEN

```
C H L O R O P H Y L L     F
E       E             V   A
L       S   C         A   T
L   N   P   Y   G L U C O S E
    U   I   T         U       C
M   C A R B O N   D I O X I D E
E   L   A   P         L       L
M   E   T   L         E   O I L
B   U   I   A   W         X   U
R   S   O   S T A R C H   Y   L
A       N   M   T   L     G   O
N               E   O     E   S
E N E R G Y   P R O T E I N   E
```

20. DIGESTIVE DILEMMA

1 CARBO**H**YDRATE
2 RICK**E**TS
3 VI**T**AMINS
4 PELL**A**GRA
5 **K**
6 ANA**E**MIA
7 **S**CURVY
8 IOD**I**NE
9 PRO**T**EIN
10 HYPOT**H**ALAMUS
11 KIL**O**JOULE
12 **M**OULDS
13 PROT**E**ASES
14 KWASH**I**ORKOR
15 IRO**N**
16 C**A**LCIUM
17 **F**OLIC
18 MINE**R**ALS
19 S**O**DIUM
20 **G**OITRE
21 **G**LUCOSE
22 ENZ**Y**MES
23 ASCOR**B**IC
24 **A**
25 DI**G**ESTION

21. FILLING IN FACTS

1 TEND**O**N
2 **U**LNA
3 **T**IBIA
4 TH**O**RAX
5 **F**EMUR
6 T**W**O
7 ABD**O**MEN
8 **R**IBS
9 S**K**ULL
10 **F**IBULA
11 TA**R**SALS
12 PECT**O**RAL
13 L**I**GAMENT
14 DI**S**CS
15 DIAP**H**RAGM
16 R**A**DIUS
17 PEL**V**IS
18 SPIN**E**
19 JOI**N**T
20 B**O**NES
21 CAR**T**ILAGE
22 HUM**E**RUS
23 VERT**E**BRAE
24 FRAC**T**URE
25 **H**INGE

22. HAVE-A-HEART

Across	**Down**
1 valve	2 vena
3 white	4 iron
5 ECG	6 cava
7 ventricles	7 valves
9 AB	8 capillary
10 plasma	12 IV
11 vein	13 lymph
14 pulmonary	15 oxygen
18 coronary	16 aorta
20 RIP	17 femoral
21 gut	19 one
22 artery	23 right
25 Rh	24 clot
26 globin	27 O
28 cell	
29 left	
30 platelets	

23. CIRCULATION CHALLENGE

1	mouth	P
2	oesophagus	Q
3	stomach	Y
4	small intestine	X
5	hepatic portal vein	G
6	liver	N
7	hepatic vein	H
8	vena cava	Z
9	right auricle	V
10	right ventricle	W
11	pulmonary artery	S
12	lungs	O
13	pulmonary vein	T
14	left auricle	K
15	left ventricle	L
16	aorta	A
17	femoral artery	E
18	leg muscle	M

Diagram is of an ice cream.

24. A BREATHTAKING MYSTERY

1 RIGH**T**
2 BRONC**HI**
3 V**E**INS
4 EMPH**Y**SEMA
5 GLUC**O**SE
6 PULMO**N**ARY
7 HAEMOG**L**OBIN
8 OX**Y**GEN
9 PNEU**M**ONIA
10 TR**A**CHEA
11 TAL**K**ING
12 ALV**E**OLI
13 MARRO**W**
14 RESP**I**RATION
15 **T**B
16 DIAP**H**RAGM
17 RE**D**
18 BICA**R**BONATE
19 THOR**A**X
20 **W**ATER
21 CAPILL**A**RIES
22 CI**L**IA
23 MUCOU**S**

25. A GROWING PROBLEM

1 CARBO**H**YDRATE
2 LIV**E**R
3 **W**ATER
4 SALIV**A**RY
5 COLO**N**
6 PROT**E**INS
7 ENZYM**E**S
8 DUO**D**ENUM
9 SPHINC**T**ER
10 AMIN**O**
11 **M**OUTH
12 **A**NUS
13 **K**
14 PANCR**E**AS
15 HEP**A**TIC
16 HYDROC**H**LORIC
17 KILOJ**O**ULE
18 **G**LANDS
19 GLUC**O**SE
20 **F**ATS
21 OESOP**H**AGUS
22 B**I**LE
23 RECTU**M**
24 MALTO**S**E
25 GLYC**E**ROL
26 VIL**L**I
27 **F**e

26. THE FACTS OF LIFE

1 ZY**G**OTE
2 F**O**ETUS
3 OV**U**LATE
4 **W**ATER
5 PLAC**E**NTA
6 OVA**R**Y
7 C**E**RVIX
8 EM**B**RYO
9 SPE**R**M
10 **O**VUM
11 UTER**U**S
12 VA**G**INA
13 R**H**ESUS
14 PROS**T**ATE
15 PU**B**ERTY
16 X-RA**Y**S
17 TES**T**ES
18 **H**EART
19 P**E**NIS
20 ULTRA**S**OUND
21 IN-VI**T**RO
22 GEST**A**TION
23 FAL**L**OPIAN
24 SMO**K**ING

27. HYBRID HUMOUR

1	23	**A**
2	0.5	**W**
3	46	**O**
4	4	**O**
5	0	**L**
6	0	**L**
7	47	**Y**
8	1	**J**
9	3	**U**
10	0.25	**M**
11	50	**P**
12	10	**E**
13	45	**R**

28. MYSTERY MONGREL

1 W**A**TSON
2 HAEMO**P**HILIA
3 CHROM**O**SOMES
4 OV**U**LE
5 M**E**IOSIS
6 NU**C**LEUS
7 PROT**E**INS
8 MEN**D**EL
9 HOMO**Z**YGOUS
10 **G**ENE
11 GENO**T**YPE
12 MONO**H**YBRID
13 DN**A**
14 MI**T**OSIS
15 RN**A**
16 X-**R**AYS
17 **R**HESUS
18 CONG**E**NITAL
19 **S**PERM
20 MUTA**T**ION
21 RECE**S**SIVE
22 ENZY**M**ES
23 DOMI**N**ANT
24 **D**NA
25 ZY**G**OTE
26 SP**E**CIES
27 PHENO**T**YPE
28 DOWN**S**

29. GENETICALLY SPEAKING

DRUG**S**
PLAN**T**
CL**O**NE
D**N**A
MOL**E**CULE
DAR**W**IN
ANIM**A**L
DI**S**EASE
MONO**H**YBRID
INHERI**T**ED
HORMONE
GEN**E**
FOS**S**IL
ENVIRON**M**ENT
OR**G**ANISMS
BR**E**ED
R**N**A
EVOLUTION
MUTATION**S**

30. IT'S A WATERY WORLD

Across	Down
1 humidity	2 detergent
3 bloom	4 oil
8 artesian	5 mercury
9 fan	6 diffusion
11 fertiliser	7 salination
12 sewage	10 bends
14 sand	13 wadi
15 DDT	16 one
17 delta	18 silt
19 oxygen	20 Nile
22 erosion	21 ice
23 tidal	
24 temperature	

31. DIRTY WORDS

Across	Down
1 lime	3 horizon
2 leach	4 phosphate
5 top	9 loam
6 humus	11 salination
7 fungi	14 nitrogen
8 silt	19 clay
10 loess	21 worm
12 pH	23 sub
13 minerals	
15 ions	
16 water	
17 tap	
18 erosion	
20 till	
22 oxygen	
23 sandy	
24 mulch	
25 basalt	

32. THE WORLD'S RESOURCES

ANIMAL**S**
ME**T**AL ORE
LE**A**D
SILVE**R**
TIN
WOOL
SOLAR **E**NERGY
CO**A**L
VEGETABLES
O**I**L
SA**N**D
GOLD
TIDAL POWER
C**H**ALK
LIM**E** STONE
CO**T**TON
ASHP**H**ALT
WIND POWE**R**
BON**E**
CL**A**Y
WOO**D**

33. IT'S ELEMENTARY

Across	Down
1 cobalt	1 C
6 Ag	2 O
7 hydrogen	3 argon
9 Ba	4 carbon
10 oxygen	5 chlorine
12 iron	8 nitrogen
13 tin	11 yttrium
16 gold	14 I
18 iodine	15 zinc
20 U	17 lead
22 Al	19 N
23 Mg	
24 Cu	

34. SEEKING A SOLUTION

Across	Down
1 suspension	2 oil
4 sugar	3 crystals
6 filter	4 saturate
8 taste	5 gases
9 ions	6 funnel
10 residue	7 two
15 evaporation	11 sediment
17 wet	12 salt
18 clear	13 solute
19 one	14 energy
20 hot	16 alcohol
21 rod	17 water
22 solution	

35. A RAPID REACTION

1 CEL**L**
2 ELECTR**O**LYTE
3 ELEC**T**RODE
4 ION**S**
5 CARB**O**N
6 **F**LUORINE
7 CAT**H**ODE
8 **O**XYGEN
9 ELEC**T**RONS
10 IONI**C**
11 COPPE**R**
12 AN**O**DE
13 PO**S**ITIVE
14 **S**ODIUM
15 **B**ATTERY
16 SULPH**U**RIC
17 CHLORI**N**E
18 ZI**N**C
19 ALUM**I**NIUM
20 L**E**AD
21 CORRO**S**ION

36. CHEMICAL CHALLENGE

	A	B	C	
1	T	F	T	**L**
2	T	T	F	**I**
3	F	T	F	**T**
4	T	T	T	**H**
5	T	T	F	**I**
6	F	T	T	**U**
7	T	F	F	**M**

37. A BASIC PROBLEM

1	**A**CIDS	11	STO**M**ACH
2	CO**P**PER	12	**A**MINO
3	ALKA**L**I	13	WEA**K**
4	INDIC**A**TOR	14	PANCR**E**AS
5	AMMO**N**IA	15	BA**S**ES
6	VIN**E**GAR	15	LITMU**S**
7	LAC**T**IC	17	SULP**H**URIC
8	p**H**	18	HYDR**O**XIDE
9	W**A**TER	19	NIT**R**IC
10	BIT**T**ER	20	CI**T**RIC
		21	C**H**ALK
		22	HYDR**O**GEN
		23	**P**INK
		24	**S**ALT

38. THE ACID TEST

1	$1H_2O$	**F**	9	$1HNO_3$	**O**
2	$2H_2O$	**L**	10	$1ZnO$	**F**
3	$1H_2$	**O**	11	$1Na_2CO_3$	**A**
4	$2HNO_3$	**R**	12	$1HCl$	**R**
5	$2KOH$	**E**	13	$3CO_2$	**A**
6	$6HCl$	**N**	14	$3H_2O$	**B**
7	$1H_2SO_4$	**C**	15	$3H_2$	**I**
8	$2HCl$	**E**	16	$1CO_2$	**A**

39. METAL MASTERY

1	DUC**T**ILE	13	**O**NE
2	LE**A**D	14	MERC**U**RY
3	NIC**K**EL	15	TI**T**ANIUM
4	MALL**E**ABLE	16	**O**RES
5	**T**WO	17	RE**F**INING
6	CAT**H**ODE	18	NI**T**RATE
7	OXID**E**S	19	T**H**REE
8	BRA**S**S	20	MAGN**E**SIUM
9	COP**P**ER	21	**G**OLD
10	HYDR**O**GEN	22	AL**L**OYS
11	S**O**DIUM	23	R**A**DIUM
12	IRO**N**	24	**S**TEEL
		25	LU**S**TRE

40. PETROLEUM PUZZLE

1	PRO**P**ANE
2	L**E**AD
3	OC**T**ANE
4	CA**R**BON
5	DI**O**XIDE
6	DISTI**L**LATION
7	WAX**E**S
8	POLL**U**TION
9	SEDI**M**ENTARY
10	VA**P**OUR
11	C**R**ACKING
12	KER**O**SENE
13	CRU**D**E
14	BIT**U**MEN
15	HYDRO**C**ARBONS
16	AN**T**ICLINE
17	SEI**S**MIC
18	TUR**P**ENTINE
19	**O**ILS
20	METHA**N**E
21	**G**REASE

41. CLUED UP ON CARBON

2	coal	1	four
5	diamond	3	limewater
7	iron	4	monoxide
8	carbonate	5	dry
9	wax	6	dioxide
10	chalk	8	charcoal
11	ink	10	CO
12	acid	14	coke
13	ice	15	age
17	four	16	six
18	graphite		
19	marble		

42. COMPOUND CONUNDRUM

1	$CuSO_4$	**H**	11	$Ca(OH)_2$	**A**
2	$NaOH$	**I**	12	NH_4NO_3	**L**
3	$C_6H_{12}O_6$	**S**	13	$KMnO_4$	**L**
4	H_2S	**W**	14	CH_3COOH	**F**
5	$NaHCO_3$	**I**	15	N_2SO_4	**E**
6	H_2O_2	**N**	16	$CaCO_3$	**L**
7	$NaCl$	**D**	17	CuO	**L**
8	KNO_3	**O**	18	CO_2	**O**
9	HNO_3	**W**	19	NH_3	**U**
10	C_3H_8	**S**	20	Fe_2O_3	**T**

43. POLYMER PUZZLE

1	**S**ARCH	15	POLYE**S**TERS
2	SULP**H**UR	16	R**U**BBER
3	MONOM**E**R	17	CA**R**BON
4	**W**ATER	18	**G**LUCOSE
5	CAT**A**LYSTS	19	T**E**FLON
6	PLA**S**TICS	20	NYL**O**N
7	B**A**KELITE	21	D**N**A
8	**P**OLYMER		
9	CEL**L**ULOSE		
10	W**A**XES		
11	RE**S**INS		
12	PRO**T**EINS		
13	V**I**NYLS		
14	SILI**C**ONES		

44. IT'S A GAS

1	carbon dioxide	F
2	helium	U
3	nitrogen	L
4	carbon monoxide	L
5	hydrogen sulphide	B
6	methane	L
7	chloroform	O
8	hydrogen	O
9	ammonia	D
10	nitrous oxide	E
11	chlorine	D
12	propane	O
13	nitrogen dioxide	N
14	oxygen	E
15	fluorine	S

45. METALS AND MAN

Across		**Down**	
1	bauxite	1	bronze
4	copper	2	iron
6	pyrites	3	ores
8	electrolysis	4	cryolite
11	lead	5	galena
12	steel	7	brass
14	uranium	9	smelting
15	lime	10	sodium
16	coke	11	stone
17	gold	13	zinc

46. $E = mc^2$

Across		**Down**	
2	argon	1	rad
7	alpha	2	Ar
9	I	3	gamma
10	uranium	4	O
12	light	5	neutron
14	air	6	tailings
15	oxide	8	plutonium
17	Sun	11	ice
18	Hiroshima	13	gas
20	Sr	16	isotopes
22	laser	19	helium
25	core	21	proton
26	ozone	23	salt
28	one	24	radium
29	Na	25	Curie
30	tritium	27	one

47. STATE SECRETS

1	L**I**QUID	11	D**I**STIL
2	MAT**T**ER	12	CO**N**DENSE
3	**W**ATER	13	**F**REEZE
4	EV**A**PORATE	14	MOL**E**CULES
5	**S**TATES	15	PRE**S**SURE
6	GA**S**	16	DAL**T**ON
7	S**H**APE	17	EN**E**RGY
8	**A**TOMS	18	SOLI**D**
9	COMP**R**ESSED	19	**C**RYSTAL
10	**K**INETIC	20	VOL**U**ME
		21	**S**MALL
		22	MEL**T**ING
		23	L**A**RGE
		24	HYD**R**OGEN
		25	FLUI**D**S

48. IN THE BALANCE

1	1,1 2,1	**C**		10	1,1 2,1	**C**
2	1,2 2,1	**H**		11	1,1 1,1	**A**
3	1,2 1,1	**E**		12	2,2 1,2	**N**
4	2,1 1,2	**M**		13	1,1 1,2	**B**
5	2,1 1,1	**I**		14	1,2 1,1	**E**
6	1,3 3,2	**S**		15	1,2 1,2	**F**
7	1,3 1,3	**T**		16	1,3 3,1	**U**
8	3,1 1,3	**R**		17	2,2 1,2	**N**
9	1,3 2,3	**Y**				

49. DIS-PLACEMENTS

1	Cu	C
2	H_2	O
3	$2AgNO_3$	P
4	I_2	P
5	$CuSO_4$	E
6	Zn	R
7	2Ag	I
8	Mg	S
9	2NaBr	P
10	Ca	U
11	$FeSO_4$	S
12	$Ca(NO_3)_2$	H
13	$CaCl_2$	E
14	2HCl	D
15	$Fe(NO_3)_2$	O
16	Cl_2	U
17	Pb	T

50. GETTING PHYSICAL

1	P	6	C	11	C
2	P	7	N	12	C
3	C	8	P	13	C
4	C	9	N	14	N
5	P	10	C	15	P

Picture is of a chameleon.

51. SYMBOL SEARCH

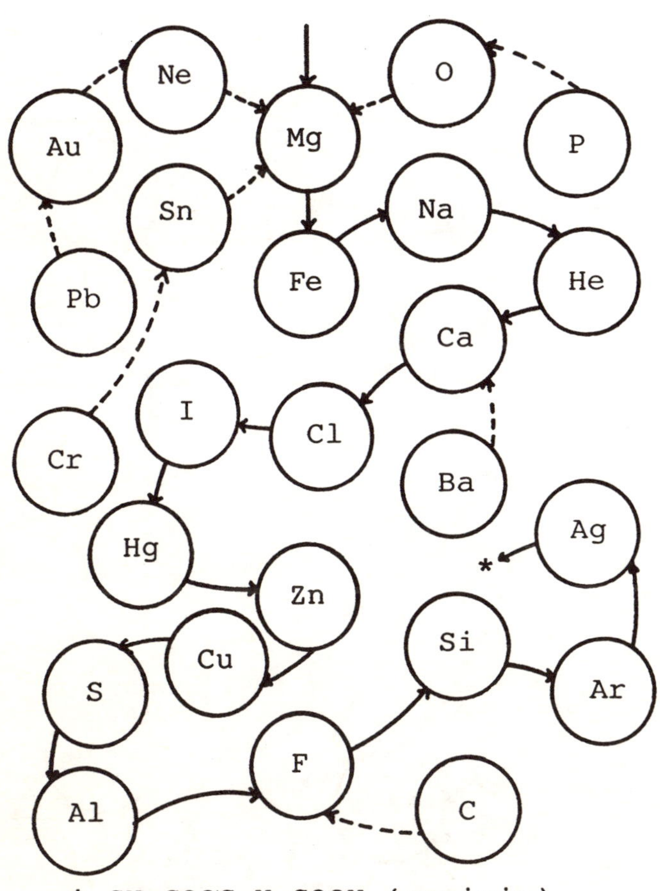

* $CH_3COOC_6H_4COOH$ (aspirin)

52. FAMILY FUN

1	Fe	**F**
2	N	**A**
3	Na	**N**
4	O	**G**
5	Ar	**S**
6	Cu	**G**
7	S	**I**
8	Pb	**V**
9	P	**I**
10	Sn	**N**
11	H	**G**
12	Ca	**D**
13	C	**A**
14	Si	**Y**

53. FERRETING OUT FORMULAE

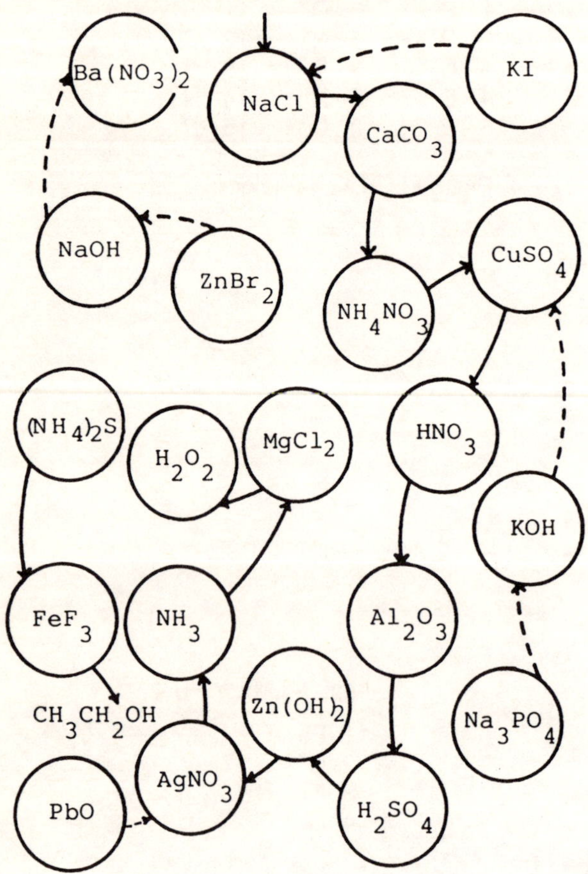

54. FORMULA FUN

Across	Down
1 KOH	1 $KHCO_3$
2 HF	3 PH_3
3 PbS	4 SiO_2
6 NH_3	5 $MgCO_3$
7 $HgCl_2$	8 H_2SO_4
8 H_2O_2	9 Na_2CO_3
10 H_3PO_4	11 PbI_2
12 Na_2SO_4	13 SO_2
15 CO_2	14 H_2SO_4
17 SrI_2	16 KNO_3
18 Al_2O_3	18 $AlCl_3$
19 O_3	21 NO
20 HNO_3	22 KF
23 $NaClO_3$	23 KCN
24 $FeCl_3$	25 H_2S
26 $MgSO_4$	

55. THE MOLE HOLE GAME

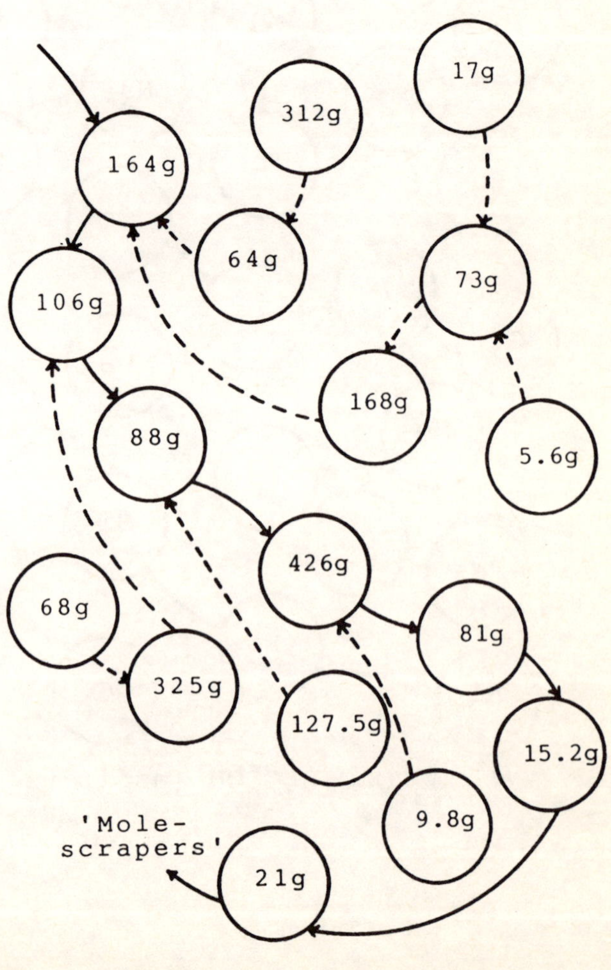

56. CHEMICAL CONUNDRUM

1	ION	15	ONE
2	POSI**T**IVE	16	NEGATI**V**E
3	T**W**O	17	PRO**T**ON
4	COMP**O**UND	18	TH**R**EE
5	MOLEC**U**LE	19	F**O**UR
6	COVA**L**ENT	20	HYDRO**G**EN
7	SOD**I**UM	21	NUCL**E**US
8	CAR**B**ON	22	DALTO**N**
9	NEUT**R**ON	23	TWO
10	ELE**M**ENT	24	S**H**ARED
11	**A**TOMS	25	NITR**A**TE
12	ELECT**R**ON	26	WA**T**ER
13	SULP**H**ATE	27	M**E**TALS
14	VAL**E**NCE	28	PO**L**AR
		29	GA**S**ES
		30	IN**E**RT

57. TOGETHERNESS

	A	B	C	
1	T	T	T	**A**
2	T	T	F	**B**
3	F	T	S	**L**
4	F	F	S	**O**
5	F	F	S	**O**
6	T	F	T	**D**
7	S	S	T	**Y**

	A	B	C	
8	F	F	T	**M**
9	T	T	T	**A**
10	F	S	S	**R**
11	S	S	T	**Y**

58. PARTICLE PUZZLE

1 ELECTRON
2 ELEMENT
3 ENERGY
4 ION
5 ISOTOPE
6 MATTER
7 MOLECULE
8 ONE
9 NEGATIVE
10 NEUTRON
11 NUCLEUS
12 PARTICLE
13 POSITIVE
14 PROTON

```
                    N
   P     E          U
 P A R T I C L E    C   N
   O     E          L   E
   T   N   M O L E C U L E
   O   E   E        U   T   L
 I O N G   N        S   R   E
     M A T T E R        O   C
         T              N   T
   P O S I T I V E          R
     N   V          I S O T O P E
     E N E R G Y                N
```

59. WATER WORDS

1 **T**ides
2 **H**umidity
3 **E**vaporation
4 **Y**awl
5 **C**ondense
6 **A**rtesian
7 **N**ile
8 **T**yphoon
9 **G**lacier
10 **E**l Nino
11 **T**sunami
12 **T**emperature
13 **H**ail
14 **E**rosion
15 **W**adi
16 **R**efraction
17 **A**mazon
18 **P**oles
19 **P**ressure
20 **I**ce
21 **N**eap
22 **G**eyser
23 **O**xygen
24 **F**reeze
25 **F**an

60. ATMOSPHERICS

Across
1 carbon
3 dioxide
6 argon
9 stratosphere
11 NO_2
12 two
13 Rn
14 acid
16 IR
18 Van
19 Allen
21 UV
23 CO
24 NO
25 ammonia
26 air
27 lead

Down
1 convection
2 red
4 ion
5 Xe
6 aurora
7 ozone
8 Torricelli
9 smog
10 SO_2
15 Pascal
17 rain
20 rem
22 vane
25 air

61. FORECASTING FUN

1	ISOBARS	16	HAIL
2	HYGROMETER	17	RADAR
3	CIRRUS	18	MILLIBARS
4	MONSOON	19	CYCLONE
5	SMOG	20	CORIOLIS
6	ANENOMETER	21	OZONE
7	CUMULUS	22	FOG
8	CONVECTION	23	STORM
9	DEW-POINT	24	TRADES
10	ATMOSPHERE	25	X-RAYS
11	BAROMETER	26	HUMIDITY
12	FRONT	27	TROPOSPHERE
13	MILLIMETRES		
14	STRATUS		
15	CONDENSATION		

62. HOT AIR

1 TROPO**S**PHERE
2 ANENOM**E**TER
3 NEO**N**
4 LEA**D**
5 HUM**I**DITY
6 DUS**T**
7 DENSI**T**Y
8 **O**XYGEN
9 V**A**CUUM
10 BURNI**N**G
11 DE**A**D SEA
12 CONV**E**CTION
13 NIT**R**OGEN
14 BAR**O**METER
15 CAR**B**ON
16 **D**IOXIDE
17 CY**C**LONE
18 PRES**S**URE
19 VOL**C**ANO
20 HE**L**IUM
21 THERM**A**L
22 STRATO**S**PHERE
23 PRIE**S**TLEY

63. A PAST PUZZLE

1 FOSS**I**LS
2 RIF**T**
3 **D**RIFT
4 SEDIM**E**NTARY
5 GALA**P**AGOS
6 PLAT**E**S
7 MAG**N**ETISM
8 BE**D**S
9 POTA**S**SIUM
10 F**O**LDING
11 SA**N** ANDREAS
12 DAR**W**IN
13 S**H**ELLS
14 WEG**E**NER
15 CA**R**BON
16 POLL**E**N
17 HIMALA**Y**AS
18 UNCONF**O**RMITY
19 M**U**D
20 WAL**L**ACE
21 CONV**E**CTION
22 **F**AULTS
23 STRA**T**A
24 GEOLOGIS**T**
25 EART**H**QUAKE
26 TE**E**TH
27 LI**M**ESTONE

64. PRESSURE PROBLEMS

1 62720 N A
2 156800 Pa N
3 490 N E
4 980000 Pa R
5 63360 kg V
6 10560 Pa O
7 1960 N U
8 90000 kg S
9 216000 kg W
10 51000 kg R
11 45900 kg E
12 50 mm of mercury C
13 1100 mm of mercury K

65. FINDING FORCES

Across
1 30 N
2 210 N
5 40 N
6 588 N
8 75000 N
10 450 N
11 1500000 N

Down
1 385 N
2 2450 N
3 10 N
4 18750 N
7 2000 N
9 500 N

66. MAD MIKE I

1 960 km T
2 10 km/h H
3 80 h E
4 1320 km D
5 0.5 m/s^2 E
6 180 km/h A
7 840 m D
8 98 m/s S
9 490 m E
10 196 s A

67. MAD MIKE II

1 3430000 N J
2 570 km/h U
3 500 km/h V
4 750 kg E
5 2.45 J N
6 4.9 J/s I
7 250 s L
8 0.5 m/s^2 E
9 3.4 m S

68. DENSITY DATA

1 1.02 kg/dm^3 L
2 342 g A
3 65 g M
4 50 dm^3 B
5 0.69 kg/dm^3 C
6 136 cm^3 H
7 97.5^9 O
8 1.2 g/cm^3 P
9 2 cm S

69. PUSH 'N PULL

1	MOVE	11	MOON
2	SLOWER	12	STOP
3	SPEED	13	START
4	GRAVITY	14	ROCKET
5	TONNE	15	INERTIA
6	FORCE	16	MASS
7	VELOCITY	17	NEWTON
8	ACTION	18	PULL
9	REACTION	19	MOMENTUM
10	DIRECTION	20	MOTION

```
            M
        S L O W E R
    G   P   V           T
F O R C E   E     V E L O C I T Y
    A   E       A       N
    V   D I R E C T I O N   M O O N
    I       E   T   N   E   O     E
  S T O P   A   I   E       M     W
    Y   U   C   O   R O C K E T   T
        L   T   N   T       N     O
        L   I       I   M O T I O N
            O   S T A R T   U
            N               M A S S
```

70. A WEIGHT PROBLEM

1	GRAVI**T**ATION	11	WEI**G**HT
2	INER**T**IA	12	V**E**CTOR
3	GAL**I**LEO	13	FRI**C**TION
4	REPUL**S**ION	14	**M**ASS
5	ELEC**T**RICAL	15	BALA**N**CED
6	CENTR**I**PETAL	16	**E**SCAPE
7	MO**M**ENTUM	17	NE**W**TON
8	MAGN**E**TIC	18	**F**ORCE
9	ATTRAC**T**ION	19	JUPIT**E**R
10	VEL**O**CITY	20	TERMI**N**AL
		21	REA**C**TION
		22	DIR**E**CTION

71. DIRECTIONAL DILEMMA

	A	B			A	B	
1	T	T	**A**	10	T	F	**B**
2	S	T	**M**	11	T	T	**A**
3	T	F	**A**	12	S	F	**N**
4	F	F	**G**	13	T	T	**A**
5	S	T	**N**	14	S	F	**N**
6	F	S	**E**	15	T	T	**A**
7	S	S	**T**				
8	F	S	**I**				
9	T	S	**C**				

Code list

A	TT	I	FS
B	TF	M	ST
C	TS	N	SF
E	FT	T	SS
G	FF		

72. A MAGNETIC MYSTERY

1	COB**A**LT	12	NE**W**TON
2	FI**E**LD	13	REVE**R**SES
3	FOR**C**E	14	**I**RON
4	DOMA**I**NS	15	COR**E**
5	REP**U**LSION	16	COM**P**ASS
6	POLE**S**	17	ELECTR**O**MAGNET
7	MAGN**E**SIA	18	COIL**S**
8	GENERA**T**ORS	19	CUR**R**ENT
9	**H**EAT	20	DEGAU**S**SING
10	NICK**E**L	21	SPE**A**KER
11	FARADA**Y**	22	JU**P**ITER
		23	ATTR**A**CTION
		24	NO**R**TH
		25	LIF**T**ING

73. 'OHM AT LAST

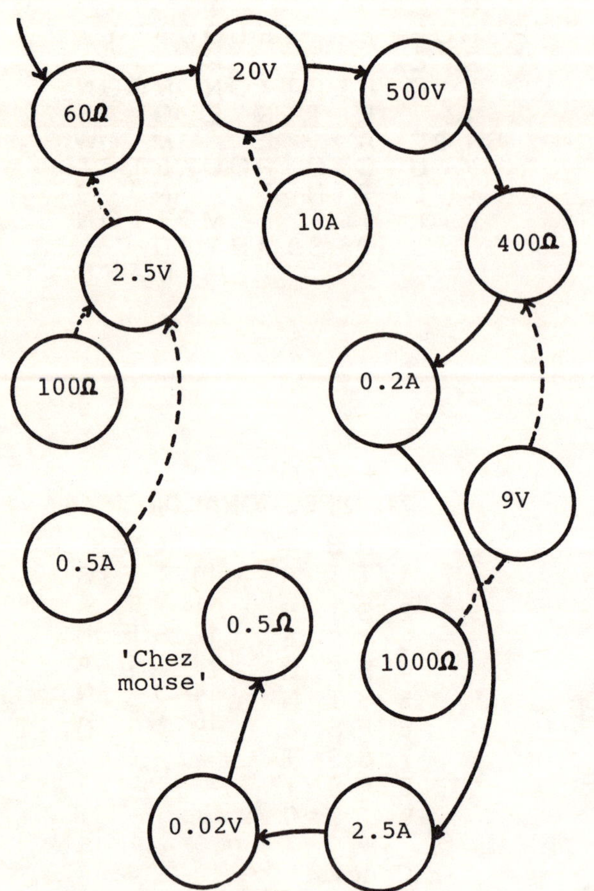

74. THE ELECTRICAL CIRCUIT

1 VOLTA
2 ALTERNATING
3 GALVANOMETER
4 RESISTOR
5 RHEOSTAT
6 TRANSFORMERS
7 SOLENOID
8 DIRECT
9 THERMIONIC
10 COULOMB
11 BULB
12 BATTERIES
13 SWITCH
14 HEAT
15 TURBINE
16 ELECTRON
17 NEGATIVE
18 ELECTRODE
19 ELECTRO-MAGNETISM
20 MICA
21 AMP
22 PARALLEL
23 LEAD
24 DYNAMO
25 OHM

75. REVOLTING RIDDLES

Across

1 electron
3 Faraday
8 iron
11 cell
12 generators
17 carbon
19 solenoid
20 core
21 heat
22 brush

Down

2 coils
4 armature
5 amp
6 magnet
7 AC
9 negative
10 direct
13 Sun
14 gas
15 Solar
16 zinc
18 ohms

76. KILOWATT KAPERS

1	48 ohms	**A**
2	0.25 amps	**V**
3	110 volts	**O**
4	2.5 amps	**L**
5	120 volts	**T**
6	1 320 watts	**S**
7	6 kWh	**W**
8	0.75 kWh	**A**
9	45 min	**G**
10	400 watts	**O**
11	0.16 kW	**N**

77. IT'S I.T.

CIR**C**UIT
SILICON C**H**IP
COMMUN**I**CATION
COM**P**UTER
RESI**S**TER
WAVE
S**I**GNALS
CAPACI**T**OR
HEXADECIMAL

DIOD**E**
CON**V**ERTOR
MICRO **E**LECTRON
T**R**ANSMISSION
BINAR**Y**
SA**T**ELLITES
SWITC**H**
LOG**I**C
A**N**ALOGUE
DI**G**ITAL

78. CROSS CIRCUIT

Across	Down
4 capacitor	1 gate
7 memories	2 ROM
8 satellite	3 disks
9 binary	5 chip
10 input	6 resistor
13 output	8 switch
14 compute	11 logic
15 microcircuit	12 stable
18 hexadecimal	16 relay
19 bite	17 RAM

79. GETTING HOTTER

Across	Down
6 convection	1 UV
9 Joule	2 ice
10 radiation	3 insulator
11 sea	4 kinetic
12 rock	5 infrared
13 dark	6 conduction
15 hot	7 gas
17 solids	8 winds
20 Sun	14 rise
21 hair	16 liquid
22 rubber	18 shiny
23 Na	19 sinks
24 air	
25 density	

For information, diagrams show:
Davy's radiation apparatus early 19th century
Dewar's vacuum flask 19th century
Crooke's radiometer 1874

80. HOT STUFF

1 HEA**T**
2 ALCO**H**OL
3 JOUL**E**
4 CLINI**C**AL
5 ME**R**CURY
6 RESIS**T**ANCE
7 TEMPE**R**ATURE
8 THERM**O**METER
9 PRESS**U**RE
10 EXPAN**S**ION
11 C**E**LSIUS
12 INC**R**EASES
13 GA**S**
14 **W**ET
15 VISC**O**SITY
16 VOL**U**ME
17 CO**L**OUR
18 **D**ARK
19 **F**USE
20 BIMET**A**LLIC
21 ME**L**TING
22 BUL**B**
23 SOLI**D**
24 C**O**PPER
25 **W**ATER
26 CO**N**TRACT

81. A SPECIFIC SOLUTION

1	190 J	A	8	5520 J	T
2	4025 J	W	9	1760 J/kg/C°	A
3	1500 g	A	10	25 g	L
4	250 g	L	11	134 J	K
5	10 g	K	12	180 °C	I
6	790 J/kg/C°	I	13	100 g	E
7	750 g	E			

82. A COOL QUESTION

1	672 kJ	T	8	28.5 kJ	W
2	12.6 kJ	H	9	23.1 kJ	O
3	31.5 kJ	E	10	566.5 kJ	N
4	42 kJ	D	11	1230.9 kJ	T
5	432.5 kJ	O	12	50.8 kJ	S
6	313.2 kJ	O	13	2066.4 kJ	H
7	201.5 kJ	R	14	608.4 kJ	U
			15	2331 kJ	T

83. AN ENERGY ENIGMA

1 X-RAY**S**
2 WI**N**D
3 KINET**I**C
4 RESPIR**A**TION
5 INF**R**ARED
6 **O**IL
7 NU**C**LEAR
8 POTE**N**TIAL
9 HY**D**ROGEN
10 CO**A**L
11 CHEMI**C**AL
12 GENER**A**TOR
13 E**N**ERGY
14 SOUN**D**
15 J**O**ULE
16 MAGN**E**TIC
17 SO**L**AR
18 TI**D**AL
19 LI**G**HT
20 **H**EAT
21 ELEC**T**RICAL
22 TUR**B**INE
23 BA**T**TERY

84. THE MEAN MACHINE

1 ROTAR**Y**
2 F**O**RCE
3 F**U**LCRUM
4 **W**HEEL
5 **O**ARS
6 P**U**LLEY
7 AX**L**E
8 LOA**D**
9 **G**EARS
10 SCR**E**W
11 EFFOR**T**
12 HOI**S**T
13 PITC**H**
14 FA**R**ADAY
15 LEV**E**R
16 WE**D**GE
17 FOR**D**
18 KNIF**E**
19 **E**DISON
20 INER**T**IA
21 NE**W**TON
22 PLAN**E**
23 PLI**E**RS
24 DIREC**T**ION

85. A SOUND SOLUTION

Across	Down
1 length	1 loud
6 hammer	2 hertz
7 auditory	3 bat
9 Rh	4 FM
11 anvil	5 ear
15 decibel	8 thickness
17 longitudinal	10 medium
19 raise	11 ABC
21 sine	12 vibrations
23 pitch	13 lower
24 drums	14 amplitude
25 tension	16 pinna
26 density	18 echo
	20 air
	22 reed

For information, diagrams show part or all of a:
Jellyfish statocyst
Moth ear
Frog lateral line system
Fish auditory apparatus
Bat external ear

86. SOUND BOX

PITC**H**
MICROPHON**E**
HEAR
E**A**R
IN**S**TRUMENT
TIMB**R**E
A**U**DIBLE
LOUD**N**ESS
N**O**ISE
ACO**U**STIC
QUIE**T**
V**O**CAL
DE**F**ECTS
VIBRA**T**ES
SPEED OF SO**U**ND
RESO**N**ANCE
WAV**E**
MU**S**IC

87. RESOUNDING SUCCESS

1 REVER**B**ERATION
2 TEL**E**PHONE
3 **C**OIL
4 V**A**CUUM
5 AMPLIT**U**DE
6 **S**OUND
7 MICROPHON**E**
8 PI**T**CH
9 CRES**T**S
10 **W**AVE LENGTH
11 E**A**R
12 RE**S**ONANCE
13 LO**W**
14 FR**E**QUENCY
15 **L**IGHT
16 OSCI**L**LATES
17 VI**B**RATION
18 SPE**E**D OF SOUND
19 FUND**A**MENTAL
20 REFLEC**T**ION
21 NOIS**E**
22 INTERFERE**N**CE

88. AN INCIDENTAL INQUIRY

1 **B**LACK
2 R**E**AL
3 CON**C**AVE
4 NORM**A**L
5 VIRT**U**AL
6 FOCU**S**
7 REFL**E**CTOR
8 PIN**H**OLE
9 CONV**E**X
10 P**H**OTON
11 L**A**TERAL
12 **S**TARS
13 NEW**T**ON
14 MIRR**O**R
15 DI**F**FUSE
16 WAV**E**S
17 PLAN**E**
18 INCI**D**ENT
19 G**R**EEN
20 **O**PAQUE
21 **B**EAM
22 **I**MAGE
23 PLA**N**ETS

89. FOCUSING FUN

Across	Down
1 convex	2 optic fibre
6 mirage	3 erect
7 lens	4 iris
9 oil	5 bend
10 prism	8 spectra
15 refraction	11 myopia
16 real	12 parallel
17 red	13 focal
19 camera	14 concave
20 eye	17 ray
21 yellow	18 dew

For information, diagrams show:
'Hooke's' microscope ca. 1680s
Magnifying glass late 18th century
Cole's theodolite ca. 1765
Galileo's telescope early 17th century
Spectacles early 19th century
Dubroni's collodion camera ca. 1865

90. SEARCH LIGHT

SHADO**W**S
PR**I**SMS
REFRAC**T**ION
S**H**ADE
PROJEC**T**OR
LIG**H**T
CONV**E**X
L**E**NSES
E**Y**E
CAM**E**RA
MIRR**O**R
RE**F**LECTION
BR**A**IN
VISIO**N**
CONCAV**E**
FIBR**E** OPTIC
COLOURE**D**
PUPI**L**
EL**E**CTROMAGNETIC

91. CAN YOU SEE THE LIGHT

1	W**H**ITE	17	IR**I**S
2	CONV**E**X	18	CYA**N**
3	S**K**Y	19	NEW**T**ON
4	R**E**D	20	**H**UMOUR
5	SP**E**CTRUM	21	VIOL**E**T
6	**P**RISM	22	BLIN**D** SPOT
7	ROD**S**	23	REFR**A**TION
8	TRAC**H**OMA	24	G**R**EEN
9	CHORO**I**D	25	DAR**K**NESS
10	LEN**S**		
11	MYO**P**IA		
12	BL**U**E		
13	COM**P**OUND		
14	OPT**I**C		
15	YEL**L**OW		
16	CONE**S**		

92. SPACE SECRETS

1	Io	12	Orbit
2	Neptune	13	Radio
3	Telescope	14	Black dwarf
4	Hydrogen	15	Infra-red
5	Eclipse	16	Titan
6	Planet	17	Uranus
7	Asteroid	18	Andromeda
8	Pluto	19	Red giant
9	Eros	20	Yellow dwarf
10	Rigel	21	Comets
11	Saturn	22	Orion
		23	Light year
		24	Universe
		25	Mercury
		26	Nebula

93. PLANETARY PROBE

1	Mars	5	Neptune
2	Mercury	6	Pluto
3	Jupiter	7	Saturn
4	Venus	8	Uranus

94. PLANETARY PROBLEMS

1	60 kg	5	9100
2	2 years	6	172321 km/h
3	4	7	10558
4	10 years	8	27000

Diagram shows a pair of scissors

95. SOLAR POWER

1	hydrogen	A
2	flares	C
3	Alpha Centauri	R
4	aurora	F
5	chromosphere	T
6	sunspots	F
7	eclipse	B
8	yellow dwarf	J
9	nuclear fusion	D
10	X-rays	W
11	corona	G
12	solar wind	H
13	spectrum	V
14	reversing layer	P
15	helium	I
16	Milky Way	S
17	Quantum	P
18	photons	Y
19	Van Allen belts	P
20	core	R
21	ozone	Q
22	light	**L**
23	convection	**E**
24	radio waves	**O**

96. A SPIRAL SOLUTION

1	CONSTELLATION	13	SPIRAL
2	NEBULA	14	LIGHT YEAR
3	ANDROMEDA	15	RADIO
4	ASTEROID	16	OPTICAL
5	DWARF	17	LENS
6	FUSION	18	STARS
7	NOVA	19	SIRIUS
8	ALDEBARAN	20	SPUTNIK
9	NEWTRON	21	KEPLER
10	NEUTRON	22	RED
11	NEPTUNE	23	DOPPLER
12	EROS	24	RIGEL

97. A SYSTEMATIC INQUIRY

1	Copernicus	2	prominences
7	two	3	rotate
8	Fe	4	infra
9	Venus	5	Pluto
13	Moon	6	Kepler
14	meteor	10	comets
17	sea	11	asteroids
18	spectroscope	12	Io
20	Mars	15	Newton
21	red	16	orbit
22	Sun	19	Eros
		20	MW

98. IT'S LUNACY

1	P**H**ASES	15	GA**N**YMEDE
2	SIXT**E**EN	16	TID**E**S
3	NE**W**TON	17	TY**C**HO
4	SEISM**O**GRAPH	18	LUNI**K** 3
5	MA**R**IA	19	COP**E**RNICUS
6	CRESC**E**NT	20	**D**IANA
7	E**A**GLE	21	**J**UPITER
8	VOLCA**N**OS	22	D**U**ST
9	G**A**LILEO	23	AR**M**STRONG
10	A**P**OLLO	24	CENTRI**P**ETAL
11	MASC**O**NS	25	CRAT**E**RS
12	EC**L**IPSE	26	METEO**R**S
13	RI**L**LS		
14	TRIT**O**N		

99. DISCOVERIES

1	Boyle	Air pressure	T
2	Curie	Radium	H
3	Copernicus	Planetary motion	E
4	Dalton	Atoms	N
5	Darwin	Evolution	J
6	Einstein	Relativity	U
7	Faraday	Electricity	S
8	Florey	Penicillin	T
9	Galileo	Moons of Jupiter	E
10	Harvey	Blood circulation	A
11	Hubble	Expanding universe	T
12	Jenner	Vaccination	Y
13	Wegener	Continental drift	O
14	Lavoisier	Chemistry of combustion	U
15	Lister	Antisepsis	R
16	Mendel	Heredity	S
17	Newton	Gravitation	A
18	Priestley	Oxygen	L
19	Roentgen	X-rays	A
20	Watson and Crick	DNA	D

100. PLANTS AND PEOPLE

Across		**Down**	
1	potato	1	papyrus
3	mango	2	taro
6	pyrethrin	3	mangrove
9	sage	4	grape
10	corn	5	weed
11	pea	7	tobacco
14	sucrose	8	rice
16	coal	12	cotton
17	hop	13	algae
18	oil	14	spice
20	tea	15	olive
21	avocado	19	teak
22	wheat		